PRAISE FOR
Less Stress, More Calm

I am so glad the groundbreaking work we began over 30 years ago on Energy Management continues to make an impact on bright leaders like Lauren Hodges. Her book is brilliant, filled with new, very practical insights, and advances thought leadership in a substantial way.

Jim Loehr
Renowned Performance Psychologist
New York Times Bestselling Author

In *Less Stress, More Calm*, author Lauren Hodges shares her deep wisdom developed through years of extensive research on what drives negative stress, and even more importantly, what we can do to manage it. No matter what your stress personality is, Lauren has a strategy to help you find your calm in the "always on" society that we live in today.

Jen Fisher
Chief Wellbeing Officer

LESS STRESS MORE CALM

LESS
STRESS
MORE
CALM

DISCOVER YOUR UNIQUE STRESS PERSONALITY
AND MAKE IT YOUR SUPERPOWER

LAUREN HODGES, ED.D.

Published and distributed by:
SOUND WISDOM
PO Box 310
Shippensburg, PA 17257-0310
717-530-2122

info@soundwisdom.com

www.soundwisdom.com

While efforts have been made to verify information contained in this publication, neither the author nor the publisher assumes any responsibility for errors, inaccuracies, or omissions. While this publication is chock-full of useful, practical information; it is not intended to be legal or accounting advice. All readers are advised to seek competent lawyers and accountants to follow laws and regulations that may apply to specific situations. The reader of this publication assumes responsibility for the use of the information. The author and publisher assume no responsibility or liability whatsoever on the behalf of the reader of this publication.

Disclaimer: This book contains information that is intended to help the readers be better informed in dealing with change and challenges in life. It is presented as general advice using the author's experience and best judgment but is in no way to be considered a substitute for necessary care provided by a physician or other medical professional.

ISBN 13 TP: 978-1-64095-479-3

ISBN 13 eBook: 978-1-64095-480-9

For Worldwide Distribution, Printed in the USA

1 2 3 4 5 6 7 8 / 28 27 26 25 24

This book is for Daniel, Jake, and Ryder first and foremost.
Thank you for being my safety rope; I love you.

This book is also for the healing inner child in us all—I
pray you learn to enjoy the detours as much as the route.

ACKNOWLEDGMENTS

In *A Gift for God,* Mother Teresa famously said, "We ourselves feel that what we are doing is just a drop in the ocean. But if that drop was not in the ocean, I think the ocean would be less because of that missing drop." I know that this book and compiled research is a drop in the ocean of knowledge out there, but I hope it impacts someone else's life the same way it did mine.

The people who have supported me on this book writing journey have been anything but a "drop" in the ocean. They have been a wealth of information, experience, knowledge, support, and guidance. So, my gratitude is abundant to:

Daniel: you're my forever safety rope. Jake, Ryder, you are my life: I'm so thankful for you. My entire family: I love you all for shaping who I am today.

My Capital F friends (Jenny, Bethany); you are everything. Thank you for dressing me, supporting me, hiking the world with me, making me laugh and drying my tears. My "work" Capital F friends; thanks for your endless wisdom, accountability, and cheerful check-ins throughout the writing process.

My publishing team, editors, mentors, and entire POP team— Where would I be without your support? You are the team I dreamed of when I first started my career.

And finally, to every client, past and present—particularly those whose stories I'm sharing in here—thank you for trusting me. You inspire me daily!

My ocean overflows because of you all.

CONTENTS

PREFACE

A little backstory on how this book came to be:

Over the past few decades, researchers have discovered some incredible, pioneering brain science around how stress impacts the brain—I stumbled across that research several years ago and fell in love with it. I've been in the human performance and well-being field for over fifteen years and have worked with some of the global leaders in human performance and well-being sciences conducting research, building meaningful learning experiences, coaching clients, hosting retreats, and performing keynote lectures and programs.

One of my clients was Johnson & Johnson's Human Performance Institute where I was lucky enough to work with the two most influential researchers and thought leaders in human performance and resilience, Drs. Jim Loehr and Jack Groppel.[1] During that time, I pored over hundreds and hundreds of studies, read many books on the subjects, and deeply immersed myself in topics around stress, resilience, well-being, purpose, energy management, nutrition, exercise, movement, sleep; you name it, I was reading about it. Jim and Jack forged the path for human performance research today—this book wouldn't be possible without their brilliance and research insights, and their work is cited throughout.

Soon after, I was brought on to the growing wellness startup Thrive Global, founded by Arianna Huffington (*HuffPost* founder), to help them create courses on well-being. One of those courses sparked my love affair with the research in this book. I was tasked with designing a mental well-being course in partnership with Accenture and Stanford Medicine. We worked with a pioneer in mental health neuroscience, Dr. Leanne Williams, who was studying the impact of clinical depression and anxiety on the brain's neural circuitry.

Our course, Thriving Mind, went on to become Accenture's most popular course in company history. It was featured in *People* magazine for its success in supporting employees during the pandemic.[2] Hundreds of thousands have completed the course thus far with life-changing, measurable results. I am incredibly proud of what we created and humbled by the lives we've impacted.

Through that process I became deeply immersed in the science— so much research abounded in the ties between neuroscience, stress sciences, human performance sciences, business performance, well-being, resilience, and so on. My journey sparked the creation of this book and the programs I and my team deliver today. I truly hope it inspires, educates, and motivates you, too.

PART I

THE

BACKSTORY

1

THE SCENE

The Great Donut Incident of 1993:
My Stress Personality Origin Story

If we were all superheroes in disguise, then when it came to our stress personalities we'd have to have a good origin story. *If* that were the case (it's not, but let's pretend it was), mine would be the Great Donut Incident of 1993. I was eleven and it was a sunny, summer Sunday morning in Miami. My father had entrusted me with a crisp ten-dollar bill to rollerblade up to the local donut shop, Velvet Creme (a long-time South Miami gem, for those who knew it), to bring back breakfast for the family. On this day I was feeling rather confident in my rollerblading skills and, on my way home from collecting a box of a dozen delicious mixed donuts, I raced down the back alleyway behind the shop at light speed. I had the box of donuts balanced precariously in one hand while my other arm swung dramatically back and forth across my body to maintain my high speed, imagining I was a speed skater in the Olympics...until I hit some gravel.

Down went my scrawny little body and a dozen delightful donuts along with me. I'm telling you, I went *flying*. Donuts scattered and rolled in all directions, spinning around on their edges before we all came to an abrupt stop on the rough pavement.

I sat there for a moment, taking it all in: it wasn't the stinging burn of the bloodied scrapes on my hands and knees or the shockingly abrupt fall that terrified me—I had a nice assortment of scrapes and bruises at all times back then, being the tomboy that I was—no, what terrified me was that I had just single-handedly ruined Sunday breakfast for the family. I didn't have enough money to go back, and I couldn't return empty-handed, either.

I looked around to see if anyone had seen my dramatic fall (the coast was clear, thank God) and slowly found my feet underneath me. I limp-rolled over to the mangled Velvet Creme box to assess the damage. About half the donuts remained inside, semi-smushed and battered. Chocolate icing was smeared across the inside top of the box. Aside from these lone survivors, the remaining dozen were scattered around the crash scene.

I tried to figure out what I should do next but at that moment, *all I wanted to do was run away and hide.* I considered taking shelter in the local park up in my favorite tree for the morning, hoping no one noticed breakfast not showing up; I also considered the possibility of running away for the next ten years and changing my name while things cooled off.

In all seriousness, I distinctly remember the fear, shame, and embarrassment I felt in that moment. Maybe I wasn't cut out for this; maybe if I was a better rollerblader; maybe I wasn't mature enough for the privilege of being out on my own, or being the one who brought home the goods…*maybe I wasn't enough…*

I didn't get angry at the gravel I hit; I didn't have any trouble thinking straight about my next steps; I just straight up wanted to run away and avoid the discomfort of going home empty-handed, and beat myself up for it. I imagined walking through the front door to see my father at the kitchen table, Sunday sports page obstructing the view of his face. I imagined him asking about the glazed donut he was so eagerly awaiting. The fear, embarrassment, and shame were persistent and immobilizing. The negative self-talk, even at 11, was real.

It surely wasn't the first time I'd felt this way, but this has always been a crisp memory; and even today when I remember that fall, as silly as it feels to put this on paper, I *still* feel the shame and embarrassment. This thought—*I'm not enough*—and those associated urges to run and avoid haunted me for years. I carried them into school (the forever perfectionist) and well into adulthood, college, marriage, business ownership, motherhood. Shoot, I even chose defensive positions in sport (defensive specialist in volleyball; defender in soccer) because I was never good on the attack and preferred hanging back and preventing disaster. Even today, that part of me shows up in moments of risk, growth, feedback, change....it nearly took my confidence, my career—even my marriage—until I finally saw it for what it was. But more on that later.

I am a Runner and a Negative Self-Talker. Though I see myself in all of the stress personalities you'll read about, just as I'm sure you will, these are the most persistent, driving feelings, actions, and thoughts throughout my life. I didn't know how to stand up for myself as a kid; confrontation and conflict made me very anxious (still do); I never quite felt like I was enough, no matter what I did; boundaries were impossible until my mid-30s. It took me many years and lots of research to figure this out and learn what to do about it.

This book is my way of helping you bypass years of heartache, self-questioning, and burnout to get to a place where you intimately know your own stress patterns, and know what to do about them.

Here's the end to my origin story:

Seeing that running away and hitching a ride to Timbuktu was not a viable option (plus I *really* needed some Band-Aids), I walked over to each donut, flicked off the gravel bits, brushed off the dirt...

...and I put them all back in the box.

And then I took them home and I *never said a word.*

Yes, my family ate them.

STRESS PERSONALITIES: THE BEGINNING

Of course, our stress personalities don't really have one singular origin story and I'm not sure about you, but I'm not a superhero—at least not in the traditional sense. However, if you were to dig deep into that vast memory of yours, my guess is you'd find an origin story or two of your own: some core memory of when your stress personality first started to show up. Heck, you might have come up with one yourself as you read about my donut debacle.

If you do have a powerful origin story memory, do me a favor and write it down. It might bring a little laughter, maybe a few tears…but it will at least start to shed some light onto a tough, deeply impactful and very human topic—stress.

Stress is one of those conversations we'll never stop having. I can't imagine a time in our future as a species when it won't be an issue. I think it's because the world has evolved faster than our brains can keep up. The pace we try to maintain in life and the demands we face have only continued to rise through the generations, and our *experience* of stress has risen with it. We've gone from stress-as-survival to stress *limiting* survival.

A recent Gallup "State of the Global Workforce Report" found that 44 percent of employees worldwide experience "a lot of daily stress."[1]

How's that for an understatement?

Here in the US in particular, we tend to stress about many things: in 2022 alone, we stressed about daily workload, balance, health, supply chain issues, the threat of cyberattacks, war, inflation; a few years ago we were stressed about Covid, hybrid work; before that, it was racial tension rising in the country and politics.[2] Even our unhappiness has been rising over the past 15 years around the world and is now at a record high.[3] People feel more anger, sadness, pain, worry, and stress than ever before.

Seems likely we won't rein in our experience of *negative* stress any time soon, which, over time and when left unchecked, takes a huge toll on our health and well-being. What I mean by negative stress is the type that doesn't lead to any growth (more on that later, but this has a lot to do with our perception of stress). High negative stress is arguably the leading cause of chronic illness and premature death in the world today: it negatively impacts resilience, happiness, immune function, weight, sleep, relationships, emotional regulation, and it even accelerates our aging process: you name it.[4]

The good news is that we're finally starting to talk about stress and burnout more, which offers researchers in the field and surrounding fields the opportunity to take take deeper dives into what drives our experience of negative stress—and what helps us better manage it.

EXERCISE: DEMANDS OF LIFE INVENTORY

Let's pause and take a quick inventory of how you measure up to the statistics. You have many demands and stressors in your life: in this inventory exercise, I want you to first rate the *importance* of the different areas of your life that demand your energy and time. How much do you value each area?

Then, I want you to rate how much negative stress these areas of life bring you—whether the actual area of your life brings you stress *or* you feel stressed because you can't seem to invest enough of your energy and time in this area. This isn't a ranking—meaning, you can rate each area of life however you'd like—they can all be 10/10 importance and 10/10 stress, for example. There are no wrong answers. Ready? Go!

Demands of Life	Importance: How much do you value this area of your life? 1 = no importance 10 = most important	How much negative stress does this area bring you (or, how much do you stress over making sure you show up at your best in this area of your life)? 1 = no stress at all 10 = extremely high stress
Family time		
Work performance/ demands		
Finances/financial security		
Physical health		
Friends/relationships outside of immediate family		
Mental/emotional health		
Spiritual health (faith, sense of purpose, giving back, etc.)		
Community		
Any other categories:		

*Adapted from a great exercise in The Power of Full Engagement by Dr. Jim Loehr and Tony Schwartz.[5]

What did you notice about your results? Again, there are no right or wrong answers here. Did some areas of life you don't assign much value to seem to bring you the most stress? Or did the areas of life you value most (family, physical well-being, for example) make you feel stressed because you don't feel you invest enough time and energy into them?

Ask yourself: *Where am I failing to invest more of my time and energy even though this is an incredibly important part of my life?*

Take a moment to reflect on your results and jot down any "aha's" that might have surfaced from this exercise. *Circle or highlight the areas you value the most—pay attention to these areas, because they'll come in handy later in the book—they are keys to busting out of this cycle.*

Here's the reason for the exercise: we all have stressors (expectations, unexpected challenges, mundane repeated tasks and responsibilities, financial worries, to-dos, health issues, relationship challenges, family drama, new opportunities, storms…*taxes*) in life that aren't going anywhere any time soon. We are busy, high-paced go-getters and the demands of life aren't going anywhere (let's be honest: are you expecting your life to be significantly less busy in any of these areas any time soon? Yea…me neither).

The point is *stress will always be there.* And that's not always a bad thing, as we'll learn in the next chapter.

If we do not manage our stress in a healthy way, it can create negative downstream impact on our ability to show up as our best in the moments that matter with the people that matter, and live our happiest, most fulfilling lives (see the categories you rated the highest in value).

There is so much at stake if we fail to take action, isn't there?

Let me tell you a story about what I mean when I say so much is at stake.

One of my long-time clients (I'm going to call her Nancy) was the first female CEO of a national healthcare facility. She's a beautiful,

beautiful soul who gives all of herself to her work. When Nancy and I started working together in 2018, despite (because of?) being incredible at her job she was a categorically hot mess in her personal life. She wasn't exercising, wasn't eating well, and she slept maybe four hours a night. She stayed up late to answer emails and was always the first in the office the next day. She worked ridiculous hours, commuting *across the country* from Monday to Friday. She was nearing retirement and still working because (a) she wanted to save more for retirement and (b) her self-worth was wrapped up in her identity at work: she knew nothing else and had lots to prove as the first female CEO.

Nancy's stress personality was the Negative Self-Talker, which we'll unpack more in that chapter.

Bottom line is, Nancy was way out of alignment with her values and she hired me to help. At first, she was a tough nut to crack; but what ultimately inspired her to make a change was her husband, a retired golf pro, and his testimony. She knew she spent *very little* time with him, but during my usual info-gathering process he shared what weighed on his heart. When I asked him to tell me what success would look like for Nancy's coaching process, he said, "I miss her. I just want to spend more time with her in our golden years." This is what snapped her out of it. She knew she couldn't continue giving her husband, the person who mattered the most to her, the last crumbs of her energy any longer.

I'll dig more into Nancy's training plan and success in a future chapter because she made some incredible strides. But right now, I want you to know the tough part of Nancy's story: two years *after* our successful coaching process, her husband died suddenly during a routine heart surgery.

Overnight, Nancy was a widow. All their future golden years together were suddenly gone, and Nancy was left to process this unimaginable hole in her heart. She carried incredible guilt that she'd let so many years go by moving through life at such a fast pace and barely coming up for air, allowing her stress personality to remain in the driver's seat for so long. She felt deep regret for how far off course she veered from what mattered the most to her: her faith and her husband. She grieved not just what was, but what could have been. I felt helpless to the depth of her loss.

In one of our conversations following his passing, Nancy reflected on the two years leading up to her husband's death: she'd done some seriously hard work on herself, getting to know her stress personality and the underlying beliefs, mindsets, and behaviors that drove her overworking, boundaryless lifestyle. She had taken control of her well-being and was much more aligned with her deepest values.

She shared the bittersweet silver lining: they'd spent two wonderful years enjoying the fruits of her efforts before he was gone. Though she wished for more time, she was thankful she had made those changes and really experienced some balance and beautiful moments with the love of her life. She decided to submit her retirement announcement and start living her golden years to their fullest in his honor.

The bottom line is this: it's not about the time we have with our loved ones and those people and things that matter the most to us; it's what we choose to do with the time we have that really matters.

FACE THE TRUTH MOMENT

Answer these questions Nancy asked herself when she faced the truth of where she was currently in life:

In the last week, how many times have you:

+ ___ Stopped to really look up and into the eyes of the person in front of you...be fully there?
+ ___ Taken a break?
+ ___ Focused on *being* rather than *doing?*

+ ____ Said yes to what fuels your joy and lightens your spirit?

+ ____ Made choices with intention and not reaction?

In the last year:

+ How would you rate the general *quality* of the time and energy you brought to the people who matter the most to you?

_____

_____

_____

_____

_____

_____

_____

_____

+ When you felt like you had nothing left to give, *what version of you showed up* and *what did you give up?*

_____

_____

_____

_____

_____

_____

_____

_____

♦ On average, which *version of you* did your family get when you walked in the door at the end of the day, or when things were hard—was it the best version of you, or the leftovers? Asked another way, what *kind of energy* did you bring to the most important people in your life on a typical day? Were you more joyful, light, engaged, present, connected? Or were you more disconnected, distant, weighted down with negative energy, anxious or uncertain, busy, or easily distracted?

_____

_____

_____

_____

_____

_____

_____

None of us know how much time we really have left to fully invest in the most important people and parts of our life. There's precious little time to waste—and lots of life left to live.

So we have to do something about this…and we can.

There is a solution: it's not a supplement, a pill, a workout plan, nor a one-size-fits-all product or process that will solve all your stress issues. You can't buy this solution, ingest it, inject it…

The solution is *you*. **You are the key.** You can let the donuts go flying and learn to get back up quickly without any physical, mental, emotional, or spiritual scars. You can take control of your stress now and not waste any more time.

This book is a journey on how to get there.

The science of stress personalities can only be leveraged with your involvement in the process. Why? *Because you are your greatest asset.* Self-awareness is the cornerstone of this book—it is the beginning and the foundation upon which you'll build your new story.

There is *strong* scientific evidence that people who are more self-aware simply have better lives: they are smarter, make better decisions, are better performers at work and in academics, raise more mature children, have better careers, are more creative, are more confident, communicate better, have stronger relationships, have more trust in their relationships at work and at home...I can keep going.

And yet, how many of us stop to do the work of getting to know ourselves, particularly around how we show up when things get hard? If you ask self-awareness experts like Tasha Eurich, there is a growing gap between how we see ourselves and who we really are (which is ironic, because most of us assume we're self-aware...currently removing the speck out of my own eye here). [6]

That's why this book is really about building self-awareness.

So, you have to be an active participant in this process—we're going to strengthen our self-awareness together around who we are under stress, why that matters, and what we can do about it.

This book is about you. And me. And all of us who understand *stress **reduction** is a myth*. We're going to take a deep dive together into the science of stress personalities, learn about our own but also others' stress personalities. And in that process, we will identify strategies to better manage our unique stress personalities so we can show up in the way we want to for the people and things we deem most precious.

This research changed my life, personally and professionally. I have a much deeper understanding of myself; my inner voice nearly did me in when I faced both the mundane, persistent stressors in life and some of the biggest challenges too. But this research found me and breathed life back into me: I'm more confident and have more moments of joy. It took some deep introspection and small steps in the right direction—steps that were too small to fail.

Because of this research I:

+ Learned how to respond to pressure and stress with more focus and intention, staying connected to my values.

+ Gained deeper understanding and love for who I am at my best and at my worst—I found *grace* for myself and empathy for others in a way I hadn't before.

+ Identified a clear process for how to be my best most of the time.

I cannot wait to dive in with you.

SUGGESTIONS FOR HOW TO GAIN THE MOST FROM THIS BOOK

It would be ironic if reading this book made you feel *more* stressed. So, here are a few suggestions on how to navigate it:

Optional strategy 1: Put this book down any time you feel exhausted by reading it. These days, we're inundated with self-help/personal development/well-being advice everywhere we turn. If we took in all of the advice we heard daily, we'd need to start our day with 60 minutes of transcendental meditation followed by 60 minutes of journaling, recite 10 positive affirmations while brushing our teeth, plan our entire day over tea, complete an hour of rigorous-but-gentle-but-high-intensity-but-flowy-but-heavy exercise, eat a perfectly balanced and nutritious meal of 1 piece of lettuce and hot water with lemon, take a cold shower, and of course find out the meaning of life before sunrise…are we for real?

Stress is a heavy subject, so I don't expect this book to *energize* you the whole way through. Let's make a deal: if at any point this book is draining your energy, *put it down* and return to it later.

Optional strategy 2: Choose your own adventure. Think about treating the book as a "choose your own adventure" where you tackle only the chapters that feel personally relevant or interesting to you. This way you read only the Stress Personalities that feel right to focus on and skip the rest. Yes, the chapters are a bit sequential in that I call back to other stress personalities or exercises the deeper into the book you get, but you don't *need* to read the book front-to-back if you don't want to.

Optional strategy 3: Treat this like a course or learning journey. Think about keeping a notebook handy and use it to complete the exercises within the book. This isn't a passive read—it's active and requires lots of self-reflection on your part. If you think about it that way, you can stop and start knowing you're going to be active in the process—it's not meant to be a "can't put it down" thriller.

Any way you tackle the book, remember this: you are in control of how you navigate all life improvement advice; you're in the driver's seat. Treat this book the same way.

Ready? Let's dive in.

Oh, and one more thing: I promise, no gravel donuts were shared or consumed in the writing of this book...at least I don't think so.

TL:DR (AKA TOO LONG: DIDN'T READ)

+ I'm not as good a rollerblader as I think I am.
+ Life is too short to allow stress to drive your life: you are the key to getting back in the driver's seat of your stress.
+ Do *not* accept donuts from an 11-year-old who has bloody knees and won't make eye contact.

2

THE SCIENCE

It wasn't until visiting New York City with my husband and two boys, ages 6 and 8 at the time, that we realized our younger son Ryder had zero survival skills. I grew up in Miami and had traveled to Manhattan (and other big cities) many times for work, so I was used to keeping my head on a swivel at intersections. Our older son also quickly adapted on the first day of our trip; but wow, if we had a dollar for every time Ryder stepped off the curb without looking into near misses by cars, buses, taxis, or bike couriers, I'm pretty sure we could have paid for our trip. Coming from a sleepy Florida beach town, I can't blame the kid: traffic and busy pedestrian sidewalks are virtually nonexistent there. Nonetheless, I found myself instinctually pulling him by the jacket hood back onto sidewalks almost at every intersection, my adrenaline rushing. Each time he'd turn and look back at me with surprise and confusion; eventually, I learned to just hold onto his jacket like it was a leash 10 feet before any curb (work smarter not harder, am I right?).

The point is, after those first few times Ryder almost got himself killed, my brain learned. When I grabbed him by the jacket, it was immediate and instinctual—I didn't pause to think about it or reflect on whether he'd look both ways this time. It was *automatic* and *non-conscious*. Why is this? Because our brain acts *without conscious thought* when it believes the matter is truly life or death. This is a perfect example of our brain's stress response system kicking into action as part of a deeper, evolutionary survival instinct to keep ourselves (or our offspring; thanks, maternal instinct!) alive. And I think that before we dive into the research behind stress personalities, it's important to start with this very basic stress science...you know, so you understand there's a biology to your quirks.

(P.S. Why didn't Ryder eventually learn? Because that's raising boys...bless their heart. Maybe if we'd been there another couple of weeks. But good news, he grew out of it...we think.)

SCIENCE LESSON 1: THE STRESS RESPONSE

Let's use another example of the stress response system we likely can all relate to, to help us go under the hood on what's happening in the brain and body during a real or perceived threat to our survival.

Picture this: You're driving down a busy highway at rush hour, minding your own business and catching up on your favorite podcast or jamming to the '80s, when out of nowhere a truck cuts you off—he *totally doesn't know you're there*—and darn near forces you off the road!

Let's pause here—mid cut-off—and examine what's going on inside your brain.

In this moment, your brain's autonomic nervous system (a system that controls our body's involuntary actions like our heart beating, blood vessel dilation, breathing...scanning for threat...) kicks into high gear and activates the stress response.

The star of the show in this moment? Our "Reptile" and "Emotional" Brains. Let me explain: Our brain could be trisected into three general areas: Reptile, Emotional, and New.

Reptile Brain

The lower part of our brain is, from an evolutionary perspective, the most primitive part of the brain, which is why it's referred to by many scientists as our "Reptile Brain." One of its most basic and important jobs is to keep us alive—it scans the world for threats, and when it detects a threat, it reacts accordingly. Fight or flight, or the stress response, originates here in the Reptile Brain.

Emotional Brain

The middle part of the brain, more commonly referred to as our "Emotional Brain" (or "Mammalian/Limbic Brain"), is where we *feel, learn, and do*—emotions and emotional regulation originate here and so does long-term memory and learning. The *limbic system* that makes up our Emotional Brain is an integral part of the stress response because our emotions are truly in the driver's seat when it comes to stress. So, here are some major players in the Emotional and Reptile Brain:

+ Our *emotions:* If our brain was a traffic light, then our emotions would be the green, yellow, and red lights (*Red light...STOP! Green light...GO! Yellow light...wait... okay, maybe go but proceed with caution...*). Our thoughts and beliefs and perspectives are all filtered through our emotions, so our emotions truly interpret and make meaning of our world and experiences and drive us to act accordingly.[1]

+ Our *hippocampus:* This is our hub for memory and learning. The hippocampus is, among other things, responsible for *remembering* and *encoding* experiences, including past stressful experiences, and use them to inform current and future experiences. So, imagine our hippocampus directing our little emotional traffic light to flash either green, yellow, or red based on how it's experienced this experience in the past: The stronger an experience and the associated emotional response the first time, the more imprinted in our memory it becomes. So, years later, a certain smell, song, sound, etc. (rollerblades or donuts, for example) could trigger our stress response thanks to the power of our hippocampus. Scientists call this *emotional tagging*.[2] This is the process of storing the memory of an event or action with an associated emotion.

- Our *HPA-axis* and *amygdala:* Our *amygdala* is largely responsible for threat interpretation and processing to tell us whether something or someone is "dangerous," but it works with the hippocampus to do so. Our hippocampus and amygdala together alert the brain's stress response system, which is known as our *HPA axis, or hypothalamic-pituitary-adrenal axis,* to come online...or not. These regions are the circuitry behind fight or flight and rest and digest.

This entire area works together like an alarm system for the brain to tell us whether an experience or person etc., is a threat to us or not—if it's good or bad, safe, or dangerous and what to do about it (*Yellow! Red! Green!*). Some consider the limbic system as the link between the "unthinking" Reptile Brain and our *conscious* thought and behaviors: the New Brain.

New Brain

Our New Brain is what makes humans, well, human. This is where higher-order, conscious, intellectual, or rational thinking like logic, reason, reflection, decision-making, creativity, innovation, active problem-solving, abstract thought, and so on, live. This is what separates us from our mammalian cousins, and how you're even able to read these words and process them. Believe it or not, we don't use this part of the brain as much as the others (and some of us even less than that…). Most of our brain's processing power lies in the Reptile and Emotional Brain—there is so much going on behind the scenes.

By the way, they call it the "Reptile" brain and "Mammalian" brain because reptiles *only* have this lower, primitive part of the brain, but all mammals can love, feel emotion, learn, etc. In other words, your pet lizard doesn't really possess the hardware to feel emotions (sorry to burst that bubble, lizard lovers). It's also why businessman and author Seth Godin coined the phrase, "Never let the lizard send an email."[3] What he means, of course, is never react, always respond—the crux of this book.

Anyway, back to the truck cutting you off: In this very moment, your Reptile Brain recognizes a threat long before you become consciously aware of it, and the stress response is immediately activated.

Fight or Flight

The stress response has two phases and is controlled by that autonomic nervous system mentioned earlier. Phase one activates the Sympathetic Nervous System (SNS), better known as the "fight or flight" stage. Phase two activates the Parasympathetic Nervous System (PNS), or the "rest and digest" stage. These two systems are like two balancing arms on a seesaw, forever working to create homeostasis in the body and keep us ticking.

The instant this truck cuts us off, fight or flight takes center stage. In a microsecond, several biological and chemical reactions fire from the Reptile and Emotional Brains:

1. Blood flow is shunted *away* from the New Brain to the primitive Reptile Brain to kick it into action. This means we no longer have the full function of our higher-order thinking (decision-making, rationale, logic, reason, focus).

This is why it's so hard to think straight, focus, or make great decisions when we're stressed. It's also why we feel like we have less control over our emotions.

2. Based on feedback and activity from the amygdala, hippocampus, hypothalamus and adrenals, the hormones adrenaline, noradrenaline and cortisol flood the body, urging us to *act*. "Acting" means different things to different people. In this case, thanks to our driver's ed classes and lots of practice, we would likely instinctually slam on the brakes and maneuver our vehicle away from the threat of an impending collision. We wouldn't have to consciously think about each step, we'd just do it. Much like my arm reaching out to grab my son's jacket as he steps off the curb and into Broadway's busy traffic, our survival instinct is in the driver's seat. The stress response should really be called the stress *reaction* because we react, not respond, to our environment—*our behaviors, thoughts, and emotions in these moments are automatic and non-conscious and not in our control*. Yes, even our emotions—that surge of anger, fear, or instinctual honking or yelling—are truly out of our control. (But! We can better train our responses, which is the entire point this book.)

3. Thanks to adrenaline, blood rushes toward the center of our body in a last-ditch effort to protect our heart, brain, and lungs and/or mobilize us to run away from the threat, so we might feel flushed or weak-kneed. The entire point of the stress response is to mobilize us to do *something*: fight, run away, etc.

4. Cortisol also triggers a rapid release of glucose from the liver (for fast energy, if needed). Frequent cortisol tsunamis are also why people with chronic stress tend to have a much

higher risk of heart disease, high blood pressure, etc. While a little acute stress like this is actually great for the heart, too much causes long-term damage.

5. On top of all of these chemical and biological actions, our digestive system and immune functions are now temporarily disrupted so that all available resources are rerouted to focus on survival. This is why, for example, you might feel the urge to use the bathroom right before running a marathon or stepping onto a stage, or feel a pit in your stomach when thinking about having a tough conversation with a loved one. It's also why chronic stress often leads to digestive issues, ulcers, IBS, suppressed immune function, and more susceptibility to disease. By the way, it's not just digestion and immune function: tissue repair and growth, reproduction, and other functions are impaired.

Okay, so back to it: this chemical cocktail flushes through our bodies, leading us to act on our instincts and habits *(Red light! Stop!!).* Without pause we slam on the brakes, swerve to avoid the truck— perhaps some of us (not naming names) partake in other unbecoming gestures and language—and the truck drives away from us.

Whew! We survived the threat.

Rest and Digest

Not long after, we come down off that adrenaline spike. Maybe we shake out our white-knuckled hands that gripped the steering wheel like a vice, or adjust ourselves in the seat, shaking out our Jell-O legs. Most of us likely at the very least release a big sigh of relief. A deep exhale like this isn't an accident, by the way; this exhale triggers the release of the neurotransmitter acetylcholine, which activates the "rest and digest" stage of the stress response. Acetylcholine lowers the heart rate in an instinctual grab for oxygen and an attempt for our nervous system to regulate.

Post-Stressful Situation Reflection

Now our "New Brain" starts to reflect and works to make sense of the situation, including our role in it. If you can believe it, unless we're pretty self-aware, in this state we are almost always the victims in our story. *It's the driver's fault and he must be a terrible human; there are too many people moving to our city; it's (fill-in-the-blank politician we hate)'s fault!* We tend to make imprecise connections and go wild with storytelling. This is because our emotions are *still* in the driver's seat, even after a perceived threat has passed, so they get the first crack at making sense of a situation and telling the story of what happened. This is probably why neuroscientist Antonio Damasio referred to our emotions as our "first brain" as far back as the early 1980s.[4]

And then, it's all over...right?

SCIENCE LESSON 2: CHRONIC, CUMULATIVE STRESS

Here's the thing: We're only built for isolated, acute, and infrequent moments of stress that last seconds, like our truck cut-off scenario.

But stressful moments don't happen in isolated, infrequent incidents in today's world. In today's world, threats are rarely true threats to our survival (predators, rival tribes, etc.); now, most "threats" are psychological or social...*and our brain cannot distinguish between real and perceived threats.*

In other words, our brain can't tell the difference between a truck pulling out in front of us, or a busy day with back-to-back calls, or a last-minute request thrown on your desk when you were supposed to leave to get your child from soccer practice, or an unexpected bill, or a wedding you're planning, or a house you're buying, or an aging parent who needs more care, or a painful past memory triggered by a smell or song—our brain hits the fight or flight button in any and all of these situations, especially if we leave them unchecked and unaddressed.

Maybe now you can see how all of these many micro moments of stress can quickly become cumulative, particularly when we unconsciously assign the idea that they're all "bad" situations and worthy of a fight or flight reaction.

There are so many types of stressors and stress, and not all are bad. To name a few:

+ *Acute stress:* See the truck example previously mentioned. Or run into a spiderweb you didn't see, and you'll quickly learn about acute stress.

+ *Emotional stressors:* Grief, loss, a breakup, relationship challenges, caring for an aging parent.

+ *Mental stressors:* Workload, screen fatigue, managing a family schedule, multitasking, learning new skills, tackling a big project, etc.

+ *Physical stressors:* Illness, injury, recovering from a surgery, chronic pain, etc.

+ *Major life stressors:* Death, divorce, moving, or having a baby; a situation seriously challenging your values; existential crises, worldview shifts, etc.

+ *External stressors* within *our control:* Applying for a new role at work; delivering a speech; buying a house; our mindset (yes, in our control); elements of our physical health.

+ *External stressors* out *of our control:* Disease or unexpected illness; trauma; sudden life changes; layoffs;

a global pandemic; racial tension and social unrest, war. Even today's technology butting up against our brain's wiring can trigger the stress response. For example, take email: We're hardwired to communicate with others as part of a group survival instinct, so to our primitive social brain, unanswered emails and texts in an inbox can feel like an emergency. Same goes with Zoom/virtual meetings: our brain hasn't adapted (thankfully) to sitting at a desk and staring at a screen or our reflections all day: doing so actually creates stress and isn't always something we can control (if you want to stay employed).

+ *Micro stressors:* Though I'm not sure I fully agree with the term "micro stressor" (all stress is stress, but I see where they're coming from), some researchers believe that the small, nearly unnoticeable accumulation of stressful moments in the day can be considered their own sneaky little brand of stress, just like deep canyons started as little trickles of water slowly eroding the landscape over the years.

+ *Learned helplessness:* Failing to show up in moments that matter triggers the stress response. For example, someone you're standing near at a party is wronged, but you stay quiet because you were taught as a child that you are meek and your words and actions won't have impact. Or, you don't speak up when someone consistently violates your boundaries or denies your needs, because you fear judgment.

+ *Internal noise and voice:* You create your own stress. We do this all the time, don't we? We worry, overanalyze, catastrophize, assume, beat ourselves up, read too much into things, etc. (See above – elements of our mindset are very much within our control.)

- *Compassion Fatigue:* If you're in education, healthcare, social work, nonprofit, long-term, or palliative care, or any other field that asks the world of you—first of all, bless you. Second, don't underestimate the powerful impact of compassion fatigue. Parents, empaths, friends of those going through hard times, caregivers of elderly parents…I'm also looking at you. This unique form of stress is sneaky and destructive.

- *Embedded/systemic stress:* Gender gaps; race gaps; ageism; marginalized voices; perceptions of law enforcement (both sides). Stress disproportionately impacts minorities, BIPOC, and other marginalized communities. One example: Women statistically work more time and put more effort in unpaid labor (housekeeping, primary caregivers of aging parents, childcare), and historically struggle to take positions of power at work and achieve equitable pay. Though it may not be on the forefront of your mind daily, the systemic stressors we all face produce a steady undercurrent of stress.

- *Economic stressors:* There's no surprise that people experiencing financial trouble or being in lower socioeconomic situations unfairly experience more stress. But, it might surprise you to know that income isn't always a predictor of stress. It's also about feeling comparatively poor, with no resources available to you, and being treated as such that really create the stress. Interesting fact: People who *perceive* themselves as poor are more chronically stressed. I find this fascinating and perhaps a reason that some poor cultures and communities have less but give more and self-report as generally happier.

- *Social stressors:* Social support (or lack of) and social isolation have a high degree of influence on chronic stress and can affect physical health and even life expectancy.

- *Gaslighting:* Needs no explanation, but here's an example: *"You're not stressed, you're imagining this and making yourself stressed,"* or *"Systemic stress doesn't exist, get over it,"* or *"At least you don't have to deal with* (insert part where I make this about me)...." Even the often well-intended would say *"Just reframe your stress/think positively and it'll go away!"* Though there is some great science to support the power of reframing and positive thinking and intention setting—we'll unpack that later in the book—sometimes it's not that easy, and this well-intended advice can send the message that whatever you're stressed about *is your fault;* ironically, creating more stress.

- *Trauma:* Traumatic experiences in your past can imprint on your brain in significant (and incredibly challenging) ways. Don't underestimate the power of traumatic experiences to influence how we experience the world today.

Imagine a day strung with these stressors, or weeks...or months. When stress becomes cumulative, it starts to feel out of our control, quickly leading to chronic stress, or burnout, or worse.

Chronic Stress

Remember, not all stress is bad. Some stress produces growth and helps us grow more resilient. This is known as *eustress*, a term coined by Hans Selye, which is moderate, maybe even high, but *manageable* amounts of stress that produce growth. Eustress is good for learning, the heart, resilience, and more.[5] In fact, other researchers theorized and later proved that low to no stress can often *hinder* our performance and happiness. (Have you ever read the 1892 short story *The Yellow Wallpaper* by Charlotte Perkins Gilman? We need some stress in our life, or we'd go mad!)

Just keep in mind that what is considered eustress in some situations can be *distress* in others or can vary from person to person. It can depend on things like how much stress we have on any given day (known as *allostatic load*, coined by scientist Bruce McEwen), how much we slept the night before, how others around us are feeling—it even depends on *how we perceive the stressor* in that moment. This is mind-bending! Dr. Bruce Perry, a trauma expert, says that stress is eustress when it's *moderate, predictable, controllable* stress—only then can stress really be growth-producing. We all have a "sweet spot."

So really, it's incorrect to think that our performance would improve if we could just...get rid of stress. It's why Hans Selye famously said, "It's not the stress that kills us, it's our reaction to it."

Perception of stress *matters*. How challenges are perceived *matters*. Allostatic load *matters*.

Chronic stress is stress that feels cumulative, out of our perceived control, unpredictable, persistent, and difficult to manage.

How do you know you're chronically stressed? Here are a few (unscientific) considerations that might help:

- [ ] The collective daily stress you face feels more than moderate, unpredictable, and tough to manage.

- [ ] You do the same thing over and over and find yourself in a loop of behaviors that lead to no solutions.

- [ ] You avoid acknowledging the stress and choose a "safer" (in the moment) route. Enter the coping mechanism—alcohol, sweets, gossip, vegging out, avoidance, shopping, conflict, exploding over something minor (Brené Brown calls this "chandeliering," exploding so badly that you hit the chandelier above).

- [ ] You're chronically sick or your body constantly feels out of whack. Chronic stress impacts the immune system, hormones, etc., so constantly feeling under the weather could be a sign of burnout or chronic stress.

- [ ] Things that used to help you recover no longer work (a good night's sleep, coffee with friends, a snuggle with the cat, a massage, etc.). You feel disengaged with the things that usually excite you (work, hobbies, etc.).

- [ ] Your *locus of control* shifts. You no longer believe you can manage your stress or start to believe you're not cut out for managing the demands you face. Or, you start to believe you no longer have choice and control in the situation.

- [ ] Your *identity* shifts. You start to speak more regularly in absolutes about who you are such as, *I'm not enough; I'm a failure; I'm not worthy, I can't do this,* etc.

☐ You've lost clarity or sight of what's most important to you or feel out of alignment with it.

☐ These feelings/thoughts go on for longer than they should—more than a few bad or rough days.

Disclaimer: Some of these symptoms of chronic stress or burnout can be easily confused with a real, actual, clinical mental health condition like depression or anxiety. If you're checking off more than a few, I highly recommend you seek professional help and make sure it's not something more serious that requires an intervention more powerful than this book could ever provide. Take care of your mental health: it's precious and you're too valuable to us not to take some action here.

We're coming full circle back to Chapter 1. When we face many demands and run at a full sprint all day, it becomes chronic, cumulative, and we slowly become out of alignment with what we value most. This can take a major toll on our health and happiness. Chronic stress is real, it's pervasive, and it's impacting many.

SCIENCE LESSON 3: A DEEPER DIVE INTO THE "REST AND DIGEST" PHASE

Like the natural world around us, our bodies are made up of rhythms, all working synchronously and harmoniously together: we blink, we breathe, we sleep, we reproduce, we digest, and our heart moves blood to and from its chambers like the reliable ebb and flow of waves on the beach. We are, in essence, made up of these rhythms.

Remember that the stress response is a rhythm in and of itself—it's a two-part show that starts with "fight or flight" and moves to "rest and digest" and back again when needed to forever balance and achieve homeostasis. It's our own built-in reminder that what goes up, must come down. And whether we're being intentional about seeking the rest and digest phase and regulating our nervous system or not, the body *will* find a way to achieve homeostasis, sometimes at the expense of our health and well-being (we get sick, injured, we burn out, we explode, etc.).

Either way, it's important to know that we are *pre-wired* to find a way to "come down" from a fight or flight moment and seek recovery.

Let's use a sports story to explain:

You may recognize the name Simone Manuel, the American professional swimmer who specializes in freestyle events. She swam for the USA Olympic team during the 2016 Rio games and 2021 Tokyo games, and she made history as the first Black woman to win an individual gold medal at the 2016 Rio games.

But you might not have heard this story, which was shared with me by a good friend and fellow coach. During training and qualifiers for the Tokyo games, Simone's performance was plummeting. She was struggling to qualify even for some of her strongest events, and she didn't know why. Her heart raced at rest, she felt intense anxiety, lack of appetite, extreme fatigue, insomnia, and muscle soreness. Even just walking the stairs to the pool left her gassed. It stumped her trainers and coaches.

Finally, doctors intervened, ran some tests, and found a diagnosis. Simone had Overtraining Syndrome; she was pushing her body too hard.

Once she stepped back from her intense training and integrated more rest and recovery into her life, her performance improved. Simone qualified for the Olympic Games in Tokyo and made us Americans incredibly proud, leading her team to the bronze in the 4x100 freestyle event. She now holds five Olympic medals.[6]

Simone trains harder than any of us could even fathom. She pushes—quite literally stresses (that's what exercise technically is)—her body in ways only a small fraction of the world can. But as any athlete can attest to and as Simone learned the hard way, training to perform at the top of her sport *requires* recovery and not just during the off season. Simone needed recovery in her weekly training and even in the workouts and days themselves. The harder Simone trained; the more important recovery became. *The cure must match the symptom.*

The point? It wasn't the training, the stress, that caused Simone's performance to plummet—*it was the absence of adequate recovery in the process.*

How many of you, like me, tell the story that we don't need a break; that to get ahead we can't stop to recover and connect; *that stress is the issue?*

I don't want you to miss this; please write this statement down:

Stress *without* Recovery = Overtraining
Stress *with* Recovery = *Growth*

The point of this book isn't to find ways to *reduce stress* in your life—that's not realistic, nor will it help you build resilience. The point of this book is to learn how to manage and better control your reaction to your stress personality, using recovery among other strategies. *Stress isn't the problem.*

Let's go a little bit deeper on this stress/recovery concept and where this theory and research originated.

Time Between Points: Stress and Recovery

Two of the greatest researchers in this space are Dr. Jim Loehr, a performance psychologist, and Dr. Jack Groppel, an exercise physiologist who co-founded the Human Performance Institute (HPI) in 1991 after meeting at the US Open tennis tournament. These two researchers spent their careers exploring and defining the concepts of stress and recovery and transformed millions of lives in the process, including mine.

In one of their experiments, they studied elite pro tennis players and noticed an interesting attribute that set the world's greatest tennis players apart from other athletes (and athletes in other sports): The most elite players instinctively used the *time between points* to maximize their recovery. Dr. Loehr realized that only about 30 percent of a match consisted of scoring points; what mattered most, what set the greatest apart most, was what the players did *in the moments between high stress moments.*[7]

Many famous athletes have infamous habits in their own "time between points" (former American football quarterback Drew Brees famously licked his fingers, for example). The point? How we choose to recover in the "time between points" (stressful moments) in our lives, matters so much to how we show up for the next "point"—so much more than we might think.

The results of Jim Loehr and Jack Groppel's work applied easily and practically to all professions—military, business, and everyday people like you and me. They formed and popularized other groundbreaking concepts we still use today—concepts I've built my career on—and that we'll unpack in later chapters.

So, back to the importance of recovery in our daily life: The funny part is, we are so good about making sure our *devices* get frequent recovery during the day, don't we? Have you ever noticed how panicked you feel when your phone battery flashes red and gives you the "low battery" signal? Is there anything more terrifying? Why don't we give our bodies and minds the same treatment? It's like what writer Anne Lamott so eloquently said in a TedTalk: "Almost everything works again when you unplug it for a few minutes—including you."

Our physical bodies are great at letting us know when we need recovery—after a hard leg workout, muscle soreness and fatigue lets you know you need a break (ever tried climbing stairs or wearing high heels after a heavy leg workout?). After a fast-food meal, our stomach might hurt or feel bloated. After a poor night's sleep, we'll feel sluggish, tired, sometimes even nauseous or have a headache.

Why can't we hear and feel those cues our minds and bodies give us under stress as well? The reasons can vary:

- **You don't know your stress personality well enough yet, so you don't recognize the cues.**

- **You know you're stressed, but you ignore it and push through to tough it out/burn the candle/hustle to get ahead or whatever other misconception or myth you've bought into.**

- **You simply don't have a system in place to respond effectively quite yet, so you move through your day reactive and disconnected from your body and mind.**

No matter the reason, recovery is a critical concept to understand. And after Loehr and Groppel, many other researchers validated the theory behind them. Rest simply makes us more resilient and productive.[8]

We need to arm ourselves with the tools and strategies to quickly reset and recover in moments of high, negative stress. Which is what this book will help you do.

SCIENCE LESSON 4: OUR BRAINS ARE PLASTIC

Ever been at dinner with a friend and their phone goes off, and they look down and start texting someone back...even if you're in the middle of a conversation?

Or, you take the same route to work every day and on the weekend need to go to the store, but accidentally take the same turns toward work?

There's a reason for these patterns—*neuroplasticity*.

And here begins my love affair with this research.

As you might already know, our brains have billions of neurons, or brain cells. When these cells "fire and wire" together they create neural pathways; there are billions of neural pathways in the brain.

Every thought, emotion, behavior, motor skill, and habit from blinking to thinking negatively to riding a bike to avoiding a collision, even our *beliefs*, are really just neural pathways that we were either born with or we've developed over the years, like billions of little rivers and streams coursing through the brain, all winding around each other in vast interconnected waterway networks.

The neural pathways we use and reinforce most often are the stronger, more resilient pathways—the wide, roaring rivers which create those deep canyons. The ones we use less often are more like trickling streams that never quite dry up but aren't used any longer.

In other words, what we feed, grows; what we don't, dries up. This is habit formation in a nutshell. *Neuroplasticity is the ability to create and reinforce new neural pathways and new habits.*[9]

For example, when was the last time you had to think about tying your shoes? Like, the literal mechanics of it? As a child learning this new motor skill, it chewed up a lot of your brain power, glucose, and mental resources; but eventually, the new hand movements became automatic, non-conscious, and effortless—a habit. These default motions now live deep in your brain and require virtually no effort to recall and apply when needed.

We're born with some of these habits (blinking, heart beating, breathing; thanks, autonomic nervous system), but others we develop over time (riding a bike, tying a shoe, writing our name, driving a car, etc.).

Do me a favor right now: place this book (laptop, device) down a moment and fold your hands in your lap. Did you notice that one thumb is laying on top of the other? Which one is it? Now try to fold your hands with the opposite thumb on top...feels weird, right? This is a great example of neuroplasticity at work.

Neuroplasticity is also responsible for non-motor skill habits and habits we do or don't want to build such as thinking more positively or looking down at our phone when we hear a ping, and away from the person we're talking to.

Neuroplasticity also influences our emotional patterns. When I was a little girl, my father lost both of his parents around Christmas time, three weeks apart. I vividly remember walking into our living room early one morning to see him leaning over his fish tank, quietly crying. I felt the sorrow that weighed so heavily on his heart at what was supposed to be such a festive and joyful time of year. Every year since, around the holidays, that melancholy follows him. What's interesting is that, every year, I also feel this sort of low frequency melancholy, yet I didn't directly experience his loss. Feeling his sadness so long ago likely imprinted a memory in me, a feeling that is a neural pathway I can't seem to shake (emotional tagging).

On a lighter note, I've had the great blessing and privilege of coaching many people to leverage the power of neuroplasticity and make drastic positive change in their lives: better managing stress, resiliently facing setbacks; losing 100 pounds; completing their first spin class;

rising to their leadership roles with confidence and clarity; weaning off of a long-time medication; learning how to share their heart with a loved one and create intimacy for the first time in years; quitting smoking and taking up triathlons; learning to set and hold boundaries to be better parents and partners.

I love the way neuroscientist and author of *Switch On Your Brain*, Dr. Caroline Leaf, puts it: "Thoughts are real, physical things that occupy mental real estate. Moment by moment, every day, you are changing the structure of your brain through your thinking. When we hope, it is an activity of the mind that changes the structure of our brain in a positive and normal direction."[10] Even learning to hope and feel more empowered is leveraging neuroplasticity for growth in your life.

Neuroplasticity is a powerful process, but it doesn't come without some discomfort. Like building any muscle, it can be tough and take time. But eventually, with practice, it becomes effortless and even unconscious…one day, it just "clicks," a deep, well-worn pattern.

LESSON 5: A STRESS PERSONALITY IS BORN

So, here's where things get really, *really* interesting. What researchers have found is that much like the well-worn patterns of thought, emotion, and behavior we have in our everyday lives—our habits—*how we experience stress is **no different**.*

Remember that I said when we are experiencing a threat our thoughts, behaviors, and emotions are not within our control…but somehow, in some situations, you still tend to show up the same way every time…or like, all the time?

Let's take my older sister, for example. Any of us family members could bet our life savings that Jen would curse up a storm if that truck I mentioned earlier had cut *her* off (that's the Miami driver in her…see and I said I wouldn't name names). It's kind of her thing, and gives me a good laugh any time I'm chatting with her on her commute home.

Or take me and my patterns: When my son walks out into traffic like a lost lamb, I instinctually grab him of course. But then, my short temper finds its way to the words coming out of my mouth no matter how patient I try to stay, followed by "I give up" childish thoughts and behavior, completed by a nice little internal self-attack on my parenting skills and self-worth. It goes something like this: *"Ryder, are you serious? STOP AT THE CURB AND LOOK BOTH WAYS! Why is this so hard?!"* (Inner dialogue: *I give up, this isn't even fun anymore, I want to go home…and seriously what kind of mother am I that this incredibly intelligent kid can't learn basic survival skills?*)

And it doesn't stop with parenting. I'm the same way *Every. Single. Time.* When work gets hard, when I have a bone to pick with my husband, when I receive constructive feedback from a colleague or friend. Every time, I avoid addressing it. It's like I'm the same 11-year-old, bloody-kneed kid wishing to run away and avoid the discomfort and shame all over again.

These *stress patterns* eventually become deeply embedded and persistent thoughts, emotions, and behaviors we default to automatically—a *stress personality*.

Over the years our stress personality develops through many variables:

- Previous heightened emotional experiences (hello, Donut Incident). Researchers have called these many names over the years: hot spots, gremlins, demons, the unconscious, patterns, emotional tags, etc. Whatever you call them— they stick (thanks, hippocampus). We all have these life-shaping moments.

- Family, parents, and caregivers—how did they model stress for us as children? This plays a *major* role.

- Community, schools, culture/geography, race, family and heritage, religion, and spiritual practices.

- Traumatic experiences.

- Education.

- Our back story (what happened to you that shaped who you are today?).

- Genetics: here's an interesting fact: Even though the other factors play a major role here, many of which are largely under our control, research on epigenetics has found that a small part of our embedded neural pathways may be related to a specific incident of stress when you were in utero, which you inherited from a parent, or perhaps even epigenetic transmission from previous generations.[11]

- Even our current and past work environments can influence these patterns. Think about bosses, coworkers, organizational culture. How is crisis, change, or urgency handled? How are you told to feel through others' actions, words, or energy? Are bosses vulnerable and courageous and open, or buttoned up and hard to read? Is the balance between work and home encouraged or discouraged?

- All this shapes how we show up under stress.

Stress personalities are a lot like (and influenced by) our regular personalities. Most experts agree that our general personality in life is developed over time through inherited traits, temperament (demeanor, energy levels, mood, whether we're extroverted or introverted), beliefs, values—who you are is a result of some modeling and reinforcement of behaviors and some innate traits.

The interesting part is, because this concept of neuroplasticity is so unique to each of our individual brains, experiences, and environments, *we don't all create the same patterns*. In other words, we don't all show up the same way when we are experiencing stress. And that's cool, actually. We perform better as individuals, teams, and organizations when we embrace our diverse stress personalities.

When we're not aware of our emotions, behaviors, and thoughts in the moment, these stress personalities of ours can impact our ability to perform at a high potential at work and at home in significant ways— not just as individuals but as partners, couples, families, and teams, and even our mental health.[12]

We're going to explore these stress personalities together, because here's the greatest takeaway about a stress personality: We *can* build our awareness of how we show up under stress and gain better control of our thoughts, emotions, and behaviors. We *can* use insight, reflection, training, and neuroplasticity to do so, and create *new* neural pathways that support better management of our stress response and stress personality.

How do you do this? How do you get to know your stress personality, and what do you *do* about it? I'm not going to make you wait—it's time in Chapter 3 to give you the solution before you even know your stress personality.

TL:DR

+ We all have a stress response: fight or flight, and then rest and digest.

+ When we're stressed, our thoughts, emotions, and behaviors are out of our control.

+ Our *habits* (including our unconscious actions, thoughts, emotions, behaviors, beliefs, etc.) are the result of neuroplasticity, or the process of creating new neural pathways in the brain.

+ Every thought, emotion, and behavior that you experience when stressed is a particular neural pathway you've developed over time.

+ We're all differently wired...we all have a different *stress personality*.

+ Learning to redirect negative energy, behaviors, emotions, and thoughts in the moment is a trainable skill that helps us get back into the driver's seat of our stress personality.

3

THE SOLUTION—
STRESS RESET

I'm going to do things a little backward and give you the solution *now* to gaining better control of your stress personality and the negative stress in your life…before you even know your stress personality.

Why?

Because I want you to have the answer in your back pocket when you dive in to discover your unique stress personality and create *your* personal toolkit as you read. Why make you flip back and forth? Let's put the cart before the horse: you can read each chapter, the solutions that work best for each, and cherry pick the ones you feel will help most.

So, here we go—*the solution is a* **Stress Reset**.

We took a deep dive into the physiology, psychology, and biology of the stress response and the stress personality in the last chapter, but here's the highlight reel:

- [ ] Our emotions, thoughts, and behaviors are *automatic, reactive, and out of our control.*

- [ ] Stress in the absence of recovery is overtraining. *We need recovery.*

- [ ] We all have unique, persistent, default patterns of emotion, thought, and behavior under stress: a *stress personality.*

Now, here's the final fundamental point:

☐ We can *train our brain* (neuroplasticity) and build better awareness in moments of stress to close the gap between reaction (fight or flight) and response (rest and digest).

But we need some sort of cue or intervention to trigger the rest and digest phase of the stress response to close that gap more quickly. Can we motivate our nervous system to regulate and come back to homeostasis? Better yet, can we use this strategy *ahead of time* to even prevent a stressful situation in the first place?

Yes, we can do both. This is where the *Stress Reset* comes in.

A Stress Reset is an action, thought, saying, regular practice, ritual, or other strategy intended to create s p a c e between your reaction to stress and your response.

It's a tool you brandish from your toolbelt right there in the moment of need to build a barrier between your stress personality and the version of yourself you hope to be in moments of stress. The Stress Reset is a direct, intentional addressing of your brain's need for balance—a way to help the brain recover more quickly.

A deep breath, a saying, an image, a walk, are all Stress Resets. Even simply *acknowledging* your stress personality is in and of itself a Stress Reset. Simply thinking, *Hmmm…I think my Runner self is coming out in this situation*, might be enough space to start being more intentional.

Some Stress Resets are habits you put into place *outside* of stressful moments to strengthen your ability to call upon them in the moment of need; others you use right in that moment.

THE SCIENCE BEHIND THE STRESS RESET

Remember, if we're going to stress (we are, it's part of life for better or worse) we need recovery. We can be intentional about it (resilience, awareness), or our body can find another way (reactivity, burnout). The science behind the Stress Reset brings our neuroplasticity conversation full-circle: we're creating a new habit—forging a new neural pathway to: 1) recognize you're stressed in the moment; and 2) take control of it through your arsenal of Stress Reset strategies. Eventually this will all happen without much effort.

In other words, we're going to *automatize resilience*.

HOW TO CHOOSE THE BEST STRESS RESET STRATEGIES

Which strategy you choose depends on your unique stress personality. Why? Because different persistent neural pathways run through and impact different areas of the brain; so, a Stress Reset might work better for one "symptom" than another.

Ever wondered why certain "self-care" or "stress-relief" strategies your friends or people on social media swear by just don't seem to work for you? I get weary reading articles or watching influencers on TikTok promise life-changing results from "this one, simple daily practice." You may have had a similar experience. You try it, it doesn't stick, and instead you feel exhausted, frustrated, and defeated.

Sometimes trying a new strategy that fails reinforces the false belief that other people can solve their stress issues, but you never will because you (insert limiting belief here: aren't enough, aren't working hard enough, aren't capable, and so on). Maybe it's not that these methods don't work; maybe they just aren't the right fit for your stress personality. Maybe they simply don't address the particular "symptoms" you're experiencing.

Some Stress Resets might be mental (retelling the story of what should be stressful in the first place) and some might be physical (I need to take a quick walk before entering this meeting with a client). The more variety, the better. The greater the alignment to your stress personality, the better—it doesn't need to be "popular" for it to work for you. And it doesn't need to be momentous (it doesn't need to be 60 minutes of meditation to have an incredible impact on your mood and energy; it can be a moment...seconds).

Remember the primary function of the Stress Reset is to *close the stress cycle (recover)* by activating the "rest and digest" phase of the stress response more quickly.

When we make a Stress Reset an automatic process, we expend much less negative energy—physical, mental, emotional, and spiritual—and we start to *expand* our positive energy through this recovery process. So, if stress is energy *out*, then our Stress Reset is energy *in*.

When we have a plan and tools to use, we don't just bounce back faster, we start to *thrive through*. We need Stress Resets that are so embedded in us that they're automatic—our go-to in between life's hectic moments.

Throughout this book, we're going to level up a bit and design *systems* in our daily life to integrate our Stress Reset strategies not only just in moments of stress but *throughout* the day so we can build our capacity ahead of time to manage all stress—good and bad.

This is why I wrote the book: to provide a way for you to collect invaluable data in your life and act on it. You'll do this by reading about how you show up under stress, and then designing systems and strategies to better manage it. You can't unlearn what you're about to learn about yourself, and, as a wise friend of mine, Bill, says: you *can't argue with your own data*.

Let me give you an example of some data I'll *never* unlearn about the need for recovery:

A few years ago, I went to the cardiologist with heart palpitations that were frequent enough to warrant a visit. After her physical exam, the doctor paused and sat back in her chair. She asked how my stress levels were. I responded with a dismissive shrug, "Normal I guess? Like everyone else, I have a lot going on. But," I told her, "I sleep well, I exercise, I eat well…so yeah, I manage it well."

She smiled one of those "bless your heart" smiles your Southern aunt gives you when she recognizes your naivety. I squirmed a bit in my paper gown, awkwardly fiddling with a crack in the vinyl exam chair I was sitting on. I felt seen.

She replied, "So many women come into my office with heart issues later in their lives because they don't acknowledge high stress, or act on it, until it's too late. I mostly see it in working mothers. Could that be it?"

Another awkward pause hung heavily between us.

She continued with such gentleness and genuine relatedness, I nearly teared up.

"Lauren, you're running a business, managing a household, raising two boys, and squeezing in time for exercise…. I don't think you realize how much demand this puts on your body. I'm right there with you; it's a lot. But we get so used to it, or feel ashamed if we complain about it, that we stop seeing it. You must see it to deal with it. Your heart is responding to the stress."

Wow. Talk about a reframe. I was stressing out my heart? *Me?* The "wellness expert" giving advice to others on stress management? (Enter the "shame gremlins."[1])

It hit me right then: I was calling my ability to "perform" at a high potential in life and not let any spinning plates drop *resilience*. But it was far from it—my inner dialogue was not in alignment with my reality. I was a literal *expert* on the subject, but that didn't grant me some de facto resilience.

I think I didn't want to admit that I wasn't managing it well; my ego got in the way. But, boy, was I missing a big piece of the puzzle: awareness and recovery. I rarely paused to check in with myself to make sure things were okay. If I was facing the truth then, I would have admitted that I never felt like I was doing enough, so to keep the plates in the air I avoided addressing the lurking burnout by calling it "resilience." Because I'm a Runner, and that's what we Runners do—avoid. I wore a portable EKG device for a month thanks to my ignorance.

It took heart palpitations and a kind cardiologist to remind me of the importance of recovery in my own life; that it was okay and normal to acknowledge high stress; that some days I had the ability and energy to manage it all, and other days I didn't; that recovery was everything, and I was currently in a pattern of not getting enough of it.

This new awareness helped me take some small steps to reconnect with myself. After some soul searching and reflection, I did two things differently: one, I bought a Whoop watch and started tracking my stress and strain and recovery real-time. And two, I started checking in with myself more often. It was the piece I was missing at that point in my life. I had simply stopped listening…to me.

It did wonders for my health to simply recognize how my body and mind were feeling day-to-day; it was the single greatest shift I've ever made for my own well-being journey.

After this experience, I sat down and created a process out of the shifts I made to share with my clients—and now with you. If you're a rule follower, a Type A, or like my husband whose love language is an Excel spreadsheet, you probably live for a process.

THE GIFT OF PAUSE PROCESS

Acknowledging stress in the moment and acting on that awareness is one of the most difficult skills to master when it comes to building resilience. I like to call this skill *The Gift of Pause*. This is the moment we *acknowledge* our stress personality and watch it play out in action, *ask* ourselves what we need, and then *act* on that need by deploying a Stress Reset type of strategy. It's tough to do, but it's not impossible.

I'll say it again in case you missed it: this is not a trait you're born with; it's a *skill*; a *trainable* skill.

This Gift of Pause builds self-awareness, the single most difficult, and important skill you can build in any area of life. Remember, there is *strong* scientific evidence that people who are more self-aware simply have better lives.

There is no more important skill, in my opinion, than the Gift of Pause. Here's the process broken down:

Gift of Pause = Acknowledge (pause, stillness) + Ask (awareness, connection) + Act (action)

Let's break each down:

Acknowledge

Acknowledging your stress means catching yourself *in a moment of stress*. This is the stillness I was seeking and trained for to better manage my heart health. If you can find this Gift of Pause in a stressful moment, you'll suddenly find yourself *observing your own thoughts and feelings*, viewing them from a 30,000-feet perspective.

Ask

Once you acknowledge that you're experiencing a stressful moment (90% of the effort), it's time to ask what's going on and what you need. This is when you *listen* closely to that inner voice of yours and get *curious* about how you're showing up and what you need. Some thoughts to observe and some questions to ask:

+ *What emotions am I feeling?*

+ *What thoughts are persistent?*

+ *How am I behaving?*

+ *What is this thought/emotion mobilizing me to do? (Stress mobilizes us to do something, right? What is it trying to tell you? Avoid, fight, be right, please, give up, etc.?)*

+ *Is this my norm? Is this my pattern?*

+ *What's different about my environment, the people I'm around, the context in which I find myself? (Notice the patterns and you will notice the personality—we'll get to that one in the next chapter).*

+ *What's the story I'm telling about this situation? Is it serving me well?*

In his book *The Body Keeps the Score*, author and psychiatrist Bessel van der Kolk says, "As I often tell my students, the two most important phrases in therapy, as in yoga, are 'Notice that' and 'What happens next?' Once you start approaching your body with curiosity rather than with fear, everything shifts."[2]

Curiosity is a superpower that we'll cover in the Thriver chapter. In this critical moment in time, we see our own needs, emotions, thoughts, behaviors, and get *curious* about what's going on around us. This small fraction of a moment where you pause to check in—a few seconds at most—is where your transformation will feel most potent.

Act

This final step is simple: once you have all your data, act. At this point, you're (hopefully) armed with pressure-tested, tried and true Stress Resets. You'll take that deep breath; call that friend; turn on that upbeat, positive song. You'll integrate whatever strategy matches your stress personality *and* your needs in the moment.

You'll repeat this process as needed until your system regulates and you'll close the stress response loop, feeling calmer and in control.

Building this Gift of Pause skill will eventually be as instinctive as tying your shoes when you have practiced it enough. I'm only breaking this down into a three-step process so you can understand how and why each stage is important. But the process is fluid, and will flow with ease (neuroplasticity, you rock) when you get it down.

In the Thriver chapter of this book, I provide additional training tools to build the Gift of Pause. With some simple, effective strategies and a little time and consistency, eventually you will catch yourself *in media res*, which is Latin for "in the midst of things." So, hang tight, this training is coming.

Exercise: Start Building Your Toolbelt

Now you know what a Stress Reset is and why it's important, and how it is formed.

So, we're going to get to work on equipping your toolbelt. Yes, before you even know your stress personality! Because I think you already have an idea of what works best for you even if you don't realize it.

Here's an exercise for you: Get out a pen and paper. When you're ready, set a timer for 60 seconds. In that time, make a list of all the ways you *currently* reset, recover, relax, etc. that work for you. In other words, what are you already doing that's working well? I'll be waiting right here.

...

The following are a few Stress Resets you might have written down:

- Listen to music
- Call a friend or loved one
- Journal
- Breathe/meditate
- Exercise
- Pet your dog/snuggle your cat
- Take a walk
- Pray
- Have a snack (healthy or unhealthy)
- Remove yourself from the situation/take a breather
- Get outside in nature
- Pamper yourself (get your nails done, soak in a bathtub, get a massage, etc.)
- Disconnect and veg out on the couch
- Watch/read something funny
- Play a game
- Read a book
- Learn something new
- Listen to a podcast

These are just a few strategies. Did you have any others?

Review the list you just wrote. See how instinctually you know how to regulate already? You already intuitively know what works best for you to recover and reset.

Like I told you before, *you are the solution.*

My hope is that, as you read this book, you identify other Stress Reset strategies that you either haven't thought of before, or haven't tried yet, or never tied to your unique stress personality. By the end of this book, you'll have the skills and training plan needed to get started right away.

Then, you'll train and practice so often that the whole process (Gift of Pause, Stress Reset) is your new default to a stressful situation.

Others' Stress Resets Can Work for You…Steal Shamelessly

One more reminder. As you dive into the main part of this book—the actual Stress Personalities—you might find that a Stress Reset recommended for one stress personality works great for you, but it's not in your chapter. Should you dismiss it? No! Try them all on for size. This isn't exact science (I'll say this often). This is fluid, complex, nuanced, and multidimensional, just like you and your stress. I base the Stress Reset recommendations in each chapter on the *most closely associated* stress personalities and associated areas of the brain most impacted—we're trying to best match the cure with the symptom. But know that you can steal ideas from any other chapters or personalities.

What works for you in one situation might not work in another; what "shouldn't" work for you might be perfect.

The goal is truly to arm you with the tools needed to find a way to quickly reset in the moment you need it and integrate these strategies into your daily life to build resilience for all of life's demands.

FINAL THOUGHTS

Bottom line: we have more control in this area of our life than we might believe. Maybe we can't always control our initial emotions or behaviors in a moment of high stress (hit brakes…get angry…act a fool…), but we *can* close the gap between our *reaction* to stress and our *response* to it. We can also gain control over our *perception* of what's worth stressing over ahead of time, which also stops the stress cycle before it even happens.

Remember, these are all *trainable skills*.

Before we dive into the stress personalities, we need to set some rules; so onto the last chapter in this section.

A quick final disclaimer and call-out: There is no amount of bio-hacks, Stress Resets, positive affirmations, meditations, emotional regulation tips, or coping tricks that will make a true threat or harmful situation feel safe. Our trauma and past experiences can leave deep, difficult imprints on our Reptile Brain, which can trigger us in ways we are often not even aware of. If you're trying a Stress Reset and still feel anxious, stressed, or unsafe, it could be something more persistent. In these cases, I highly recommend seeking professional help like a mental health counselor or psychologist. As we talked about in Chapters 1 and 2, there is stress and then there is "more-than-stress."

I also highly recommend the book *What Happened to You*[3] by Dr. Bruce Perry and Oprah Winfrey to learn more about how trauma can influence even the chemistry and biology of the brain. Just keep in mind that sometimes "doing the work" or "not doing it right enough, the way the influencers say to do it" isn't it at all—sometimes our brain is reacting to a true and real threat, doing its job to keep us safe. *Your body is never working against you*—so listen when it speaks.

This doesn't mean the tools and strategies in this book can't help, so keep trying on different Stress Resets and practicing this Gift of Pause.

Do the work of getting to know yourself under stress. It certainly can't hurt—and is a great practice to share with your therapist, by the way.

TL:DR

+ A Stress Reset is an action, thought, saying, ritual, or other strategy intended to create space between your reaction to stress and your response right there in the moment of need.

+ Some Stress Resets work better for our stress personality than others; the following chapters outline those for you.

+ We are meant to move between periods of stress (high demand) and recovery throughout our days. We actually perform better when we do (what we do in the "time between points" matters a lot when it comes to our performance and resilience).

+ We already have Stress Resets that work; we worked to write them down.

4

THE RULES

The following chapters will explore each stress personality in depth: the different areas of the brain most impacted, the predominant emotions, thoughts, behaviors, challenges, etc. Then, we will explore which Stress Resets work best for those personalities.

Before you navigate the Stress Personality chapters of the book, I want to establish some rules to play by as well as do a quick exercise to help you clarify and narrow down your stress personality.

RULE 1: LOOK FOR THE PATTERNS

This is an important rule—this is where you start. As you read through the Stress Personalities (in any order), *look for the patterns—where your mind, emotions, and actions go **first and most often**.*

You may be thinking, *What does she mean by where my mind goes first and most often?*

On a high stress day, you likely experience *all* of the different stress personalities…maybe even in a matter of minutes! But remember that neuroscience tells us we all have predominant, default patterns—neural pathways—of thought, emotion, and behavior, even beliefs, under stress that we've forged through years of repetition.

For example, I might be angry and irritated (Fighter), I might emotionally shut down (Freezer), or I might be pretty darn resilient and self-reflective (Thriver).

You'll likely see yourself in *all* these stress personalities; but if you spend some time reflecting, you will likely see the patterns emerge around one or two. These are your default—the place you most often go, or the place you tend to go first. Your job is to figure that out.

Exercise: Stress Audit

Part 1: Getting it All on Paper

Let's do a quick exercise to get you started. Take a few minutes and journal about some stressful moments in the last 6-12 months.

Look for memories big and small: both really challenging moments (up for a promotion and didn't get it; a painful divorce; an unexpected financial setback on your goal to buying a house), and the everyday, mundane stressors (how you handled your son's latest detention; your toddler's temper tantrum this morning; your coworker's temper tantrum this afternoon; the long wait at the bank; the rude fan at the football game; the latest request at work from the same person who tries to push extra work your way to get it off his plate; having to call your insurance carrier three times to try and get a prescription covered; *TAXES*).

We're not necessarily looking just for the big, life-shifting or traumatic events, because this book is really about how we show up and manage the everyday stressors of life, the acute and chronic stuff. But we need to think about the big things too. All of it builds awareness.

Let's do some reflection now. Answer these questions:

+ **When you think about moments that really pushed you over the edge, was it the big things that really got you? The little things adding up?**

+ What resources or skills did you use to get through?

+ What gaps do you still have?

+ What stage of life are you in right now? Anything major going on? Are you working? Retired? A new parent? Newly married? Just starting college? Transitioning jobs? Making a move across the country? All of this can influence or at least highlight our stress personality.

+ What are your circumstances? Let's name some realities: How are your relationships? What are your main interests, talents, and skills? What are some limitations you've been facing lately? How is your financial situation? How's your family dynamic? How is your work dynamic?

+ What cross have you been called to bear? What I mean is, looking back on your life so far, what have been the moments of deepest pain and challenge? How did they shape you? How did you change as a result?

Whew! Yes, these are big questions. But they help us better capture the big picture of how you are showing up today, and possibly why.

Part 2: Narrowing Down

Now pick a few of those stressful moments and let's get granular about them. Spend time on this one. When you journal about these moments, *really* take yourself back to each moment and try to recall the details about how you showed up. Bring them back to life: who was there, what time of year was it, how did the room smell, what other situations were you dealing with at the same time?

The following are some prompts and things to consider when journaling:

+ How did you FEEL?

What were the persistent emotions? Try to get *really* specific. For help with this, see the emotion wheel referenced at the end of the book.[1]

+ **How did you ACT?**

What were your behaviors? Did you lash out, throw your hands up? Yell and scream? Slam something down? Walk out of the room? Sigh loudly so that everyone could hear? Retreat or shut down? Lean in and seek to please? Cry? Growl? Put your hands over your face? Grab a snack? Grab your phone and check out? Look for someone to argue with or point fingers at? Stuff it and tell yourself you were being ridiculous? Another way to ask this is, *What did you feel mobilized to do?*

+ **What did you THINK?**

What were the persistent thoughts? Were your thoughts *outwardly* focused on others or more *inwardly* focused on yourself? *He's such an idiot* versus *I'm such an idiot.*

What was the *tone* of those thoughts? Were you encouraging? Discouraging? A coach? A critic? A champion for yourself or others? Were your thoughts rife with *hyperboles and absolutes?* (*I'll **never** be able to get this done; I'll **always** be struggling with my finances; Why does this **always** happen to me?!; Why does he **never** call my name when I raise my hand?!*). One thing about stress personalities in general: you'll likely hear a lot of hyperboles in what you say to others or what you think. You'll likely find yourself thinking and talking in absolutes. And, like politics, religion, diet trends, and other subjects we love to fight over, hyperboles and absolutes are red flags (probably why Obi-Wan Kenobi says in *Star Wars:* "Only a Sith deals in absolutes").

When you hear hyperboles in your thinking or what you say to others, pause and pay close attention: this is your stress personality showing its face. In this moment, you are most likely feeling threatened and in fight or flight. We tend to default to binary, limited, or exaggerated thinking in moments like this. Why? Because our brain can't tell the difference between a saber-toothed tiger and getting stuck in a traffic jam: a threat is a threat. So, look to a variety of memories to really hone in on the patterns. Is there a pattern you can see in different memories/situations and how you thought about them?

+ **What PUTS you into these spaces?**

Another strategy is to ask what triggers you or puts you in these places. Answering this question might help you see some patterns. For example, I really, *really* hate being interrupted; it feels like my voice is being devalued. Being interrupted or ignored puts me immediately into fight or flight mode and rather than speaking up, I tend to back away and not even trying to make myself heard. It triggers my own deeper limiting beliefs of low self-worth, insecurity, and feeling like I'm not enough.

That's just one example but there are many out there: a certain person at work or in your life; a time of year; a holiday; a location; a situation or condition (work deliverables butting up against personal to-dos, an important meeting overlapping your wife's birthday dinner); kids.

What puts you in these spaces and what can that tell you about yourself?

The following are some sample journal entries from clients, used with their permission:

Journal Entry 1: I avoided confrontation with a coworker today...again. He continuously refuses to complete some paperwork for me that I've asked for several times. Eventually we're going to miss our submission deadline because of him. But, instead of confronting him and delivering the right feedback, I avoid, ignore, push off and sometimes do it for him...why on earth would I do that? Fear? I know I need to handle it but I just avoid the situation. I do the same thing when it comes to addressing my high blood pressure. I'm supposed to make an appointment with a nutritionist the doctor referred me to, but I haven't made the appointment yet. I see the pattern here. I've also been working on a slide deck for an upcoming presentation and I can't seem to get it finished. Every time I open it, I see more more that needs to be done with it and I walk away again. I feel like it's not good enough. Perfectionist much? Avoidance much?

Journal Entry 2: I went off on my sister at our parents' house on Thanksgiving. She refused to help with the dishes after the meal and didn't tell her children to help, either. She just sat out back watching her kids toss a baseball and scrolled TikTok like a zombie. I felt frustrated and resentful. I went out back and questioned her parenting and her manners as a guest in our parents' house, and we didn't speak for a week. At the time, Dad was dealing with a biopsy on his pancreas and we were all scared—I felt bad after she left. I was up to my ears in budgets at work and short staffed. I regret how I treated her. I do this all the time—yell first, ask questions later. Always followed by regret and guilt whether I'm in the right or wrong.

Journal Entry 3: Last month I sent a condescending, patronizing email to a coworker and copied the whole team, including our boss. She continued to pass off poorly reviewed, barely edited drafts to others because she knew we'd take the time to polish them up before sending them to leadership. I was angry and felt used and unappreciated. Not just by her but by my boss who never sees her half-assed work. Her laziness is our burden to carry. I regretted sending the email, though…and copying the whole team, especially our boss. I was overloaded with work at the time and my dog was just diagnosed with an untreatable cancer—not only was I having to come to grips with what that meant, I was facing a few thousand in emergency vet bills.

Journal Entry 4: I lost my cool with my husband last week, and my kids. I screamed at them all when I got home and dinner wasn't cleaned up. I felt irritated and unappreciated. At an earlier board meeting, another board member was very disrespectful to me yet again. She questioned my leadership abilities without saying so directly and patronized me for the umpteenth time. I just sat there, like a deer in headlights; just sank lower into my seat and took it. I felt ashamed and inferior. The entire drive home, I questioned my abilities as a leader. I remember I drove slowly and didn't listen to music. I was consumed by self-doubt. Maybe I'm not cut out for this position…maybe I have low self-worth and that's why I can't speak up for myself. But if that's the case, then why did I lash out at home and have no problem exploding on my family?

The more detail you can bring to these memories, the better. Remember, we're searching for clues, gathering data in our own lives.

Keep these journal entries handy—they will also clue us in during Rule 2 and later in the book when we look at how our stress personalities clash with, work with, and interact with others—and where our superpowers lie (yes, we have superpowers in our stress personalities…more on that later).

The goal is to be a Sherlock Holmes in your own life, looking for patterns in the way you showed up in these memories. Remember, you can't argue with your own data.

When you're done journaling, I recommend taking 24 hours away from your journal entries and this book. Sleep on it. When you return, take a high-level look again: which patterns feel more like outliers, and which feel more familiar? Notice the patterns and you'll notice the personality.

One more suggestion: ask your VIPs to give more color to those same memories or offer up new ones. They may not see the whole picture (see Rule 3) but they might help offer a new perspective or surface memories you've forgotten. This might take some vulnerability and courage, though, so be prepared for that conversation. Be mindful that feedback and conversations like these can retrigger our brain's stress response so take lots of deep breaths and breaks if needed; keep an open, curious mind.

RULE 2: STRESS PERSONALITIES ARE OFTEN CONTEXT DEPENDENT

It might sound like a contradiction to Rule 1, but stress personalities are very often *context dependent*. What I mean is, certain people, environments, situations, or even *intensities* of stress might bring out different patterns and personalities.

Why does this happen? Remember the process of emotional tagging? This is when your brain attaches certain emotions to certain memories, for better or worse. This can lead to misleading patterns for future experiences because we start to tell a story about how we should feel in certain situations, and those stories can become powerful influencers of our behaviors. For example, if my first trip to the airport resulted in flight delays and cancellations, the next time I had a flight to catch I might arrive at the airport in fight or flight before I even stepped into the terminal. Or, if I had a bad experience with a coworker one time, I might feel triggered and anxious every time I was around that person thereafter.

Here are some questions to consider:

+ How do you respond to conflict/crisis/change at work versus at home?
+ How do the people around you influence your behavior, thoughts, or emotions (if at all)?

- Are there situations or intensities of stress that cause you to show up differently?

- What's different in your environment? Who are you around or what are you doing in this memory versus others to cause you to show up differently?

Revisit your journal entry memories and ask yourself these questions. Look for differences, if there are any, and similarities. Here are some examples in my life:

- I tend to question my abilities as a business owner when I'm alone but not when I'm with the team—I feel much more resilient when surrounded by others.

- I tend to shy away and "run" rather than face confrontations with family but not as intensely with acquaintances or strangers (Great Donut Incident of 1993 case in point).

- "Big" stressful events rarely faze me, but the smaller things trigger me like crazy (in other words the intensity of the event has a strangely inverse relationship to the intensity of my stress personality). When my son broke his arm at the skatepark, I was focused, action-oriented, and cool as a cucumber. If we're moving, or traveling overseas, I'm good. But if a client asks for a sudden large request and I have three other urgent tasks at the same time? My heart rate goes through the roof and I emotionally flee faster than Roadrunner.

- One of the women I work with is calm and collected when it comes to managing her team, but when one particular person—a peer—shows up to a meeting, she immediately starts to second guess her abilities and competency; her resilience flies out the window. Strangely enough this person never did anything to her—the peer is lovely, capable, confident, and thriving (the Thriver personality triggers this colleague of mine and her insecurities).

+ A client of mine was a very different person during the pandemic—composed, focused—but emotionally shut down in order to lead her team; normally, though, under everyday stress she's completely different. We learned this through our work together.

This isn't always the case: I have other clients and friends who are the *same exact stress personality* whether they're standing on a stage in front of 500 work colleagues or at home with family or finding out their flight was canceled. Some people have the same stress personality no matter their environment or what's happening around them; we're all different.

Just remember that the goal isn't to box yourself into one personality, it's to find patterns based on where you are, who you're with, and what is happening around you. If that's one stress personality, great; if it's two or even maybe three, okay then. Don't forget Rule 1: look for the patterns and where you go first and most often.

My suggestion is to try to narrow it down the best you can. Think about a variety of memories in different contexts and see if you can identify some patterns. My guess is one or two are likely your default.

RULE 3: DO NOT DIAGNOSE OTHERS

This is a tough one.

Trust me. It will be *so* tempting to run to your partner in the other room and shove sections of this book in their face (*Oh, my gosh, LOOK, this is so YOU!*) or to snicker at the thought of a coworker you are just *convinced* is a Fighter, and all you want to do now is impart your newly acquired wisdom and show her the way through some Stress Resets for Fighters.

Hang on there, Yoda.

One of the greatest traps of the mind is believing what our eyes see. Our brains have an incredible ability to tell stories and fill in missing gaps in information, whether the stories are true or not (we'll hit this one hard soon).

Though we can learn a lot from someone's actions, how someone behaves on the outside doesn't always betray how they feel and what they're thinking on the inside.

Think about it: How often do you mask how you're feeling and thinking around others; *especially* at work? How often do you have a tough day and decide it's not worth bringing it up to your spouse?

We can't possibly know how others are feeling and thinking unless they talk to us about it. So, focus on yourself.

Okay, and maybe your partner and your best friend. I'll allow it.

My suggestion? Read this book through, *then* talk about it with the VIPs in your life. Better yet, read it together. Get a friend group or work group to read it together and talk about it. The more you talk about and engage with the content, the deeper you'll learn it and the more you'll learn about yourself, and others too, in the process. It's a win-win.

RULE 4: ENJOY THE PROCESS!

This one is simple: This is meant to be awareness-building and *fun*. You may not spot your stress personality right away. Don't stress it! (See what I did there?) *This isn't an exact science—it's meant to be fun, fluid, low-stress, and reflective.* If there was a clear-cut answer, it would be out there in the literature, and there would be a quick fix that worked for us. But no—we are so beautifully nuanced and complex. This is more about the journey than a destination. My hope is that you have fun reading this, learning about yourself, and then continue to notice, process, reflect, learn, and notice some more after you finish.

HOW TO USE THE NEXT SECTION

Okay, that's it! Short and sweet. The following chapters detail eight Stress Personalities. This isn't an exhaustive list; there might be other personalities, so there's a chance yours isn't quite in one of these eight. Who knows, you might invent one along the way! If you do, I want to hear about it.

Navigate these personalities at your own pace. You can read straight through, or you can flip first to the ones which feel right. Each has their own Stress Reset recommendations and takes a deeper dive into brain science.

Each chapter has the following sections:

OPENING

Defining the Stress Personality. What emotions, behaviors, thoughts, etc. are most persistent.

UNDER THE HOOD

Getting to the root of the brain science behind this stress personality.

EXERCISES

Short, awareness-building exercises to get to know this personality, especially if you think it's you!

STRESS PERSONALITY SUPERPOWER

This one I need to break down. Remember that stress is neither good nor bad. *Stress is simply our brain's reaction to a perceived threat.* It can be good, or it can be bad; the same experience can be perceived as a threat to me, and an invitation for growth to someone else. Heck, I can see the same experience differently based on the day, right?

My point—the goal of these chapters isn't to call out how messed up and broken we are under stress and pick us apart. Quite the contrary—the goal is to build *awareness* of who we are under stress so we can work to better control how we experience stress and close that gap between reaction and response.

With that in mind, consider this: *What if there were parts of our stress personality that could actually work for us? Could this be considered our stress personality superpower?*

Two questions to ask yourself during this discovery are:

1. What is my stress personality mobilizing me to do?

2. What superpower lies within my stress personality?

If you spend time thinking about it, you'll discover the great power behind your stress personality and the value you bring to those around you not despite your stress personality, but *because* of it.

So, each chapter has a section on superpowers. They might not be exhaustive, but I hope to at least get you started on thinking about your own unique superpowers.

WATCHOUTS

This is where your stress personality might get you in some trouble with yourself or others, and how we might justify our stress personalities to others.

STRESS RESETS FOR YOUR PERSONALITY

This section unpacks Stress Reset strategies that work best for your unique stress personality. The goal of this section is to highlight the Stress Resets that work best for this Stress Personality. If it isn't your stress personality but you're reading the chapter anyway, these Stress Resets can also work for you! But based on the research, they are well-suited for this Stress Personality.

Just like the sorting hat ceremony at Hogwarts, it's time to find your stress personality. And now, the book really begins.

Enjoy!

TL:DR

- ✦ Stress personalities can be context dependent; look for patterns but also for how you might show up differently based on context, environment, people, places, situations, or intensities of stress.

- ✦ Behaviors on the outside don't always reflect what's going on inside; don't diagnose others.

- ✦ Enjoy the process of self-discovery.

PART II

STRESS

PERSONALITIES

5

THE FIGHTER

Imagine you're on the board of a local nonprofit you care a lot about, and you were assigned as the committee chair for a big annual golf tournament. You've spent the last several months finding sponsors, designing the website, securing donations and raffle prizes, organizing volunteers, developing and implementing the day of operations and schedule for the week leading up to the event.

Now you're two weeks out: your committee team is *exhausted*—they were stretched to begin with, all having their own jobs and lives on top of this event, but this big push toward the end nearly put them over the limit. You're at work and it's the end of the day when you jump onto the board meeting call to present your plan. Things should be smooth sailing from here...except they're not. The board responds that they aren't satisfied. They want you to make several changes this close to crunch time *and* cut your budget. They give you a laundry list of recommendations for changes to the master plan.

You are *furious*—your face flushes, your heart races, and you're shaking with anger. Why didn't they give you these recommendations *months* earlier and not at the last minute? You're short and rude with the board the rest of the meeting. The committee is texting you on a sidebar conversation with angry face emojis and choice words; it's all you can do to remain composed.

On the way home, you feel frenzied and in a hurry. You honk at cars and mentally draft an angry email to your board president. You arrive home to find that your teenage son hasn't done his chores—and he receives the wrath you intended for your board president. You struggle to focus through dinner and are short with the entire family all evening. In fact, you take your anger out on everyone in the house at one point or another, and they start to tiptoe around you the rest of the night. You go to bed that night heavy with guilt, shame, and exhaustion; you wish you would have handled the whole afternoon better.

This was the story of a former client. Though this story involves a last-minute change that totally justified her anger, what she noticed after we talked it through was that she showed up this way in most situations that didn't go her way and *even when the fault was her own*. She simply got *angry* and she lost control of her behavior. Interestingly, most of the time she could stay relatively buttoned up in a professional setting, but often took it out at home on those she was most comfortable with or in the form of gossip, back channeling, and passive aggressive behaviors at work. In fact, she realized she had regular friction or issues with others at work. Her husband's main gripe at home was her short fuse and quickness to blame and finger point. She really wanted to change all of this.

She was a Fighter.

If you have a Fighter Stress Personality, the focus of your emotions, thoughts, and behaviors is likely *outward* toward people or things around you. You don't run from stress—you face it, but not usually in a mindful or compassionate way. Sometimes anger is misdirected when you can't express it directly to the people you want to (like this frustrating nonprofit board), and sometimes it's expressed in other more subtle but still harmful ways.

Anger is the opposite of a Freezer or Runner. There is a strong urge to *act* and squash the threat by any means necessary. Whether we feel irritated, full of rage, disgusted, or bottle it all up...we are *acting*. I think of the old cartoon character Katie Kaboom from the animated Animaniacs Warner Brothers show. Katie was a teenage girl whose anger would build and build, and her family tiptoed around her emotions until something set her off—then the entire house and neighborhood would explode in a mushroom cloud.

I think we've all been there. But for the Fighter, this happens more often than the rest of us; it's their first line of defense.

EMOTIONS OF A FIGHTER

The primary emotion of a Fighter is usually anger, and that anger can range from mild irritation to complete lack of control, fury, and rage depending on the person or the situation. A Fighter also tends to feel emotions like *short temperedness, resentment, vengefulness, or aggression* when stressed. In those moments it probably becomes hard to practice empathy, compassion, active listening, introspection, or curiosity and understanding. Fighters can also feel secondhand emotions like *sadness, embarrassment, guilt, loneliness, or regret*—as well as feeling dramatic, temperamental, or out of control.

THOUGHTS OF A FIGHTER

If you think you may be a Fighter, my guess is your *thoughts* are more self-protective in nature. You may think, *It's not my fault, it's yours and here's why, or why does this always happen to me?* My guess is you are usually the victim or the one who's right, and the rest of the world can buzz off.

In a fight or flight moment your worldview can get very small and leave little room for gray areas or nuances. This is where justifications and stories can push through. So you might think or say things like:

+ **There is injustice here and I aim to prove it.**
+ **I need to defend (this person or myself).**

- You want to challenge me? Bring it on!
- You want to criticize me? Let me tell you something about you…(rolls up sleeves, puts on boxing gloves).
- Don't tell me what to do!
- Something isn't aligned with my values therefore I need to make it right or call it out.
- Not my problem—you handle it.
- Just do it my way and there's no issue.
- Why can't you be more _____ (like me, of course)?
- I can do what I want and no one can tell me otherwise.
- You wouldn't understand (or other comments to push someone away).
- Because I said so.
- Prove it (that you're on my side).
- You're with me or against me.
- I don't trust you.

BEHAVIORS OF A FIGHTER

Here's what you might do when you're stressed:

- Yell or scream
- Use passive aggressive language or "cold shouldering" to get your point across
- Throw your hands up
- Slam doors, slam things around
- Bottle it up inside and explode later

- Feel tense, anxious, have a racing heart, elevated blood pressure, shakiness…"seeing red," as they say.
- Act impulsively
- Speak up, blame, shame others, or bark back without thinking
- Make decisions you later regret
- Assume the worst
- Deflect blame or responsibility
- Brood and stay quiet
- Play the victim or martyr
- Push people away, pout, sulk
- Justify
- Covet, compare, pick apart, or break someone down
- Gossip

Fighters aren't bad people and they can be angry for a good reason. Contrary to what you might think or how they come across, Fighters are usually *very* anchored in a sense of right and wrong, clear on their values, and justice is important to them. So you also might zero in and get fixated on making things right for others or making sure others feel you're right.

Fighters can also be Type A personality types who get "more-Type-A-ish" under stress. Not necessarily angry or aggressive, but uptight, irritated, and have trouble calming down. They might not be angry per se, but will buzz with high negative energy nonetheless.

The fight response is *so* intense and *so* powerful that our thoughts, behaviors, and emotions are totally hijacked, which can drain us physically, emotionally, mentally, and spiritually. *Fighter personalities tend to expend large amounts of negative energy, often followed by a crash, or feelings of guilt, regret, or exhaustion.*

These are the types who end up with heart disease, by the way. I read a fascinating story about the "Type A behavior" in one of my favorite books on stress, *Why Zebras Don't Get Ulcers: The Acclaimed Guide to Stress, Stress-related Diseases, and Coping* by American researcher Robert Sapolsky. He shared the story of a cardiologist in the 1950s by the name of Dr. Meyer Friedman who was spending a fortune having the chairs in his waiting room reupholstered. For some odd reason, the armrests and seat cushions were torn and tattered on every chair, as if patients were sitting on the edges of their seats fidgeting and clawing at the armrests. The upholsterer noted to Dr. Friedman he'd never seen anything like it—chairs don't typically wear out that way.

At first Dr. Friedman brushed it off, but a few years later he realized just how insightful the upholsterer's observation was—"Type A" people were on the edge, irritable, and chronically stressed, which had a direct link to their inevitable cardiovascular diseases and landed them in Dr. Friedman's office.[1]

So, Type A personalities out there: Are you a Fighter? Can you see yourself in that chair when you're stressed?

One more thing: Fighters usually prefer the company of Pleasers or Runners—those who would rather avoid or oblige when stressed (because otherwise it's WWIII if you confront a Fighter in the moment, right?).

THE FIGHT PERSONALITY: UNDER THE HOOD

What's the brain science behind a Fighter personality?

Remember that, like all stress personalities, being a Fighter is a *learned* reaction. Things like past experiences, genetics, culture, geography, modeling, you name it, may have taught this personality to fight in order to protect itself and those around it.

Recall that every time our brain experiences a threat, our stress response (fight or flight response) is activated. When a Fighter experiences a perceived threat, though, the fight response is exacerbated or is harder to shake because for whatever reason, "fighting" becomes their default reaction to threat.

The main characters in the fight or flight response are the amygdala and hypothalamus, (two specific areas of the Reptile/Emotional Brains triggered when we perceive a threat). Now, we didn't go too deeply in Chapter 2, but as part of the stress response, catecholamines and hormones like adrenaline, noradrenaline, and cortisol are released to give us a burst of energy to help us *take immediate action*—in the Fighter's case, well, fight.

Where does the Fighter personality come from?

The Fighter personality may be more hereditary than we think, but that doesn't mean it's *predominantly* hereditary. Like many (maybe all?) of the stress personalities, it likely develops because of modeling in childhood and/or deep-rooted fears, identities, or beliefs that drive behaviors to self-protect and attack.

If I had to guess, I'd imagine many Fighters grow up in a Fighter home or have faced some difficult circumstance or circumstances that have shaped and molded their personality through the years, but I have no research to support that except my many conversations with Fighter personalities. Perhaps they:

- Grew up in an unsafe environment or experienced trauma as a kid; fighting is a way to feel safe and squash the threat.

- Have parents who were Fighters and they are modeling what they see.

- Have parents who were less involved, self-centered, negligent, or maybe just worked a lot and weren't really around, so the Fighter became temperamental as a strategy to be seen and heard and in control in an environment where they were invisible, neglected, or felt unseen.

+ Could be reactive to rejection, judgment upon them, exclusion, or isolation.

+ Are fiercely protective of others, possessing a keen eye for injustice and wrongdoing.

If you look at the research on anger, anger is often an emotion triggered by some deeper (possibly perceived) violation of our values or beliefs; when we simply cannot get something we feel we should have (connection, respect, validation, justice for ourselves or others, etc.). We also express it when we're fixating on others because it's easier than dealing with the discomfort, fear, uncertainty within; we tend to lash outward and seek to blame others in a state like this.

Think about it: here are some deeper beliefs or identities that could be driving a Fighter to default the way they do:

Belief	Reality
The world is out to get me.	You learned this from your parents or caregivers.
Perfection is a non-negotiable.	You self-protect for fear of judgment or being really "seen."
I alone am responsible for fixing the world's problems. No one will help me, and I can't trust them to.	Strong urge to fix a situation, and quickly, for others or yourself (learned from parents/caregivers/past experiences of being hurt or betrayed).
I need to hurt people before they can hurt me.	Because hurt people hurt people; this is self-protection and an attempt to control the situation. Vulnerability or connection is too difficult (this is a difficult truth to face. If this one gave you a bit of a gut punch, pause and process).
It's all their fault. Everyone else is wrong (if they don't see it my way) and I need to prove that they are.	You are avoiding discomfort so you fixate on others instead of dealing with your discomfort because that feels easier. Self-protection from Imposter Syndrome, lack of self-awareness, fear of judgment, deeper insecurities, etc.

	Reality check: You think they're better than you because you feel that way deep down. And
The world is after me; people think they're better than me.	that is hard or impossible to process. So, the story spins.
There is a true and real and justified reason for my anger, and I need to offload it.	There really is a true and real and justified reason for your anger and you need to offload it (yes, this can be true!).
No belief; simply high anxiety bubbling up.	High arousal, high negative energy needs to go somewhere so you release it as anger and rage.

Do any of these resonate with you/your thoughts?

Again, we've all been here at some point. It's important to call this out: being angry here and there *doesn't make you a Fighter.* Losing your cool after a long day *doesn't make you a Fighter.* As the profoundly wise Austrian psychiatrist and Holocaust survivor Viktor Frankl said, "An abnormal reaction to an abnormal situation is normal behavior."

Blowing your top is sometimes exactly what is needed—that's not what we're dealing with here. The difference is for Fighters, this reaction is what they default to: where they go first and most often, and for situations which don't always justify it.

Regardless of the backstory, your brain sends the message to be angry, or challenge the person or circumstance; to live in a hyper-aroused, panicked "fight" state. After all, fear shrinks the brain, which isn't a very productive place to be. Why? Because anger creates disconnection, hurt, and disengagement, and leads us to behave in ways we don't want our children or employees to model.

EXERCISES TO UNDERSTAND THE FIGHTER PERSONALITY

The following are three exercises to help you build awareness and get to know your Fighter personality a little better:

Exercise 1: What's Under Your Fighter Emotion?

Pull out the exercise I asked you to complete in the previous chapter where you looked for patterns in past stressful experiences. If you believe it was a Fighter personality coming through, let's go deeper.

Fill in the sentence stem: *"I feel angry, but the truth is I also feel*

_____

_____

_____ *."*

See if you can find another emotion lurking underneath. Can you get closer to the root of *why* you're feeling that Fighter emotion? Don't forget: sometimes, we're simply upset, and that's okay too; it can be *yes, and…* you'll hear me say that a lot.

You can use the following list of emotions[2] to fill in the sentence stem:

+ Anxiety

+ Fear

+ Rejection

+ Loneliness

+ Depression

+ Embarrassment

- Humiliation
- Overwhelming stress
- Helplessness
- Outrage at injustice
- Jealousy
- Shame
- Guilt
- Isolation
- Sadness
- Hurt
- Grief
- Confusion
- Frustration
- Worry
- Disappointment

Exercise 2: Shame Gremlin Mining

In her book, *Atlas of the Heart*, Brené Brown has an eye-opening exercise which I think applies well enough to the Fighter personality, because the fight response is often so closely related to fear and shame.

Fill in the sentence stem: *"It's really important for me **not** to be perceived as* _____ *."*

When I completed this exercise, my words were "selfish," "inept," and "unempathetic." I realized I worry about being perceived as uncaring, incompetent, or not smart enough. These are obviously triggers for me that could spark my stress personality (a Runner).

Exercise 3: Values Mining

Here is one more exercise to unearth some additional insight:

Fill in the sentence stem: *"The two core values most important to me are:*

_____

and

_____."

What are two values—such as integrity, honesty, thoughtfulness, relationships, etc.—that matter the *most* to you?

Then, think about the last few times you were set off and ask yourself, *What was the reason for my anger? Did someone or something violate or butt up against my values?*

For example, my two core values are *service* and *relationships*: both are an important part of my life and guide how I run my house, my business, friendships, and so on. So, it's no surprise when I experience friction in my world, I usually feel like these values are being compromised or challenged. But here's the thing: sometimes I also *unfairly judge* a person's actions *because* my values don't align with theirs. I assume that everyone should value service and relationships above all else or my vision of serving others might not look the same as theirs, which is unfair for me to judge.

Here's a good example of values being challenged:

I had a participant (let's call her Mary) in one of my workshops who valued accountability and integrity but worked with someone (let's call him Carlos) who valued connection and relationships. Mary and Carlos were both leaders on the same team and they had a new hire who was making a lot of mistakes in her first months on the job.

Mary believed that to help the new hire, feedback and accountability needed to be direct, quick, and exact. Carlos, on the other hand, believed that help should look like continual conversations and connecting on a personal level with the new hire to help her feel included and, therefore, more committed to performing at a higher level.

Neither is wrong; both are right. But clearly Mary, who was thankfully brave enough to bring up the situation, was frustrated, irritated, and resentful of Carlos's leadership style. This generated a table discussion between the two and some "aha" moments and brainstorming on how to integrate *both* their value systems and leadership styles to tackle the problem. It was a moment of deeper connection between them.

Knowing your values also helps you process difficult emotions including anger, fear, and hurt. I take all my clients through this exercise, but I placed it here in the Fighter chapter because I believe that Fighters are likely some of the most highly values-driven people. Am I wrong?

WATCHOUTS

Take caution with this stress personality: Fighters can easily disconnect themselves from others in a several ways:

+ **Words *hurt*. Often in a high negative state, Fighters can forget the power of what they say and do and end up having to pick up the pieces. This can create tension, disconnection, strained relationships, distrust, and a whole lot of regret. For my client mentioned at the beginning of the chapter who unloaded on her teenage son because of her nonprofit board, she was unintentionally straining her relationship with her family.**

- As an unchecked Fighter, you might quickly become the one who:

  » Is defensive and unwilling to receive feedback
  » Isn't willing to learn, grow, or admit when they're wrong
  » Snaps at others
  » Jumps to conclusions
  » Gives others the cold shoulder because of assumptions or to make others feel bad
  » Is the rude or inconsiderate person in the room
  » Quickly becomes the gossip, tattletale, or makes others feel they can never measure up
  » Could be known as uncooperative or unproductive, too focused on being wronged
  » Could become known as unreliable or untrustworthy

If this happens, don't give up—as much as words and actions can hurt, they can also heal. There is something very powerful in a little vulnerability, acknowledgment, and ownership. Apologizing and talking through how you're working to improve in this area of your life can reconnect you to the people you might be unintentionally hurting—and it models this behavior for others, especially useful if you're a parent or partner.

FIGHTER SUPERPOWERS

One of the most important things to know about your Fighter personality is that it's not something to be ashamed of or to "fix." *You're not broken*. I think that of all of the eight stress personalities (and others I don't know about yet), Fighters get the worst rap, but have the best intentions.

Fighters are:

+ Fiercely loyal and protective

+ Values-driven and are seldom swayed from those values

+ Knowers of what is right and wrong

+ Seekers of justice

+ Defenders of those who can't defend themselves

+ Great at thinking under pressure

+ Independent and action-oriented

+ Go-getters and go-doers

The following is an example of a real-life Fighter superhero I'm glad to know:

Amber is a client of mine. She runs an alternative high school in California where the most vulnerable, marginalized, and potentially aggressive students are given their last chance before being locked up. These students often come from violent, poverty-stricken, difficult backgrounds and often are either expelled from or have left other schools in the area. Some are teenage parents and most qualify for free lunch; many come from drug or gang backgrounds; and nearly all face or have faced trauma, abuse, and violence in their homes and neighborhoods.

When we started working together during the Covid shutdown, students at Amber's school were in lockdown like all others. But lockdown looked different for these students than it did for most US kids. For many of her students, home was *not* their safe place: home often meant no access to food, exposure to more violence, getting back into former gangs or dangerous circles. For many students, *safe* was school.

So, Amber and her staff would go out of their way on their own personal time and expense to check in on students and their parents and deliver meals as often as possible. Her challenge was more than adjusting instruction plans and ever-changing Covid procedures: it was keeping her kids fed and out of immediate danger.

During that shutdown, Amber was *furious*. She was told at one point she couldn't visit homes nor use funding or school transportation to deliver meals (she did anyway). She was angry at the limitations of the lockdown, and about the lockdown itself...the state of the world. Who wasn't?

When I started working with Amber, we learned very quickly that she was a Fighter. Amber would get *so angry* at anyone who risked getting in the way of her students' access to support and a fair opportunity. She was angry at the way her students are marginalized and treated, at the social unrest and prejudice in our world today, and at the cards her "kids" have been dealt. But it bled over into other areas of her life; whether it was the board cutting budgets, a staff member unfairly doling out punishment, a peer looking at her wrong in a meeting, a district leader disrespecting or undermining her leadership or decisions, a parent failing to show up for their kid, she would see red and act before thinking—and that reaction would get her in trouble.

Let's peek under the hood of what was underneath the anger for Amber: Amber grew up with trauma, abuse, and violence in her own life. Fighting was all she knew. Fighting and defensiveness were a *safe* place for her, and connection, vulnerability, and self-awareness were the unsafe place, just like her "kids." In fact, Amber often seemed to *like* to fight and debate and be angry because it was safe and familiar. When we peeled back the layers, we realized that she also had some deeper feelings of inadequacy in her role—she felt that others didn't respect her authority because she ran an alternative school (notoriously regarded as "inferior than" in some circles and often given less attention, funding, and respect).

Imposter Syndrome was another culprit. Generally, Amber didn't like to be told what to do and felt she needed to hustle for her worth and prove herself. Her path to leadership and a stable life was incredibly difficult; and she used it as a defense shield, particularly toward those in power above her.

When it came to other stressors in her personal life—her children, her marriage, her physical health—she was a Freezer personality. She simply shut down at the thought of connection and intimacy and didn't want to deal with it. So her stress personality was also context dependent.

Knowing all of this, tell me Amber is an "angry person;" tell me she acted irrationally breaking the rules and bringing food and support to her kids during the shutdown.

Of course not.

Amber is a great example of a Fighter personality superpower: she's highly regarded as an incredible leader in her area who fights fiercely for her kids to have a chance in life. Her school has seen an incredible transformation under her leadership.

Amber used her anger during the Covid shutdown to *act*. She channeled it for good and her behaviors were in support of her deepest values—her superpower.

That doesn't mean her quick temper doesn't get her in trouble. She was regarded as a fiercely protective, incredible leader by her staff, but feedback from her superiors revealed that she lacked patience, had trouble holding her tongue, and was too quick-tempered.

So, Amber had work to do. Through some deeper work together and months of insight, reflection, and conversation, Amber realized that her Fighter personality was triggered when her most precious values were threatened—sometimes that didn't serve her well, and sometimes it did. It helped her get out of poverty and violence, attend college, rise in the ranks, and today she continues to excel at her job in so many ways. She's learned to harness anger for good by really connecting with her values, but also learning to create pause between her reaction and a response. More on that soon.

So, before you write the Fighter personality type off as someone you don't want around, keep in mind, this personality is a *go-getter*. People with this stress personality fight for what they need and are often quick on their feet in a confrontation. Thinking quick on your feet is a great feature for a Fighter, someone we need on our side to support, protect, and *do* rather than *avoid*.

The lovely movie *A Beautiful Day in the Neighborhood* is about Lloyd Vogel, a broken, angry investigative journalist interviewing the one and only Mr. Rogers. Throughout the movie (spoiler alert) you learn that at a young age, Lloyd's father abandoned him, his sister, and his dying mother, and he carried the hurt and anger of it into his adult life. He is skeptical and frustrated with Mr. Rogers's relentless positivity, joy, and uplifting spirit.

Lloyd is a Fighter.

In one scene in a restaurant, Lloyd tells Mr. Rogers he is broken.

Mr. Rogers shares a heartwarming reply: "I don't think you're broken, Lloyd," he says. "I know you're a man of conviction. A person who knows the difference between what is wrong and what is right. Try to remember that your relationship with your father also helped to shape those parts. He helped you become what you are."

What a beautiful thought—the pain, trauma, hurt, fear, uncertainty, and discomfort we carried through life can also be the superpowers you give back to the world.

One of my favorite quotes about anger is from the book mentioned earlier, Brené Brown's *Atlas of the Heart*. She writes, "Anger is a catalyst. Holding on to it will make us exhausted and sick. Internalizing it will take away our joy and spirit: externalizing anger will make us less effective in our attempts to create change and forge connection. It's an emotion we need to transform into something life-giving: courage, love, change, compassion, and justice."

So, how can you transform your Fighter personality in such a way that it catalyzes growth, connects you to your values, and can be your superpower most of the time?

It starts with recognizing when your anger is serving you well, or not. In fact, it's a good general rule for every stress personality:

Is my stress personality serving me well at this moment, or not? If not, how can I transform it?

If you're a Fighter, remember that fighting *is also your superpower*, but it doesn't always serve you well. There isn't a sweeping rule—every decision requires intuition and thoughtful reflection. Sound familiar? This is your Gift of Pause process, applied.

Major disclaimer on emotional regulation and "fixing" negative emotions: I want to be very, very careful here not to send the message that anger is an emotion we *shouldn't* feel. "Should" is a dangerous word, a word that too often our inner voice will throw out to reinforce self-limiting beliefs about ourselves and the world. Quite the opposite—anger is very useful. It's a mobilizer and often justified; sometimes it mobilizes us for worse, sure, but sometimes for the better.

Please know this and don't miss it: *All emotions are valid.* And the skill and promise of better "emotional regulation" is *not* learning to generate positive emotions to *replace* negative emotions with more calm, joy, peace.

No, no, no. Just no.

Rather, the word *regulation* implies control. So, emotional regulation is really the skill of learning emotional *awareness* first, then having *choice* and *choosing* calm, joy, peace, etc. after acknowledging your negative emotion. I hope that distinction is super clear. Anger mobilizes.

What's it trying to tell you, my amazing values-driven, justice-seeking Fighter?

STRESS RESETS FOR THE FIGHTER

The good news is, with some awareness and training, Fighter types can be tamed. Let's unpack some of the better Stress Resets for a Fighter:

Physiology First

Remember, our brain is like a toddler having a tantrum when it's in fight or flight. It's typically easier to calm the body than to calm the mind. Closing the stress response loop is vital before you try to do anything else, so hack your biology as quickly as possible. Here are a few suggestions:

Breathing

Your breath is arguably your most powerful resource when it comes to stress. Science and personal experience tell us that the most stress relieving component of deep breathing lies in the exhale because it slows the heart rate and brings us back to a balanced place. A deep, long breath (or several), can immediately create space between our Fight response and the situation.

The US Navy SEALs, an elite special operations force, use a technique known as "box breathing," designed to train their recruits to stay calm and in control under extreme stress.[3] Imagine a square box and think about each breath representing a different side of the box. Here's how it works: Exhale for four seconds. Hold for four seconds. Inhale for four seconds. And hold for four seconds. Repeat as many cycles as needed.

*Important: You're not breathing to move **past** the tension, you're breathing to move **through** the tension. Don't underestimate the power in acknowledging tension and honoring where you are in the moment…*

Movement

Movement is a powerful antidote to stress. Why? Because movement also triggers rest and digest. Mechanically speaking, movement and short bouts of exercise trigger the release of regulatory neurotransmitters like serotonin, norepinephrine, and dopamine which disrupt the stress response cycle and regulate the nervous system by re-regulating blood flow to the New Brain and appendages.[4] So, try movement of any kind:

+ Walk (There is power in a brisk walk to relieve the tension of a Fighter stress response, or any personality for that matter.)

+ Exercise (A set of jumping jacks, squats, arm circles, and so on—microbursts of movement can improve mood, energy, and help regulate the nervous system.)[5]

+ Dance!

+ Shake out your hands, feet, and body.

+ Ignite your inner hulk. If you're in a controlled environment, not directing it toward others, and it feels good…release it! Scream, cry, throw a pillow, take a kickboxing class, lift heavy weights, swing a rope in the gym, do sprints, swim fast, etc.

How we channel these big emotions matters, so when possible recognize anger and release it safely before it does any damage.

MENTAL AND EMOTIONAL STRESS RESETS

+ 1-Minute Mr. Rogers Exercise: In that same restaurant scene, Mr. Rogers asks Lloyd to spend a minute thinking about all the many people who "loved him into being." I loved this scene; it brought me calm, it made me tear up, and it filled me with immense gratitude. Try it for yourself. Who loved you into being?

+ Meditate: As mentioned earlier, breathing is powerful. Structured and intentional breathing like meditation is an incredible Stress Reset. We'll cover this in many chapters—particularly in the Thriver Accelerators section—because it applies to all Stress Personalities, but consider a short, guided meditation to focus on your thoughts.

+ Visualization and Imagery: Focus on an image, memory, or ideal state of being (calm, focused, etc.) and visualize a relaxing experience from your memory or imagination.

+ Check In with a VIP: Ask someone you trust to help you talk (maybe even breathe) through your anger. You will receive support and hopefully a new perspective.

+ Laughter: Text your funny friend or watch a funny dog or cat video. Laughter gives you a boost of serotonin and dopamine to trigger rest and digest.

+ Focus on I Statements: Check in with yourself (*I feel* _____.) Try to redirect any "other focused" thoughts and focus instead on yourself. *Sit with the discomfort:* rather than search for calm, learn to ground yourself in the instability, and calm will follow. Sit with it; notice it; acknowledge it.

- Change Your Environment/Location: If you're in a direct confrontation with someone, take a quick timeout before even speaking to the other person to create the space needed to regulate your nervous system first. Sometimes changing your environment will help you do that.

- Go Under the Hood: Use one of the exploratory exercises to try and unearth what's beneath the anger. Ask yourself what's really behind the Fight: what values are being challenged? What's the second layer emotion? If you're angry with someone, gently question what you see in them that you also see in yourself. What insecurity could be masked?

AMBER'S STRESS RESETS

Let's go back to Amber one last time. Her go-to Stress Resets: she learned quickly to pause when she felt angry and take *deep, long breaths*. She also used an *affirmation* tied to her story along with the breathing—she repeated, "I am safe" several times. Breathing was her signal to stop, get to the root of her anger, and decide what to do next; repeating "I am safe" reconnected her to the present moment, tempering her "trauma brain." She also really connected to the *values* exercise, so part of her "Gift of Pause moment" was to ask whether she felt her values were being threatened in the situation. Often, this was the case. And when possible, she took *quick walks* to calm down.

With training, Amber learned to catch and redirect her anger and negative energy before she responded, and it was life-changing. She learned empathy for her board, her team, her children, and herself— she grew as a leader, mother, and wife in so many ways. I'm proud to say that she also finally agreed to get professional help with a psychologist to face her trauma and start to reconnect with herself, and subsequently her daughters and husband. Now she's on a path to earn her doctoral degree to affect change at a higher level.

FINAL THOUGHTS

Fighters: I see you! You are the protectors of the rest of us. Your hearts are massive, your values are strong, and you care so very much. Your superpower is to be decisive, values-driven, quick on your feet, and the one in the room who speaks up when the rest of us freeze, run, or self-doubt. Don't apologize; don't try to "stop" it. Feel through it and learn to tame it. You. Are. Amazing.

TL:DR

+ If you have a Fighter Stress Personality, the focus of your emotions, thoughts, and behaviors is likely *outward* toward people or things around you.

+ You likely tend to feel emotions like anger, irritation, or aggression when stressed.

+ My guess is your *thoughts* are more self-protective in nature.

+ Fighter personalities tend to spend large amounts of negative energy, often followed by an energy crash, and feelings of guilt, regret, and exhaustion.

+ The area of the brain most impacted is your Reptile and Limbic brains: the stress response/fight response areas.

+ This is a mostly learned personality modeled by past environments, but some research suggests there is a stronger hereditary component than we thought.

- Researchers debate whether anger is a core emotion or if it masks other emotions like fear, shame, hurt, etc. Getting to the root of your "fight" response can yield deeper insights about yourself.
- Move *through* anger, don't try to move *past* anger.
- Stress Resets that work best for Fighters are:

Physiology First

- Breathing work
- Movement
- Grounding/Body Scan
- Let it out!

Mental/Emotional

- Meditation
- Visualization/Imagery
- Laughter
- Language check-in
- Get to the root emotions

6

THE RUNNER

When I was in Houston a few years ago for work, I left my phone in the backseat of an Uber. I realized it after the driver dropped me at the airport and drove out of sight. He had my only means of communication and my boarding pass—and my flight was taking off in an hour.

Let me tell you a little bit about how I showed up in that moment— it wasn't pretty. My emotions, standing at the departure lane staring off into the ether, were my norm: I felt completely *overwhelmed* and filled with *intense anxiety*.

My immediate thought at that moment was also my norm: self-blame: *Lauren, you doofus. Why do you **always** do this? Why can't you be more careful? Why do you **always** have to chat up the drivers and get distracted? And by the way, why are you even here? You **should** be home with your kids being a mother rather than playing business owner all over the country. If you were truly a good mom…* you get the point.

The way I acted? Also my usual: I felt a sudden urge to run away, give up, and hide my head in the sand. I question why I even try. I don't like emotional discomfort, so I lean away from it and hide (not much has changed since 1993 and the donut incident, apparently). In this case, I threw my hands up and Chicken Little'd my way through a pity party. I walked in circles. If I had been home, I would have crashed on the couch and hid behind a Netflix documentary for a while. Instead, I literally put my hands over my face trying to hide.

Notice the hyperboles? The harshness and a cruelty I would never use with my worst enemy? The "shoulds"? The self-attack? The Imposter Syndrome? Did you notice I retreated from stress and others rather than leaning in and toward?

You've had one of those moments, right? Those "I'm over it all" kinda moments when you fantasize about quitting your job and leaving the country? If so, welcome to the Runner's world—this is how we react almost every time we feel stressed. And run we do—physically, emotionally, mentally. Because Runners are the *flight* in fight or flight.

Like I said, I'm a Runner, through and through.

EMOTIONS OF A RUNNER

Unlike our Fighter friends, the energy and direction of thoughts and emotions of a Runner are more *inwardly focused*. We tend to feel *overwhelmed, panicked, anxious, question our abilities*, and mostly we seek to *avoid or run from discomfort*.

THOUGHTS OF A RUNNER

Runners tend to think in flight-focused, retreat-or-avoid thought loops. Often Runner thoughts are much like a Negative Self-Talker— self-deprecation, self-blame, or insecurity. They can also be like a Worrier—unsure, uncertain, rolling situations around. Or they're simply and totally overwhelmed. Their thoughts are often *scarcity*-focused versus *abundance*-focused when stressed (*I'm not enough* versus *I have everything I need to get through this*). Usually thoughts like this are triggered by some cumulative experience of stress or someone causing us to experience emotional discomfort: a longer to-do list, multiple competing priorities, someone challenging our position, a fight with a friend…you name it.

Following are some persistent thoughts of a Runner:

+ *I give up.*
+ *If I avoid this, maybe it'll go away.*
+ *I have too much to do/too much going on and I don't have the capacity to handle it.*
+ *I can't even…*
+ *I'm not enough. I'm not capable. I can't do this.*
+ *I'll just push this off for later and deal with it then.*

BEHAVIORS OF A RUNNER

The major behaviors of a Runner under stress are to *avoid, push off, retreat, procrastinate, and so on.* I imagine the inner voice of a Runner and a Negative Self-Talker are very similar. The difference is that *Runners often confront negative self-talk by avoiding, pushing away, retreating, and wanting to be left alone when stressed.* I'm not referring to thoughtfully taking the time to process, which by the way could be a superpower of a Runner if we reframed it the right way…but we'll get to that.

Runners may not want to deal with something or someone for a few reasons:

+ Fear
+ Overwhelming feelings/accumulation of multiple negative stressors

- Inability to deal with difficult emotions (Freezers, you feel me)

- A way to create space between anxiety and action to buy time; a coping strategy for anxiety.

- They might be Runners because they're stress junkies. No, seriously. Interestingly, some people procrastinate because they actually need to get stressed to focus and be productive. They thrive off of the last-minute urgency (but then often continue to complain about the after-effects like exhaustion, fatigue, anxiety, physical ailments, etc. Distracted, you might be in this camp too).

- They might be *conflict-averse*. Runners don't usually *want* to lean in, talk things through, or argue…at least not right away. So, they aim to create space between themselves and the threat. This could be for many reasons:

1. They don't know how to communicate effectively.

2. They haven't learned how to deal with emotional discomfort so they delay or avoid.

3. They don't want to let someone down or fear not measuring up.

4. They inherently don't believe confrontation is worth it, which conditions them to avoid or deescalate conflict by non-confrontation, or they've learned to push off as a way of delaying or avoiding.

5. They're simply overwhelmed, anxious, and struggling to think straight (aka, a *capacity* issue).

For me, it's a little cocktail of it all. I wasn't raised in a home where conflict was managed well: my parents divorced when I was young, and despite their best efforts to help support us kids through that transition (therapy, lots of love, and really impressive co-parenting), I wouldn't say that communication and relationship conflict management were strong suits for either back then.

My two sisters and I all seemed to develop different ways of managing stress over the years. Personally, I learned to stuff, avoid, and retreat inward—maybe it was the middle child in me, but this felt safer and easier. And it unfortunately followed me through my life in moments large and small. I still avoid difficult conversations with others because I don't like the discomfort and fear I'll let someone down or they won't like me (though I'm getting better). I often won't send a meal back, even if there's an issue with it. I spill donuts and don't fess up…

Runners can be Runners in so many ways, in so many areas of life.

ADDITIONAL BEHAVIORS AND THOUGHTS OF RUNNERS

There are other ways a Runner might show up under stress:

+ Trouble paying attention/sitting still. *I'm so overwhelmed I can't deal with this.*

+ Perfectionist tendencies. *I'll just push it off because everything must be perfect.*

+ Sadness or loneliness. *I'd rather avoid connection or intimacy, but then I feel alone in the world* (like a Freezer personality).

+ Overthinking/Overload. *I have so much in my head because I keep avoiding dealing with it all* (so it builds and builds, so unlike a Worrier who leans *into* overthinking, Runners overthink because they stuff it all and let it build up until their head bursts).

* Giving up. *I'll never fix this; I'm not enough; I'll never be able to be everything for everyone.* (Even in writing this book, I spent many, many hours walking away and even debated walking away from this project a few times, because why would anyone want to read a book like this? What would I be offering that isn't already out there?)

* Retreat inward. *I just won't say anything. I don't want to stir the pot or deal with the response* (also the Pleaser and Negative Self-Talker).

* Feel out of control. *I'm so overwhelmed because there's too much to do/too much out of my control.*

* Conditional thinking. *If I can get through this, then I'll be able to relax and be happy.*

* Toxic positivity. *I'm fine, everything is fine* (like a Freezer maybe…a strategy to avoid discomfort).

Many experiences of a Runner can also be experiences of other stress personalities. Intention and motivation underneath the feelings play a *major* role in determining what your stress personality is and where it comes from.

ANXIETY VERSUS OVERWHELM

Anxiety and feeling overwhelmed are both strong characteristics of a Runner. Though the lines might blur, there is a difference between feeling overwhelmed and feeling anxious, so it's important to distinguish between the two to get to know yourself better.

Anxiety can be thought of as *intensity* of stress. This emotion is prevalent in so many of the Stress Personalities, maybe all of them:

* For a Runner, anxiety is avoidance and running away from discomfort.

* For a Fighter, anxiety is lashing out and leaning into discomfort. Or avoiding discomfort by fighting/arguing instead because hurt people hurt people.

* For a Worrier, anxiety is overanalyzing through the discomfort.

* For a Freezer, anxiety is compartmentalizing or shutting down.

* For a Pleaser, it might be overcommitting, saying yes more often.

* And so on…

Overwhelm is a *way* that anxiety shows up for some. It can be thought of more in terms of *perception of quantity of stress or anxiety*. Where anxiety is the intensity of stress in so many ways (including overwhelm), overwhelm is a type of anxiety that feels like so much is being asked of you or is in your field of vision that you're unable to function. Overwhelm is also about *perception of control.*

The less you feel in control of your circumstances—the psychological term for this is having a high *external locus of control*—the greater the feeling of overwhelm. When feeling overwhelmed, we don't process emotions as well and don't make good decisions; we stop feeling like we're capable of handling things so we might shut down (Freeze) or we might run (Runner), and so on.

Imagine this scenario. *Anxiety* is when your car alarm is stuck and blaring and screaming. *Overwhelm* is not being able to deal with it, running inside and hiding under a pillow instead of trying to turn it off.

THE RUNNER PERSONALITY: UNDER THE HOOD

What's the brain science behind a Runner personality?

You need this knowledge for many of the Stress Personalities, so let's take it back to high school science for a moment and look at the basic function of a few key players in the brain on a *normal, non-stressful day:*

The CEN, DMN, and Salience Network: Our "On" and "Off" Switch

Our **Central Executive Network (CEN)** is responsible for higher-order thinking, tasks, and decision-making; it's like our brain's control center. This is where *willful* attention and focus lives—where we regulate our thoughts, actions, and emotions.

The CEN isn't all New Brain: it works with our Emotional and Reptile Brains to help us do many things like accomplish tasks, remember phone numbers or grocery lists, do math equations, make decisions, consciously choose how to behave next, and so on... self-awareness lives here.

The *opposite* of the Central Executive Network is the **Default Mode Network (DMN), or mind-wandering state**. This is another network of interacting brain regions that are active when we are not focused on the outside world or actively focused on anything at all— like sitting at a traffic light, taking a shower, sitting in a boring meeting, going for a walk, etc., and allowing the mind to drift.

The DMN is where we are most creative, innovative, and often unintentionally go to process difficult decisions, emotions, or problems (this is why we get our best ideas or remember our to-do list in the shower!).

Our **salience network (SN)** is like a mediator between the CEN and DMN,[1] sort of regulating how we move between being "on" (active thinking) and being "off" (mind wandering).

How do these areas tie to our stress personality?

Why break these three general areas down so intricately? Because here's the thing: When we pile enough on our plates (high stress day, multitasking, tackling our mile long to-do list, etc.) and push our CEN into overdrive, our salience network can become dysregulated and fatigued; like a dam breaking, suddenly *everything* rushes in and starts to feel like it's relevant and in need of our immediate attention. This can quickly set off alarm signals causing us to feel overwhelmed, anxious, and in the case of a Runner, can induce flight and fear-based behaviors like avoidance and procrastination. Dam breaks. Floodgates open. Thoughts and emotions rush in. This is why when we have too much going on, it's hard to focus on anything at all.

Here's an example:

I had a client (I'll call her Marcy), who was the epitome of "letting it all in." She had a high-paced job with lots of responsibility for people's safety, and often took on other people's work out of perfectionism, a need for control, and to prove she was a great leader.

Marcy was a Runner through and through: she really struggled to let things go. Her signature move was avoidance. When work was especially busy or she had a difficult decision to make and too much on her plate, her go-to was to move away and avoid it all—to the point where she became paralyzed with indecision, fell behind on work, and would withdraw from her friends and colleagues. She also overate because, well, everyone knows that chocolate = anxiety relief. Staying focused and feeling in control would suddenly become impossible. Once Marcy recognized her patterns, she worked to integrate some new Stress Resets. I'll share those shortly.

Another client (calling her Trisha) would skip our meetings and avoid conversation and connection when life got stressful. Her signature move was avoidance as well, but it was more about retreating inward and closing off connection with others. I knew things were getting stressful and she was feeling overwhelmed when she'd reschedule coaching sessions, or she'd show up but was distant and much less engaged in our conversation. Her primary feeling was overwhelm. She couldn't let things go and would essentially say, *Screw you all, I'm out. I can't do this.* Trisha was a tough cookie; it took a long time to recognize her stress personality, but once she did, she took small steps to tackle it. I'll share those shortly, too.

Other Reasons Runners are Runners

Sometimes a Runner simply lacks the skills to lean into discomfort so their initial reaction to a "threat" would be to run and avoid.

And sometimes, they aren't intentional about staying organized, letting things go, managing their everyday life, tasks, to-do's, or building awareness of where they might be unintentionally driving their focus. All of this could play key roles in a Runner's stress personality and ability to better manage it.

Perception of Control

One more interesting piece of psychology we should cover for a Runner, although it relates to all the stress personalities, is perception of control.

Consider this: In World War II during the onset of the Nazi invasion in downtown London, bombings were like clockwork at night. In the suburbs of London, however, bombings were more sporadic, occurring perhaps once per week. Given the immense stress of impending bombs, there was a significant increase in ulcers in the English population at the time. So, who do you think had the higher incidence of ulcers: The people living in downtown London or the suburbs?

The answer? The people living in the suburbs. Interesting, right? Why is that? Although all the bombings were obviously stressful, because they were less frequent in the suburbs, they were *less predictable.*[2] Sound familiar? In Chapter 2 we talked about how stress that is *moderate, predictable, and controllable* is growth-producing and not as harmful to us. A lack of predictability and control leads to a different experience of stress.

Even in our jobs, a sense of control trumps occupational stressors. Those in occupations with a high degree of stress but a lot of control (think of an air traffic controller, trauma surgeon) experience *less stress* than those with lower stress jobs but no control (think of an assembly line worker).

Amazing, isn't it? I think this would apply to any stress personality but is perhaps amplified for some over others. I can only speak for myself as a Runner when I say that there is very little that gives me anxiety more than being out of control of my situation—like leaving my phone in the backseat of an Uber.

As we have and will continue to unpack in the book, psychology and perception play critical roles in our experience of stress and the onset of these stress personalities.

Exercises to Understand the Runner Personality

Here's a quick checklist to consider if you think you might be a Runner:

- [ ] Do you lean into challenges, storms, or change—or do you move away? (I mean this both literally and mentally/emotionally).

- [ ] Is your inner voice full of hyperboles (like *always* or *never*) when things get hard or you mess up?

- [ ] When you're stressed, do situations feel impossible rather than possible? Runners often feel as if the world happens to them, not the other way around.

☐ When you feel overwhelmed or like you have too much on your plate, do you question your inherent capability? (This could also lean toward Negative Self-Talker).

☐ Do you believe in yourself when you're feeling stressed? Runners often struggle with *self-efficacy* or belief in their abilities to do even the smallest things when stressed. Even if in our normal, everyday lives we can remain empowered and positive, when life gets hard we can shift, turn about face, and run the other direction physically or emotionally.

☐ Do you avoid, push off people or tasks, or procrastinate on your to-do list when you're stressed?

☐ Do you avoid conflict with others, or seek it?

☐ Do you often think, *This is too much; I can't handle this; I'm out of here* etc., when you're stressed?

☐ Do you *choose* to avoid, or does that feel like something you do whether you want to or not?

☐ Do you sweep uncomfortable feelings/situations under the rug and pretend everything is okay? (This could also be a Freezer.)

☐ Does retreating, avoiding, or pushing off usually make things better, or worse? (Temporarily it might feel better to run, but often it doesn't solve the issue.)

☐ If you checked off more than half, you could be a Runner.

WATCHOUTS

There are some dangers, of course, to an unchecked Runner stress personality:

An obvious watchout is *regularly avoiding conflict* and not dealing with it. This can quickly lead to burnout or a mental health crisis, or even physical manifestations of stress surfacing—illness, disease, disintegrating relationships. I've never heard of bottling up emotions being a productive habit.

Watch out for *stressors piling up* to the point of boiling over. Runners can easily become overwhelmed, leading to a loop of negative thoughts, second guessing, and avoidance.

Watch out for *disconnection*. Although they often want to be alone, Runners can start to make a habit of leaning away from connection with others when stressed, which can lead to strained relationships, loneliness, or difficulty managing conflict in a healthy way.

Procrastination and avoidance can impact *productivity, integrity, and trust* with others.

Runners can very easily mistake avoidance and procrastination as being *thoughtful and cautious*. Though these can be Runner superpowers, it's critical to know when we're using them as a crutch. My "work bff," Karen, and I have this conversation often. We are both Runners by nature, and both of us admittingly sometimes conflate being "cautious" with avoiding challenge or discomfort. Being aware of the difference is a big watchout. How can you tell the difference? One intention leads to *peace* and *focus* and the other leads us right back to more discomfort. If your actions lead you to feel more unsettled and anxious, then clearly the story you're telling isn't serving you well—and it's time to rewrite it.

RUNNER SUPERPOWERS

Runners aren't all panic and retreat. In fact, Runners are a great asset to any team; because when we're using these traits well, we're pretty thoughtful, careful, considerate, and non-confrontational people.

Like the other personalities, the defaults that we struggle with can be leveraged for growth. For example, we will never be the ones to act without thinking, yell, scream, or attack. We're a little less reactive in that sense. It's likely we won't be the hasty, snappy, impulsive ones in the group.

Runners are often card-carrying procrastinators, but another way to look at this is that Runners are more adept at requesting and protecting space. We'll be the first to say, "I need a minute," where others might instead say yes too quickly (Pleasers), argue and confront (Fighters), mentally shut down (Distracted), or emotionally shut down (Freezers) in the face of the same stressors. If Runners can wrangle in that tendency to avoid, we can use the space to create tight, protected boundaries to process, consider, and then act wisely.

Think about this, my Runner friend: How can you use your knack for creating *space* between you and what brings you stress and discomfort to actually *grow and thrive*? How can you "run with intention"?

Another superpower of a Runner is they often place high value on getting things done right rather than getting things done quickly. If this doesn't devolve into perfectionist tendencies, a Runner is likely the one you want to go to when you need a careful, thorough, high-quality project completed.

It's also highly likely that you are great at working under pressure because you are so used to pushing things off. Is that the case for you? And as mentioned earlier, have you unintentionally learned to thrive off of procrastination? If so, add it to your Watchout list. If not, great!

STRESS RESETS FOR THE RUNNER

Let's explore a few Stress Resets that work well for a Runner.

Do nothing to do something.

Yes, I recognize that this is an oxymoron. But what if Runners did *nothing* to stop that Runner urge when we felt it? If a Runner's superpower is the ability to create space for themselves between their reaction and response, even if this doesn't always serve us well, we can leverage it for good. What if we leaned into our nature temporarily and embraced doing *nothing*, until we felt ready to do *something*? Perhaps this small act of letting go of expectations will be enough to ignite action.

This comes in handy especially when we are feeling overwhelmed. It's important to use the word "overwhelm" the right way. Sometimes when we're feeling stressed we might say we're feeling overwhelmed, when in reality we're not truly overwhelmed; we're still functioning and can manage the feeling of anxiety. We can even avoid, procrastinate, push off and still not feel overwhelmed; there is a difference. If you feel overwhelmed, it's important to honor that feeling and *do nothing* until you feel ready to do *something*. Your brain and body are screaming for space, so give them what they need. Take a walk, go hide in the bathroom, lean back from your desk and stare out the window, go for a drive, do a quick stretch—anything to honor that space of doing nothing.

A go-to of mine is to take a drive or get out into nature. I *like* to be alone when I'm feeling stressed because I crave space to process. One time, when I was going through an incredibly hard time, I took a girls' trip with my best friends for the weekend thinking that the connection with them would help, as it normally does. But I left midway through the weekend to go home and instead drove the four hours home as slowly as I could. I needed the space: the quiet drive was the most helpful part of the weekend. In that case I was not "running" from my stress. I used this long car ride and the '80s Pandora radio station to process better than I would have by trying to ignore the stress and have a good time.

A quick note: This might be an issue when you need to make quick, in-the-moment decisions. If this is the case, I have a training solution for you in Chapter 14 (see the strategy Training Under Pressure).

Lean into discomfort with baby steps.

Remember the early 1990s movie *What About Bob,* starring Bill Murray and Richard Dreyfuss? Dreyfuss plays a successful psycho-therapist who loses his mind after one of his most dependent patients, an obsessive-compulsive neurotic (Bill Murray), tracks him down during his family vacation. In one hilarious scene, Dreyfuss gives Murray the advice to just take baby steps toward managing his anxiety and OCD...and Murray takes the advice literally. He takes baby steps out of Dreyfuss's office and all the way to the elevator...and all the way home...and then later all the way to Dreyfuss's family vacation home. The movie is hysterical, and it reminds me of this great stress reset—lean into discomfort using baby steps.

Remember Trisha, my client who was skipping meetings? One of the Stress Resets that worked well for her was pausing to feel her feel-ings and honoring her discomfort. Then, she'd take *one* small baby step *toward* the discomfort. These baby steps were nothing monumental: maybe writing one sentence as a journal entry, or a text to her coach (me) or a loved one or best friend to share her feelings. Sometimes it was just pausing to notice the discomfort and saying hello to it. Other times it was making a list and checking off one item.

For Marcy, my client who tended to withdraw from colleagues and avoid making decisions, this baby step analogy worked well for her, too. Except for Marcy, like Bob, she leveraged this using mindfulness.

She *literally* focused on her next steps forward, even if it was her literal steps out of the office and into the office supply room and back. She noticed the sound her feet made on the carpet, or focused on the filing cabinet she was headed toward and the way the papers felt on her fingers as she shuffled them. This little strategy helped take her mind off the overwhelm she was facing for a moment and helped her lean into the present moment, which calmed her stress response and helped to regulate her anxiety. Then, she returned to face what was bringing her the feeling in the first place, a little calmer this time.

Remember, discomfort-type emotions (well, all emotions really) are like signposts—they're our inner voice trying to guide us. When we ignore them, stuff them, avoid them, or try to sidestep them, we usually end up causing ourselves more stress and discomfort. Recognizing and acknowledging discomfort is a huge step toward managing it (Gift of Pause, right?).

Allow your mind to wander.

For a Runner, having so much swimming around in our heads is where overwhelm or generally feeling anxious can take hold. Allowing the mind to wander (aka, get into that mind wandering space) is a powerful strategy. This goes hand in hand with our "do nothing" Stress Reset. Whether it's coloring, play, taking a few seconds, minutes, hours or even a whole day with no agenda, or a few moments of nothingness, the goal is to focus on nothing at all, giving yourself a bit of a break.

Get curious.

Move from avoidance to curiosity; rather than ignoring what you feel, get curious about it. How do you feel? Why? What's the trigger? What helps you get out of that? Ask, ask, ask.

Let go of the overwhelm.

Mindfulness thought leader Cory Muscura says that the moment before we let go is often when we grip the hardest. Isn't that the truth? If possible, don't run from emotions; rather, let them flow through you. Let go of the unproductive emotions and thoughts and release the weight of them off your shoulders. This is a great meditation activity.

Control what's controllable.

Try to control the controllable to alleviate some of the anxiety and overwhelm you might be feeling. Here are a few suggestions:

+ Make a list of what is within your control right at that moment. Studies have shown that even the smallest of things you control like the direction of your thoughts or getting a glass of water can help you feel more in control in general. When I feel especially overwhelmed and like everything is out of my control, I do the smallest things that make the biggest impact.

+ Make a list of what is causing you stress: perhaps it's a to-do list, an uncomfortable decision or conversation, and the like. Then, triage what you can chip away at first (I do this nearly every morning now when I start working, and it works wonders). Tackle small challenges and set reasonable goals that push you, but don't feel impossible. Each time a micro-goal is met, celebrate those small successes. Note: For some, making a to-do list could make things much worse, so recognize if this Stress Reset would work well for you or not.

+ Try to think of "the big picture." Take a 30,000-feet perspective on longer term goals to minimize the perception of importance of smaller challenges and setbacks.

+ Do things you're already great at and build your confidence in them. For example, I love to cook—the aromas, the sounds, the joy of playing with flavors and spices is like a sensory experience and a stress reliever at the same time. But cooking also gives me a sense of control. Are there any habits you already have in place that help you feel a sense of control? Swimming laps, painting, playing music?

+ As part of my natural coping process for moments of high stress or extremely challenging times, I literally run—as fast as I can. I run a mile and sometimes bring myself to the brink of exhaustion. So, my stress personality takes a literal turn under extreme stress. Then, I come back and try to sort out why I'm feeling the way I'm feeling. Try it out—it sure beats emotionally running away.

Seek feedback.

Challenge yourself to seek feedback on what you can do differently. Ask a trusted someone to help you work through stressors you tend to "run" from—and be ready to accept the feedback. For example, you might receive feedback that your actions are causing others more work; someone might urge you to take the next step on a project you've been avoiding; you might get feedback that your procrastination creates a bottleneck and further confusion. My guess is you also get encouragement that you're fully capable and wonderful and just need to trust that—our inner voice is our own worst enemy.

Swap language.

Mind your language. Journal how you feel and look for places where you can swap limiting or avoidance language for more empowering language. Some examples:

+ *If I can get this paragraph right, then I can finish the paper* versus *I can finish this paper without having to get everything exactly right.*
+ *I hope to be more capable and confident* versus *I am capable and confident.*
+ *I have no control and I can't do this* versus *I am capable and there are many things I'm still in control of in this situation.*
+ *I'm not good at this* versus *I'm not good at this yet.*

Reframe.

Part of many of these Stress Resets is the power to reframe obstacles that get in the way. You can also work to reframe what's worth your stress in the first place. For me, this go-to is simple but powerful.

Clear is kind.

When interacting with others, keep this advice by Brené Brown in mind: clear is kind. Work on being direct rather than avoiding the discomfort of interacting with others.

More than likely, you are already kind so that's not an issue (as it might be for a Fighter). For some Runners, even asking someone for help can bring uncomfortable emotion. To build this muscle, try being clear and kind with smaller things (like declaring what you want for lunch) and notice how it feels to sit with the discomfort before moving on to bigger interactions.

As for my phone being left in the backseat of an Uber in Houston? Here's how I used some of these Stress Resets mentioned:

1. I *did nothing* for a moment and created space to breathe. After my little pity party, I took a moment, and took a few deep breaths. Like a Fighter, I knew I needed to tackle physiology first to regulate my nervous system.

2. Then I *reframed* the situation. Here's my usual go-to reframe: I ask myself, *Is my house on fire? Are my kids safe?* This sounds overly dramatic on paper, but there's a good reason—one of my two greatest fears is, one, a house fire (after seeing a few families in our 1960s Space Coast neighborhood experience this and lose everything). And two, infinitely worse than that, in 2011 two of our friends lost their daughter Hailey to cancer when she was 7 years old. Losing Hailey rocked them and our community, and changed our friends forever. Watching them go through that experience changed me—it changed the way I saw what was worth stressing over. It's been twelve years since she passed, but when I feel overwhelmed or things aren't going my way, I still ask myself if my kids are safe—and it immediately shifts my perspective.

3. I pulled a Bill Murray and took baby steps. I asked myself what the *smallest* step forward would be. At that moment finding a phone was the logical next step. And, lo and behold, a kind baggage attendant nearby lent me his phone. After a few calls, my knight in a shining Toyota Corolla was back in the departure lane with my phone, and I made my flight just in time.

This simple, three-step process took less than a minute—when you train with intention, it eventually becomes second nature. I'm often at the point these days where my Runner personality only steals but a moment or two of my day.

FINAL THOUGHTS

Runners, you are the careful, considerate humans we need in our life. You're the opposite of impulsive, and you help us all learn to take more pause when processing difficult emotions. With a little training, you can use your Runner qualities to find focus, control, peace, and productive action.

TL:DR

- The emotions, thoughts, and behaviors of a Runner are more *inwardly focused*.

- Runners usually feel overwhelmed, panicked, anxious, or question their abilities. Runners avoid or run from discomfort and are the *flight* in fight or flight.

- Runners tend to be conflict-averse.

- Anxiety is about intensity of stress and showing up differently for different personalities; overwhelm is about capacity and lacking a sense of control.

- For Runners, everything can start to feel relevant and in need of their attention, leading to overwhelm. Runners can also avoid discomfort out of fear or lack of tools needed to manage discomfort.

- Stress Resets that work well for a Runner:

  » Do nothing to do something.

  » Lean into discomfort with baby steps.

  » Allow your mind to wander.

  » Get curious about what's causing you discomfort.

  » Let go of the overwhelm.

  » Control what's controllable with lists and tackle one thing at a time.

  » Seek feedback.

  » Swap "if-then" language.

  » Reframe obstacles.

  » Clear is kind.

7

THE WORRIER

Have you ever worried about something so much it was hard to think of anything else or go about your daily routine?

Me too.

Now imagine every time you felt stressed, this was you: your mind a hamster on a wheel, spinning in endless circles at a furious speed, unable to get off. Your ability to think clearly, make decisions, focus, stay present—all hijacked by this hamster wheel of thought and worry.

You've just entered the mind of the Worrier.

EMOTIONS OF A WORRIER

Worrying and anxiety go together like peas and carrots. Remember that anxiety can take many forms, and worry is one of them. In other words, *worry is the persistent experience,* but we can experience it in many ways. Worry can feel like *uncertainty, unease,* or *fear* (fixation on the future) or *rumination* (fixation on the past).

But it can also feel like being *unsure,* feeling *tense, regretful, hesitant,* or *overwhelmed* (yes, like a Runner), *indecisive, unsettled, scared, confused, anxious in anticipation of the unknown,* a feeling of *foreboding,* or even *shame* or *embarrassment* (if your go-to is reflecting on past failures, mistakes, or painful memories).

Brené Brown, one of the leading experts on emotion doesn't consider worry an emotion but rather she refers to worry as "the thinking part of anxiety."[1] And this makes sense; remember, where a Runner might process anxiety by avoidance or a Pleaser by leaning in and taking on more, a Worrier processes stress as overthinking and over-analyzing. Worrying is giving way to anxiety in a sense—dwelling on the anxiety, like rubbernecking on an accident you can't seem to look away from. Worry, in a way, is how Worriers process surrounding emotions.

THOUGHTS OF A WORRIER

Your thoughts are likely *loops you repeat: replaying past experiences; catastrophizing; anticipating the worst case scenario; thinking about all of the ways things could go wrong or have in the past; looking to the negative first.*

Perhaps you believe that worrying about something will prevent it from happening, or that worrying helps you better manage anxiety (aka, *Let me just think this through…* news flash—it doesn't help). Where a Freezer might suppress negative emotions and a Runner might run from them (both of which, ironically, reinforce more worry), a Worrier wants to play that scary movie over and over in the hope it doesn't come true or to try and solve it or simply because they can't help it. The problem is, we can't *prove* that something won't happen in the future, so we continue to worry about it.

Negative self-talk can easily creep in for a Worrier or can be an underlying cause of worry.

Side note: See how these personalities are so interrelated? There's no rhyme or reason with these personalities; they are fluid. The point is to ask yourself: What is most persistent for you? Where does your stress originate—chicken or egg? What triggers it, and what drives it?

If you're a Worrier, you can likely relate to getting stuck in these cycles of rumination, fear, and uncertainty. The worry could be *inwardly* focused—maybe about your health, your capabilities at work, feeling antsy about an upcoming meeting. Or *outwardly* focused, like worrying about your family's future, mulling over an awkward or tough situation. I would venture to say there are different types of Worrier personalities within the Worrier personality.

Think about it. There may be:

+ The Worrier who is a silent sufferer, who leans toward anxiety and processes it alone.

+ The Worrier who is highly productive and *doesnt want to miss out*, or fears not getting it all done, or is a control freak so takes it all on, or worries others won't measure up, or fears messing up.

+ The Worrier who worries about everyone else; thinking their worrying will keep others safe and attempts to temper their anxiety that way.

+ The Worrier who's unsettled and never satisfied; you might avoid positive feelings out of a fear of them: scared to feel settled, content, or joyful because you're rehearsing disaster or waiting for the other shoe to drop.

My guess is if you're a Worrier, you probably even worry about your worry! Here are some thought loops you might recognize if you're a Worrier type:

+ *Why on earth did I just say that? Why did she look at me that way? How can I ever figure out this situation? (Aka, you can't turn off my brain.)*

+ *If I just think this through, I can figure out a solution and let it go.*

- *No one will do this like I can, so I must do it all.*

- *I have to do all the things or I might miss out/make a mistake/miss something/others will think less of me.*

- *I am so worried about screwing up/something going wrong, I can't get anything done.*

- *Worrying about you means that I care about you; not worrying about you means that I don't.*

- *If I let my guard down, I'll make a mistake.*

- *If I don't worry about this, people will think I don't care.*

- *If I replay the worst thing that can happen in my head, it won't happen.*

- *Remember the last time I did this? I totally messed up. I'm going to mess up again, I just know it.*

If that's you, all aboard the rumination train!

BEHAVIORS OF A WORRIER

What about behaviors common to a Worrier? You probably *lean toward* stress and discomfort. But, unlike a Fighter, it's not to attack first and ask questions later, it's to lean in and process your stressor ad nauseam in an attempt to squash it. You might lean into the stressor physically—making lists, talking to people, acting right away in a hurried, fear-driven way—or perhaps mentally/emotionally you struggle to process your worry but you're *doing* a lot mentally to work through it. In other words, *your brain won't turn off* and you have trouble shaking the associated negative emotions.

My guess is you love to *talk things through* with yourself or others to weigh all those options, catastrophize, or replay those past failures.

But not always. Some Worriers like to keep it to themselves, which means they can easily become *distant and disconnected.*

Productivity? Again, that might depend. Sometimes they can become quite *unfocused* when stressed and productivity suffers; sometimes they're quite productive and *doing, doing, doing,* but are emotionally a bit more disconnected or productive out of a fear of failure, etc.

Much like a Distracted personality, Worriers really struggle to *shut off their mind and stay present,* and often feel *foggy-headed* and *easily distracted.* But for the Worrier, this isn't only a case of being at cognitive capacity (like a Distracted stress personality), it's because they can't shut off that worry and uncertainty.

THE WORRIER PERSONALITY: UNDER THE HOOD

What's important to understand about worry is that the *function* of worry is quite neutral—worry, like stress itself, is at its most basic neither good nor bad. Like any emotion, worry plays a role in our survival—a signal pointing us toward the fact that a threat is coming (perceived or real) and we need to pay attention. Worry can quickly demotivate us, paralyze our productivity, derail our mental health, and prevent us from being present with loved ones and connecting with others. But worry can also motivate us to take productive action (see Worrier Superpowers).

So, Worriers, how's this reframe: how you perceive your worry might help you process it better.

When we worry, it's primarily our Default Mode Network (DMN)[2] that is impacted. Remember the DMN is essentially our mind-wandering state—where we go when we're not focused on anything, or daydreaming, or when we drift off. One unique feature of the Default

Mode Network is that it's also the hub for innovation, creativity, and problem-solving (not actively problem-solving, but rather letting a problem simmer and process in the background, which is quite productive when you're stuck on a problem and walk away from it).

But here's the thing. Sometimes a Worrier can get *stuck* in this mind-wandering place and struggle to come out of it and back to the present. Studies have found that when we're experiencing high negative stress, there is increased activity in the salience network and Default Mode Network. Many Worriers don't just get paralyzed with indecision, uncertainty, or worry in a moment of stress, they can get *stuck* in that state much longer than expected. Finding their way out of their mind-wandering place becomes quite difficult.

Isn't it interesting that a Runner needs to seek more time in the DMN, while the Worrier gets stuck there? This is another reason I suggest that Stress Resets need to match our unique stress personality.

Our hippocampus—the hub for our long-term memory—plays a role in worry, too. How? We use our past experiences to anticipate or ideate our future, which is why we replay past experiences over and over (it's also the same reason why we learn so much of life's lessons from the tougher parts of our past, for better or for worse). So, a Worrier will make assumptions around what to worry about based on the past in an attempt to prevent the worst from happening again.

Our higher-order thinking and New Brain also play a role in worry too, of course. Worry doesn't just happen subconsciously; our brain diverts resources like attentional control and expends energy focusing on what could go wrong, what went wrong, etc. Experts call this *conceptual elaboration*. We chew up lots of cognitive resources on worry, which then intersects with our emotional reactivity to the situation, and soon boom—all areas of the brain are commandeered by worry.[3]

EXERCISES TO UNDERSTAND THE WORRIER PERSONALITY

So, you're a Worrier, or this is one of the dominant stress personalities you identify with. Let's get to know that side of you a bit more now. The following are journal prompts to think through and make notes on what kind of worrier you are, how it shows up, etc.

Journal about following questions:

1. Do you often feel indecisive and conflicted about personal or work-related decisions, leaving you feeling stuck or paralyzed?

2. Are you generally risk-averse when it comes to making decisions? Or do you fixate on the potential consequences?

3. Do you worry about preventing the worst from happening?

4. Do you worry about what other people think of you?

5. On a scale of 1-10, how in control of your worry do you feel?

6. Do you worry more about yourself (health, well-being, financial security, relationships), or your family (their health and safety, etc.)? Or is it more about your professional relationships?

7. What are the body sensations you feel when worrying?

8. What are the *other* emotions attached to your worry (fear, shame, uncertainty, confusion, anticipation, etc.)? Generally, are you aware of your emotions in those moments?

9. On a scale of 1-10 how comfortable are you sharing your opinion…or is that what is keeping you in a worry loop?

10. Are you more of the Silent Sufferer, the Over-doer, the Other-Focused, or the Unsettled and Never Satisfied type of Worrier? In other words, how do you behave?

WATCHOUTS

There are relatively obvious negative impacts of *persistent* worry on our everyday lives. Let's explore a few:

Excessive worry can impact mental health.

It should be no surprise that extreme levels of worry are associated with poor mental and physical health. Extreme or automatic worry that becomes constant and hard to control can quickly lead to depression, obsessive compulsive disorder, or generalized anxiety disorder.[4]

Managing worry before it becomes extreme is certainly worth working toward. Recognizing you are a Worrier personality is a huge step toward better managing it.

Excessive worry projects the wrong messages sometimes.

Be cautious about what message worrying puts out into the world—especially if you have children, a partner, or you are a leader of a team. What's the unspoken message behind frequent worry? That happiness is conditional? That you don't trust others to support you and do a good job? That the world is unsafe? What's the perspective you want to put out into the world for those around you? For yourself?

Excessive worry leads to sacrificing today for yesterday and tomorrow.

Worry can make it incredibly hard to stay present and connected. With a fixation on the past and future, a Worrier can easily miss what's right in front of them. Think about the impact of worry in life's most precious moments: a child telling you a story; your partner sharing a tough part of their day while at dinner; missing key information in a meeting. These smaller moments can quickly build to larger feelings of disconnection, inadequacy, and questioning competency or capability.

Like a Negative Self-Talker, Worriers naturally focus on the negative, which unintentionally redirects attention from the positive, both for themselves as well as for the people around them. *Don't let excessive worry make you miss what's going right.*

Excessive worry begets other negative emotions.

Worry can lead to other heightened negative emotions that can easily dominate your life. Here's an example. You mull over an incident at work with a coworker that was a simple misunderstanding, but you overthink it and struggle to let it go. This leads to shame, or perhaps anger and resentment, or irritation. Soon every time you see this person you feel this same irritation, shame, or other negative emotion. You take those emotions home with you to your family; you bring that irritation to standing in line at the coffee shop the next morning; you carry the load of that shame with you into your next performance review.

Negative emotions are contagious and build upon each other. This is an important reframe covered in the Negative Self-Talker chapter.

Excessive worry can drive undesired behaviors and habits.

Worrying often leads to behaviors we wouldn't normally exhibit. As we're about to explore, worry can easily motivate us to take meaningful action in different areas of our life; but how thoughtful will we be when we're taking that action? Action driven by worry can sometimes lead us to act *out of alignment with our values, beliefs, and our purpose.* When that happens, our behaviors can easily go awry, such as overextending ourselves, working later than we should, hurrying and rushing, staying up later and sacrificing our sleep, skipping workouts, multitasking, and so on. Though we might be well-intentioned, our behaviors can quickly derail us from what matters most in our lives.

As Lao Tzu said, "Nature does not hurry, yet everything is accomplished."

WORRIER SUPERPOWERS

Don't get me wrong, not all worry is a bad thing. Worriers are powerful assets to any team, family, or community. Why? For so many reasons.

Worriers are often highly productive and action-focused.

Worry can motivate us to take productive action and create opportunities for us to rise to the challenges and storms of our life. In some studies, worry led to better academic performance, greater likelihood to make big life changes such as quitting smoking and inspired better preparedness for the future.

Think about this: what if you could make your worry *work for you?* What if you can use your worry to inspire the change you need in your life to take it to the next level?

Worriers are risk-averse, careful, and considerate.

Worriers are often risk-averse and great at considering all possible outcomes. Because worry is often future-focused and originates from deep within our memory banks, Worriers can be great at being adaptive to change and challenge, know how to anticipate things going wrong, and are more likely to act than the rest of us.

Worriers tend to be organized and detail-focused.

Worriers also tend to be better list-tacklers and more detail-oriented. Their mental muscle of tackling to-dos and checking off boxes is much more developed than the rest of us.

Worriers are great problem-solvers.

Worriers are great people to have on board when you need to prepare, plan, and problem-solve. Unlike our flight-risk Runners or unreliable Freezers, they won't shy away from what must be done; and unlike our reactive Fighters, they won't act without thinking. A Worrier anticipates all risks, notices every detail, and prepares for every outcome. Worriers are excellent planners and often excellent communicators. Know any attorneys or actuaries? I'm willing to bet they're Worriers.

Of course, there's often an interesting inverse relationship between worry and performance: too much worry, and you're paralyzed with helplessness, lack of action, or paralysis by analysis; too little and there's no motivation to act. Not everyone is a "go get 'em" type of Worrier; creating balance and leveraging worry for productive action is a thin but possible line to ride.

STRESS RESETS FOR THE WORRIER

The Worrier is a popular stress personality. The good news is that because of this popularity, there's lots of great research around minimizing worry in your life. If you're one of them, I recommend a few key practices:

Be mindful of danger, but not consumed by it.

I would never tell a Worrier not to think about what could go wrong. But, detaching from the fixation on what could go wrong is a great and tough skill to learn. Recognize that worrying is different from being *driven by* worry. Try to detach yourself from your worry by *observing* your worry.

Schedule worry time.

Scheduling worry time is a great way to reduce the amount of worry in your life and observe your worry at the same time. Yes, literally pencil in time for worry on your calendar. Sounds silly, I know, but studies show that over time you'll notice less intensity and frequency of worry.[5]

Scheduled worry time can look like whatever you want it to, but here's a recommended process:

1. Catch the worry. Recognize when you're experiencing worrying thoughts through mindfulness.

2. Set them aside—the hardest part. This will likely create anxiousness and *more* worry of course, so this will take some training to let go of it.

3. Honor your worry time. Re-engage with those worrisome thoughts at the dedicated time. Hopefully by this point, the intensity or amount of worry has reduced.

Think about what Dr. Susan David, an emotional agility expert, says about fighting our worry:

"We feel angry at our anger, worried about our worry, and unhappy about our unhappiness. It's like quicksand: the harder you struggle with your emotions, the deeper you sink."

It makes sense—the more we fight these emotions and try to shut them down, the more we worry about our worry. So why not get it out on paper?

When you do sit down to write in a worry journal, try working through it a bit by asking yourself:

- *What is true? What do I know? What are the facts?*
- *What's directly within my control?*
- *How does this align to my values?*

What's the benefit of focusing on what we don't have control over? Obviously, nothing (easier said than done). Remember that your emotions drive you to act but can often derail you from what's important and toward things that haven't even happened, or happened in the past, both of which you have no control over.

A worry journal can help you navigate these big thoughts. By the way, you might notice a central theme of these Stress Resets throughout the book—naming and claiming emotions is a powerful remedy for stress. Getting our emotions on paper has been shown to decrease the intensity of the stress response and anxiety, and even reactivity. I highly recommend getting into a regular journaling practice as a Worrier. You don't have to write a book—even listing worries on a Post-it note can be a cathartic, stress-alleviating experience.

Guided meditation.

Meditation is an incredible skill to hone, and *how* you meditate matters. Here's what I mean: imagine telling a Worrier to go be alone with his or her thoughts (often the strategy of unstructured or open-monitoring types of meditation). How do you think that would go? Allowing your mind to wander as a Worrier isn't usually the greatest idea. Where a Runner might benefit from unstructured meditation, a Worrier would likely not.

So, try strategies including thought prompts, focused breathing, body scans, or other forms of guided meditation to help redirect worrisome thoughts and connect back to the present.[6]

Productive meditation.

In his 2021 book *Deep Work: Rules for Focused Success in a Distracted World*, Cal Newport shares a training strategy called productive meditation. The goal, he says, is to take a period in which you're already doing something else (preferably something automatic and not cognitively taxing, like walking, running, driving, showering, etc.), and use the time to focus your attention on a single issue or problem (or worry?). He uses this strategy to improve his focus and mental performance, but I think it would be a great strategy for a Worrier.

No one type of meditation is better than another, but some work better for one stress personality than another. My suggestion? Try them all and see what fits.

Don't rehearse disaster.

There was a famous 2007 Harvard study on musicians who played piano for five weeks, resulting in the part of the brain that controls movement increasing in size.[7] What does this tell us? That energy goes where attention flows—so don't rehearse disaster, or behaviors will follow. Like a toddler, your worrying brain occasionally needs redirection. This is where guided meditations or mindfulness activities come in.

As Michael Jordan famously said, "Why would I think about a shot I haven't taken yet?"

Be the Chinese farmer.

There's a Taoist parable titled Sāi Wēng Lost His Horse, which is about a poor Chinese farmer. It goes like this: A long time ago, a poor Chinese farmer lost a horse, and all the neighbors came around and said, "Well, that's too bad." The farmer said, "Maybe." Shortly after, the horse returned bringing another horse with him, and all the neighbors came around and said, "Well, that's good fortune," to which the farmer replied, "Maybe." The next day, the farmer's son was trying to tame the new horse and fell, breaking his leg, and all the neighbors came around and said, "Well, that's too bad," and the farmer replied, "Maybe." Shortly after, the emperor declared war on a neighboring nation and ordered all able-bodied men to come fight—many died or were badly maimed, but the farmer's son was unable to fight and spared due to his injury. And all the neighbors came around and said, "Well, that's good fortune," to which the farmer replied, "Maybe."

And so the story goes.

In China, when something bad happens people will say, "Sai Weng Shi Ma" (Remember The Old Man Who Lost His Horse) to remind themselves and others that, sometimes, "bad" things happen that carry a silver lining—and that it's often in the way you look at things that determines their power over your spirit. It is a caution to all not to get too attached to what happens to us, good or bad. This is a very Taoist tale indeed—themes of yin and yang, balance, peace, pacifism, openness, and receptiveness.

In such a binary culture these days, it's tough not to get attached to things being "good" or "bad"—because that's easier for us, isn't it? It is easier for our psyche to accept good and bad rather than, well, "maybe." But there's such peace in "maybe" when you really think about it; there's a peace in not attaching to an outcome.

This is, of course, easier to do when you are on the fortunate side of fortune. But when things go south in your life, or you come across a conflict or struggle at work, the ability to perceive your situation in an unattached, objective "maybe" way brings the promise that, at the very least, clarity, insight, and wisdom will follow you out the other side.

When you're feeling worried, be the Chinese farmer and say "maybe" rather than worrying about what could be or what has been. There is no one way to find calm, hope, and happiness; these don't come from rules, but often from learning to flow with what is, rather than focusing on what was, what isn't, or what's to come.

Mindfulness cues.

A contemplative neuroscience researcher at the University of Miami by the name of Amishi Jha conducted several studies on military personnel involved in combat to explore mindfulness and its impact on what the military term "VUCA" situations: Volatile, Uncertain, Complex, and Ambiguous situations, or extremely high stress combat situations.

Dr. Jha and her team took participants through several weeks of mindfulness training and, interestingly, found that during these times of extreme uncertainty, participants were able to recover more fully from the extreme stress.

Can mindfulness or some other type of meditative practice help you reduce worry and rumination the same way?

Here are a few mindfulness strategies:

Be where your feet are.

One of my favorite former clients is a healthcare executive named Bob, and his favorite saying when challenges surfaced was to "Be where your feet are." He stole it from former New York Giants football coach Tom Coughlin and shared it with me during a leadership retreat on a sunny Chicago spring day a few years ago. "Be where your feet are" was Bob's cue to stay in the moment and not think about past failures or future worries.

Bob is a Thriver: let's clear that up. He is no Worrier. But I loved his advice so much that I had to include it here as its own Stress Reset. Reminding yourself to stay in the moment and "be where your feet are" when you feel worried, or any other associated emotion is a great prompt to direct your mind to focus on the present moment.

Look up, notice the world.

Let's practice mindfulness in the moment, right now. Stop reading for a moment and look up. Look around you. Notice the smells, the sounds, the air on your skin. Find something beautiful near you—a picture, a scene, a leaf—let the awe and wonder of the present moment consume you. This is such a valuable skill to hone. Imagine the time and energy you'll get back from worry robbing you of life's greatest joys.

Three things exercise.

Here's another mindfulness cue that's one of my favorites. Get comfortable in a chair or lie down on the floor and take a few deep breaths. Then, take notice of the room around you and find:

+ Three things you can *see*.

- Two things you can *hear*.
- One thing you can *touch*.

These quick, easy mindfulness cues are just a few of dozens. But they're so simple and effective at recentering us in the present moment and away from unwanted wandering thoughts. They're great "adult timeouts" and even better for kids. (I use the 3, 2, 1 exercise often: to stop myself from screaming at my boys, between meetings on hectic days, and even sometimes in the driveway when I arrive home to recalibrate before walking in the door.)

Take a walk in nature.

If nature is sparse around you (urban setting, for example), go for a walk and *find* nature. A tree, a flower, a shrub, a plant store, a local park. Researchers have found that taking a walk in nature reduces anxiety and rumination. Connect with the natural world and soak it in.

How to make decisions when you're stuck in a worry loop.

Worriers tend to overrely on either too much emotional thinking or too much logical thinking when making decisions, or they get spun up in a mixture of both, not knowing which to trust. When we get stuck and can't make a decision it can quickly lead to fear, not taking risks, missing opportunities, and can often impact our productivity, trust in ourselves, our reliability, and so on. So how do we make better decisions, or decide at all, with minimal worry?

Don't underestimate the importance of emotion in decision-making… and, sometimes our emotions can deceive us. (I'm not helping with this subtitle, am I?) There are very few (if any) decisions made in the absence of emotion, but often we discount our emotions as irrelevant or interfering with "the facts" in the decision-making process. We think our emotions are deceiving us. However, our emotions can provide us clues, like little red flags, or green lights, that whisper things like:

This isn't right…move on…

or,

This feels exciting…proceed with caution…

But sometimes our emotions can also lead us astray. The decision-making process is really two processes: pattern recognition (mentioned earlier) and emotional tagging (mentioned in Chapter 2), which is when your brain "tags" certain emotions to experiences in your memory bank.

You can probably imagine that, sometimes, our emotional tags or distorted patterns lead to poor decisions. For example, previously you were burned by a contractor who failed to finish a home renovation after you paid him in full. The contractor was a tall man with dark, wavy hair. Now you're looking for a new contractor and the best guy for the job happens to look just like the previous crook. Emotionally, the guy just rubs you the wrong way, but you can't pinpoint why and don't want to move forward with him.

Okay, so our emotions can deceive us, so we just stick with the facts? After all, logic, the facts, and what we know to be true and accurate is a huge part of the decision-making process and should remain so. Right?

Yes, and…

There *is* a connection between logic and our emotions: it's called the *orbitofrontal cortex* and it's highly involved in integrating intellect and logic with emotion. Our brain works to balance them together when making decisions, interpreting a threat, and acting on it.[8] So, we should too. In fact, research shows that when we're unable to tap into our emotions, even if our logical thinking is intact (Fighters, Freezers, you listening?), our decision making skills are impaired.

Now let's layer in clarity of our values. Having the ability to connect with our emotions on a decision *and* our values at the same time is the skill of *intuition*—intimately knowing your inner voice and even how your body responds to situations. Tapping into our emotions is part of intuition (in the Negative Self-Talker and Thriver chapters we take a deeper dive into intuition and how to strengthen it).

Bottom line: we need all three. Most experts on decision-making agree that the best way to make decisions (even from a place of worry) is to *balance logic with emotion and connect to our values.*[9] This can help you stay decisive and action-focused, values-driven, and take risks with authority and facts, not impulsivity.

Remember:

- **Emotions are in the driver's seat and are trying to mobilize you to *do* something.**
- **Logic grounds you in the facts.**
- **Values keep you oriented to what's most important.**

If making decisions is hard for you, start with smaller, less life-impacting decisions to practice. Create some space or pause to reflect on the decision—this is important…you can't be busy, distracted, or have other input coming your way, especially if this is a big decision. Go back to your worry journal, focusing on how you feel, what is true, what you know, and how it connects to your values.

From there, make an informed decision to the best of your ability. And then? *Move forward.* Embrace the discomfort that might come with moving forward from a decision—it's normal. Decision by decision, the discomfort will lose its grip over you.

FINAL THOUGHTS

Worriers, you're the detailed, considerate, cautious, and action-focused friend we need when life gets hard. When some of us are impulsive, fearful, numb, overzealous, you're the one who steps in and tells us to stop, think, consider, process, anticipate, and plan. How can you use your Worrier superpowers to motivate, inspire, and act? How can you design systems in your daily life to pause and stay in the moment, so as not to miss the beautiful parts of life, and even stress itself? Thank you for being the friend, teammate, and partner we need.

TL:DR

+ The Worrier personality gets stuck in a cycle of rumination, fear, and uncertainty. The worry could be inwardly focused or outwardly focused; it can be more rumination on past events or worry and uncertainty about things that haven't happened yet.

+ Worrying and anxiety go together like peas and carrots: some experts consider worry an emotion, and others believe it's the "thinking part of anxiety."

+ Worriers experience thought loops such as replaying past experiences, catastrophizing, anticipating the worst-case scenario, thinking about all of what could go wrong or has in the past, or looking to the negative first.

+ Sometimes worry is a demotivator, can paralyze our productivity or derail our mental health, prevent us from being present with loved ones and connect with others; but worry can also motivate us to take productive action.

- Extreme levels of worry are associated with poor mental and physical health, and can quickly lead to depression, obsessive compulsive disorder, or generalized anxiety disorder. Worry can also lead us to behave in ways out of alignment with what matters to us: our values, beliefs, and sense of purpose and meaning.

- Some Stress Resets for a Worrier include:

  » Be mindful of danger, but not consumed by it.

  » Journal; schedule worry time (*What is true? What do I know? What's directly within my control? How does this align to my values?*)

  » Guided meditation.

  » Don't rehearse disaster.

  » Be the Chinese farmer (it is what it is...maybe).

  » Be where your feet are (stay in the here and now).

8

THE FREEZER

Recently I spoke to an acquaintance about this stress personality research. He's been a first responder for the past 15 years and spends his life moving in and out of incredibly intense, crisis situations. When there's an emergency—a high speed crash on the Interstate, a cardiac arrest, an overdose patient—like all first responders he has the incomprehensible ability to stay calm and laser-focused thanks to his training and thousands of hours of practice.

The problem, he reflected, is that in a way his emotions are non-existent in those tense moments; but often afterward, he struggles to reconnect to his emotions and process it all…especially if the emergency involved children or resulted in the person losing their life.

As we talked a bit more, he realized that he often brings that "mental training" into his parenting and relationships: he'll shut down when there's confrontation or tension, growing cold, singularly focused, and blunt. His wife said it's like he's devoid of emotion.

My friend is a Freezer.

My guess is that if you're a first responder, healthcare worker, physician, nurse, military, law enforcement officer, educator, social worker, or someone similar, you can relate. In fact, post-pandemic many more people seem to relate to this stress personality—they found they needed to shut down just to get through.

Freezers are exactly what the name implies. They simply freeze in one of two ways: they freeze with inaction or freeze emotionally.

Either way, they check out. Let's call them the Productive Freezer and the Unproductive Freezer.

EMOTIONS OF A FREEZER

Emotionally, both kinds of Freezers (Productive and Unproductive) might feel emotion*less*—so it's not that there's a persistent negative emotion associated with stress, but rather little to no emotion at all. They might struggle to feel *joy*, *empathy*, or *compassion* or anything at all (Productive).

Or sometimes they do feel: they feel *drained*, *sluggish*, *indifferent*, *apathetic*, or *disengaged* (Unproductive).

THOUGHTS OF A FREEZER

What about the thoughts of a Freezer? This is a tougher one. Productive-type Freezers often *don't think* through their stress and discomfort as much as the other stress personalities; they *compartmentalize*, intentionally *blocking negative thoughts* to self-protect. Some are quite lucid and able to focus on the task at hand; but they don't allow themselves to think through what they're really feeling inside or deny the stress altogether.

Other Freezers (Unproductive) might have negative and self-directed thought loops such as *I'm not cut out for this, so I'm going to give up*; or exhaustive, self-protective thought loops like *I'm not going to deal with this right now* or *I can't do this right now* or *I'm done*, and physically freeze.

It's not that Freezers run, but they don't lean in, either.

My favorite thought of a Freezer? *Stress personality? What stress personality? I don't stress...I'm definitely not a Freezer.*

Okay...sure.

BEHAVIORS OF A FREEZER

Freezers can often come across not-so-pleasantly from the outside looking in. They might come across *highly focused*; but others as if *they don't care* or seem *disconnected*. They can be *curt, blunt, short,* or *callous*, but also perhaps *extremely productive* and task-focused—this is the type of Freezer who lowers their gaze and goes through the emotions. This is the person who can skillfully *compartmentalize* their negative emotions or stress and get through the day. They make important decisions, lead teams, excel (on paper) at work or as a parent, friend, partner...but over time, the price they pay is an inability to effectively connect with and manage their emotions, or connect with others as a result. Like a Runner, this type of Freezer can practice *toxic positivity* and might not even realize they are Freezers in the first place. Their way of coping with stress might be to wear a smile, pretend it's all okay, block the negative, and move on. They might try to stay as busy as possible to avoid those negative feelings and thoughts. This is the Productive type.

Other times (Unproductive type) they might struggle with *productivity* or find themselves *glued to the couch*, mindlessly scrolling social media rather than tackling their to-do list. They might literally feel *stuck* or *paralyzed with inaction* (like a Worrier) and procrastinate and avoid (like a Runner). In times like these they might come across as if they're *not paying attention, forgetful* or *spacey* (like a Distracted).

It's not that Freezers don't care or are bad people; far, far from it. They're just stuck...checked out.

One consistent feature of both types of Freezers is that *connection* feels difficult when they're stressed, including connection with themselves. This could be because of a fear of connection, past trauma, or just a result of persistent compartmentalization. They often retreat and disconnect from others.

Do you remember my client Amber, the Fighter, who runs the alternative school and fights for her students daily, sometimes at the expense of her patience? Amber's childhood was rife with trauma, abuse, and violence. What's interesting is that she grew up both fighting for herself and her safety, but also dissociating and shutting down in her later years when it came to connection in her personal life or in some work relationships. She was both a Freezer and a Fighter depending on the situation.

For Amber, connection that didn't involve a student in need was unsafe. She struggled with intimacy with her friends, partner, and coworkers. She would fight like crazy for her daughters, students, or staff—but froze when it came to opening up and sharing with others.

Often a Freezer's stress personality shows up in non-Freezer ways—a sudden blow up, getting sick more often, *over-productivity* by keeping themselves busy (*just don't think about it*), over-judging others or projecting. In fact, overdoing pretty much anything might be a key attribute of a Freezer. To *feel* anything at all, they might overeat, overwork, overindulge, overdo social media, or gossip (see Under the Hood section for why this happens).

One of my clients mentioned in an earlier chapter, a superintendent of schools, was a Freezer during the pandemic. When it came to normal, everyday stress she was not a Freezer; but when the pandemic hit, she emotionally shut off to make incredibly challenging decisions and thoughtfully respond to the rapid, incessantly constant changes in protocol and policies.

She led her team with such grace, wisdom, and courage that her team would have followed her anywhere during that time. But the consequence of blocking out the fear, uncertainty, and high stress to stay focused and quick-thinking was that she started to struggle to connect with her own emotions and with her family. At the end of the day, she'd be so checked out, her husband started to worry. She couldn't turn it on and off.

THE FREEZER PERSONALITY: UNDER THE HOOD

How does a Freezer type become a Freezer? So many ways: upbringing, line of work, experience, a trying time in their life or career, and so on.

Freezers are born this way.

At its most basic, Freezers could be Freezers simply because they're wired that way right out of the womb. In a stress response situation, our reactions don't actually stop at fight or flight: "freeze" and "appease" are the other two ways we can react to threat. When we freeze, we aren't preparing for action, we're preparing for injury. Freezing is like curling up and bracing for impact, like a turtle retreating into its shell. This can be a trained response, but we can also be wired this way.

Freezers are reacting to deeply embedded memories or upbringing.

As we explored already, our hippocampus is great at memorizing facts, faces, languages, and capturing and recording experiences even when we're not actively trying. We know that a smell, a song, the mention of a name, even a time of year can produce a surge of feelings like melancholy, joy, sadness, or loneliness because at some point or another we assigned importance to these stored experiences, told our version about what happened, and stored them as memory. If you've watched the movie *Inside Out* (highly recommend), you learned this concept.

Trauma can have the same effect. According to Dr. Bruce Perry, a trauma expert, *all* of our brain regions get involved in situations like this (I mentioned his book earlier for those who experienced trauma in the early part of their life.). Sometimes, negative past experiences leave memory traces and powerful associated emotions without our conscious awareness, but we react to these triggers nonetheless in weird, often unproductive but self-protective ways.

Sometimes, this can explain how a Freezer becomes a Freezer.

For example, let's say you grew up in a tough home. Stress was modeled by explosive rage, passive aggressiveness, demeaning words, dominance, control, or abuse. You, as a young child, learned quickly to stay quiet, compartmentalize, and numb to stay physically or emotionally safe. It would make sense, then, for you to identify with the Freezer personality in your adult life, right? Yelling, frustration, and conflict would trigger those deepest memories, and subsequently stress response would whisper to your heart and head, *Hide...don't move.* So, you hide. You shut down.

Disclaimer: Not all Freezers have trauma in their past. Let's be careful not to make that assumption. Nonetheless, many Freezers do, and if this is you, I see you. I'm so very sorry. And I hope this book helps you make sense of these patterns.

What about non-trauma related pasts shaping the Freezers of today? Let's say you grew up in a home where children were to be seen and not heard. Your parents were Type A, had high expectations of children, were perfectionists. Speaking up, having a voice, taking up space was not the norm; the norm was *shut up, do what you're told, respect authority, and earn your keep.* It would make sense that, in the face of stress as an adult, you think that *less of you and just keep your head down* is the best way to handle stressful situations.

Another note: just because your parent/partner/caregiver etc. played a role in your Freezer personality doesn't mean they intended to; I'm not suggesting you look for a person to blame here. Perhaps they were simply too busy earning enough to put food on your table to be there emotionally, or they were hurt themselves and you understand that now. You don't have to have a toxic relationship with someone to realize they might have played a part in how you show up under stress today.

American stress researcher Robert Sapolsky identifies a personality type called the "repressive" personality. This is a person who, in all areas of life, is careful, a planner, is structured and plays by the rules. On the outside he is calm, collected, and calculating. He sees the world in black and white and keeps a very, very tight lid on his emotions. He wouldn't be considered depressed or anxious, but he shows a strong aversion to expressing emotion and a limited emotional vocabulary.

Studies have revealed that this type of person has a chronically activated stress-response. Why? Because they stuff, avoid, divert, redirect, and generally "freeze" when it comes to processing stress... so they get stuck in a perpetual stress response. This might also be the type who showed up in that cardiologist's office and tore up the waiting room chair armrests (remember them, from the Fighter chapter? Maybe they weren't Fighters but Freezers?). So, like a blocked pipe, suppressed emotions build and build, and one day...boom (literally, their arteries could be a metaphor for their emotional blockage).[1]

A Freezer is *is trained* to be a Freezer as an adult.

Here's another example. You're a trauma surgeon who had a great, positive, supportive upbringing and stressed was modeled superbly for you. But during your years in med school, rounding, residency, and so on, you were trained to make very quick life-or-death situations. Emotion *cannot* be part of your decisions (like my first responder friend). You must stay focused, objective, and able to make a quick decision under immense pressure. After some years, you unintentionally take that incredible ability to compartmentalize home with you to your family or into workplace relationships and get feedback that you're "robotic" when you're in conflict with others, or apathetic, indifferent, or callous when interacting with coworkers. I worked with a group of physicians for a while, and those who moved on to leadership and admin roles in their hospitals really struggled with communication and connecting with their teams for this reason. Likely, many are Freezers by training, not by upbringing: their brain is conditioned to compartmentalize, at the expense of emotional intellect.

Dopamine and a Freezer

Dopamine (a type of neurotransmitter and hormone) is highly involved in regulating the way we think, feel, act, and even learn and motivate ourselves. This is one way we experience pleasure and reward and regulate our behavior.

Here's the thing, though: chronic stress often blocks or reduces dopamine production, and this pathway can quickly become underproductive. This might be because we're repeatedly and intentionally compartmentalizing and blocking emotion, or perhaps this repeated "freezing and protecting" nature through the years has led to dopamine suppression. Either way, under stress this person has trouble *feeling* emotion…even positive ones (aka, the dopamine hits). Chronic dopamine suppression might explain why both types of Freezers unconsciously seek a "dopamine hit" in other ways when stressed, like overeating, a third glass of wine, gossip, overdoing social media, overexercising, over working, oversleeping, and so on…they're simply trying to *feel* anything at all.

Compartmentalizing and a Freezer

The psychological principle of compartmentalizing is important to understand because many Freezers (mostly the Productive types) do this. Compartmentalizing, like stress, is neither good nor bad. Technically speaking, the purpose of compartmentalizing is to avoid what's known as *cognitive dissonance*, which is when we experience situations, people, beliefs, or ideas that aren't in alignment with our own expectations, beliefs, values, or assumptions.[2] Sometimes people compartmentalize so they don't have to face their choices, and then they create a story to make it okay (*I took someone else's cab, but that's okay because another will come and I was really late*). Others compartmentalize to get things done and focus under pressure (military, first responders, mental health counselors…those stoic trauma surgeons).

Turning off emotion is how Jocko Willink, a retired Navy SEAL officer, was able to lead his team to do incredible, courageous things. Willink led SEAL Team 3's Task Unit Bruiser in the Iraq War battling against Iraqi insurgents in Ramadi and has a unique approach (that I consider a Freezer mentality) to handling high stress situations: he takes stress by the horns. His approach is a mindset shift of radically taking ownership over every stressful thing happening in your world and attacking with fervor. I see this less as a Fighter mentality and more as a Freezer—he blocks all emotion and then charges forward.

But hey, it works: Willink led his SEAL Team to become the most highly decorated US special operations unit of the Iraq War; and it is how my friend, the first responder, and the trauma surgeon save lives and get through situations the rest of us could never handle. It's also how many of us got through the Covid pandemic.

My point? Not all "freezing" is bad—but it should come with a warning label. There are risks to putting your head down and charging through if you're not careful to stop and check in with yourself here and there.

EXERCISES TO UNDERSTAND THE FREEZER PERSONALITY

Here are some questions to consider if you think this might be your stress personality. Some of these might be emotionally charged, so buckle up and take space to walk away if you need to.

Do you connect with any of the following thoughts on a regular basis when you're stressed?

+ *I have too much going on—so much that I am at my breaking point.*

+ *I'm not cut out for this, so I'm going to give up.*

+ *If I feel, I'll get hurt.*

+ *I can't deal with this right now.*

+ *I don't need anyone; I'll just do it all myself.*

+ *This is how I shield my heart from any further betrayal, abuse, disappointment, or neglect.*

+ *This is how I prevent being hurt again by my absent/busy parent/partner.*

+ *This is how I prevent anyone from hurting me again with false promises or making me believe I have value but are actually taking advantage of me.*

+ *This is how I prevent people taking more from me than they give.*

Do any of these resonate? Hurt? Trigger painful memories?

Remember, it can also come from conditioning and training: aka, *This is how I do my job.* Nurses, doctors, social workers, firefighters, military, I see you.

If you don't connect with any of those, but still think you're a Freezer, do you resonate with the following?

- *I can't emotionally connect with others when I'm stressed; it's too draining or challenging.*

- *Emotion needs to be left out of this decision, so I need to not feel to get through.*

- *It's impossible to recognize and name my emotions when stressed.*

- *I have received feedback that I'm not empathetic, a good listener, or seem absent when stressed.*

- *I can quickly let things roll off and move on, but I don't quite feel settled after.*

- *I sit on information for a long time and don't know what to do with it.*

- *To get things done I just have to put my head down and power through.*

- *People follow me because I get things done and can operate under pressure; I don't see anything wrong with that. However, I'm difficult to connect with; people say I'm distant or cold when things get hard.*

- *When I have too much on my plate, I totally shut down.*

Make your own Freezer personality.

You might not resonate with any of the above prompts, but still feel like a Freezer personality is your default. Or you might be in a time in life where you feel more like a Freezer. If so, here's what I'd like you to do: fill out the following sentence stem to try to get to the root of it.

I know I'm a Freezer personality because I feel _____

_____ .

Lately, I've been dealing with (example of stressor/ circumstance). I usually think/my thoughts are usually

_____ ,

and I behave by _____ .

What insights did this exercise unearth? Hopefully you're a bit closer to understanding your Freezer personality.

WATCHOUTS

Mental health is at risk.

I mentioned that an approach like Jocko Willink's should come with a warning label…I wasn't kidding. Freezers above all others should take caution because there is certainly harm in stuffing emotion or disconnecting from others when you're feeling stressed. Of all the stress personalities, this is the most volatile and risky. Why? Because a Freezer can quickly disconnect from themselves and others when stress becomes cumulative, chronic, or too intense. Burnout, or a mental health crisis like depression, isn't too far away if you're regularly numb, indifferent, or paralyzed with inaction.

If this persists, eventually you'll learn to numb out to *all* tough situations, or at the very least avoid stress by disconnecting and folding into languish, disconnection, and disengagement. It's a matter of when, not if.

You're not on an island, Freezers—*all* the stress personalities run the risk of burnout or a mental health crisis when leaving chronic stress unaddressed. However, I'm sure you can see the risk in stuffing emotion.

Don't use this book to self-diagnose a mental health concern. If you're regularly shutting down, feeling indifferent, apathetic, or disconnected, I highly recommend seeking professional help and reaching out to the VIPs in your life for support.

Let's touch on a few other watchouts, outside of the most obvious risks already mentioned.

Watch out for overdoing.

Remember that under stress this person has trouble feeling emotion because that dopamine pathway is blocked or disrupted. For this reason, a Freezer might unintentionally seek a "dopamine hit" in other ways. Be wary of overdoing, overindulging, addictions, etc.

Check in with any unhealthy habits you might default to under stress: consider your diet, social life, and physical activity first, which are obvious casualties of chronic high negative stress. And by the way, exercise and other healthy habits *can* become a bad thing if overdone. I once worked with a phenomenally fit personal trainer who overtrained to the point she suffered a nearly catastrophic injury; she was quite literally stuffing her psychological discomfort with rep after rep at the gym to the point it nearly cost her life. She healed after finally accepting help from a therapist.

Unproductive productivity.

Another watchout is knowing the difference between disconnecting to get things done to stay connected to your mission—and disconnecting from your emotions and the people/things that matter to you. Be wary of the *cost* of your productivity. Again, compartmentalization in and of itself isn't dangerous or unproductive—sometimes, a singular focus is exactly what you need to fully engage in the most trying of times to achieve incredible things. This kind of compartmentalizing leads to fulfillment and alignment with your purpose and values.

Other times, it's not. And sometimes, it can do both. *Know the difference between compartmentalizing and disconnecting.* The difference is key—one creates connection with yourself and others—the other does not.

FREEZER SUPERPOWER

I think you might have just read between the lines on a Freezer's superpower. Read those last two paragraphs again. Remember my superintendent who did incredible things when she put her head down and charged forward through some of the most difficult moments and decisions of her career? And Jocko Willink, the Navy SEAL, who remained composed in extreme combat situations?

Freezers are quite resilient, or have the capability to be. Here are some Freezer superpowers:

- They can get along with coworkers they don't like and still get the work done.
- They can go through a tough divorce or cancer treatment but keep smiling for pictures and stay present for their kids.

- They can make decisions under pressure that the rest of us cannot.

- They can practice self-care even when demands are high. How? They know how to shut it off and focus on themselves when life demands exceed their capacity (I'm so envious of people like this).

- They can be excellent leaders through transitions, big changes, layoffs, staffing shortages, buyouts, major organizational changes.

- They can create and maintain boundaries to function well at work or at home.

- They unapologetically take the time to disconnect when the world gets overwhelming; they can couch surf like the best of us when needed.

Just be wary: Are you creating connection, or creating disconnection? Are you effectively recovering from the times you needed to keep your head down and power through? See the Stress Resets for a Freezer to know what I mean.

Here's another interesting and related Superpower of a Freezer. Dr. Bruce Perry, mentioned earlier, studies the brains of babies and children who have been through traumatic experiences, and he wrote something that stuck with me: he worries about these children finding peace and connection in life, but he also worries about children who grow up with *frictionless* lives, where they cruise through life without a care in the world. He says that children who have no experience falling and getting back up again tend to have lower resilience later in life and a tendency to have a fixed mindset rather than a growth mindset.[3] He calls them "invisibly vulnerable high achievers."

How many people do you know like this: who struggle with feedback, criticism, challenge, or even the smallest things like not getting their way in an argument?

The Freezer has usually seen and has *been through some stuff*, or they've chosen a field that requires them to make big, high pressure, and quick decisions or presses them to dig deep and perform at a high potential with high risk and cost. If that's you, pat yourself on the back: you are here, you're still standing, and you're stronger because of your path in life.

STRESS RESETS FOR THE FREEZER

What are some Stress Resets for a Freezer? Let's focus on the most important first.

Connect, connect, connect.

If disconnection is the primary outcome of a Freezer's patterns, then we must find a way to create connection. *Connection is single-handedly or easily the greatest antidote to negative stress for every stress personality.*

How can you find a way to reconnect with the people and things that matter to you when you feel like shutting down? Whether it's a trusted advisor, best friend, partner, therapist, or anyone else who can support you, find that person or persons and put them on your short list of VIPs.

Speaking of that short list, have you ever heard of a "Capital F" friend?

Before I define a Capital F friend, I have a job for you: find a piece of paper (yes, real paper), and write down the names of your top 5-10 closest friends/confidants/trusted advisors (I'll be waiting here…).

When you're finished, look at that list and circle the one or two names you consider your very best, closest friends. Don't read the next paragraph until you have this list.

Ready?

Now, look at that narrowed list very closely—this one or these two people could be your Capital F friend(s).

The brilliant, wise, Christian theorist and thought leader, Gordon MacDonald, writes about Capital F friends in his book *Ordering Your Private World*.[4] MacDonald says that we only get a few of these Capital F friends in our lifetime; sure, you can value other friendships, and even spend more time with other friends than these special, rare souls, but a Capital F friend is different. This is the person you feel most connected to and comfortable with. This person knows your heart and you know theirs. They regularly spend time and energy on you, take initiative to connect with you, hold you accountable to your values, and know when to offer advice and when they just need to listen. You may have only one, two, or possibly three of these rare friends in your lifetime.

I am deeply grateful to have two Capital F friends in my life. These ladies are there for me in every area of my life: always present to listen, support, and celebrate my success. They know my values and hold me to them. I can share the worst parts of me without fear of judgment, which is rare these days.

Not everyone is worthy of your vulnerability and courage to connect, so choose wisely.

Who are your Capital F friends? Can you leverage them to find connection with yourself and others?

We all *need* connection; humans are wired for it.[5] But that doesn't mean we are to be walking open books or seek intimacy every day, or in every relationship. If that's not your nature, don't stress it; the dose is different for everyone. Some of us are energized by being around others, and some of us are drained by it, and some of us are somewhere in the middle. I'm often drained by casual social interaction, but I also love getting to know people, speaking to groups, and my job is *highly* people-focused.

Freezers might need some time alone to recover, reflect, process (like a Runner). Take this Stress Reset with caution and use it when it feels right. There's no right amount of connection, there's only what feels right at the time—and connection with yourself is your priority.

Reconnect to your purpose and values.

Remember in the Fighter personality chapter I asked you to make a list of your core values and identify which were most precious to you? Return to that list; if you haven't made the list yet, go to that chapter and complete the exercise. Try to connect to your values and what brings you meaning and purpose. Why? Because there is a profound link between purpose and motivation.

Need a little additional help with this one? Answer the following questions:

1. Who or what matters the most to you in your life? What makes life worth living?

2. Who are you at your very best? List three words to describe that person.

3. Who are you when you're most proud of yourself?

When you tap into and connect with what's most important to you, you're more likely to be goal-directed, more resilient, more productive, more decisive, and better able to use those challenges to take your next steps forward.

Remember my mantra: *Is my house on fire? Are my kids safe?* This reframe mentioned in the Runner chapter is my way of reconnecting to my values when I feel the urge to run, avoid, or self-protect. *Nothing matters more than my children.* For a Freezer, this same reconnection to values and what's most important can be the spark that lights the flame within.

Get to know your thoughts again.

Freezers often find themselves totally disconnected with their thoughts and emotions, more so than other personalities. Creating space to examine your thoughts is useful for all personalities, but it's particularly helpful for Freezers to flex that mind muscle when feeling emotionally or physically shut down. The following are a few questions you could ask yourself, should you find yourself stuck, numb, disconnected, checked out, languished, or burned out:

1. How did I get here?

Fear? Exhaustion? Too many things on my list of to-dos? Too much to face at once? Something scaring me on that list? Is this just a habit now?

2. What's the risk of staying here?

I won't get done what I need to get done; I'm wasting precious time disconnected from my family or friends; I'll lose energy and focus on my goals; I'll pull my team/others down with me; my confidence and motivation is at risk.

3. What's possible if I take a small step forward?

I will achieve the things I want and need to do; I will build a stronger positive self-image; I will grow a stronger connection to my purpose, passion, values, and skills; I will motivate myself and others; I will build resilience.

Extreme ownership meets strategic recovery.

Jocko Willink's "extreme ownership" approach could be considered a Thriver strategy as much as a Freezer strategy…but it very much depends on how we *recover and reset* from those moments.

Whatever you call it—extreme ownership, compartmentalizing, powering through, braving the chaos, yada yada—it can propel you to do great things. The caveat to preventing emotional disconnection or burnout is to match that action with intentional recovery. If you powered through for several weeks, take a couple of days off. If you powered through a tough morning, go to lunch, and fully disconnect. Every situation differs. One way or another, check in with yourself: How are you feeling? How was that experience? What were the emotions you felt? What do you need *right now* that would help you move forward?

A caveat: I'm not suggesting you *stuff the hard stuff and pretend it's not there*, nor just whitewash your struggles and challenges. Sometimes, this extreme ownership approach simply isn't appropriate. But sometimes in life, it's just what you need. Regular self-reflection will help you know the difference.

Try mindfulness to bring you back to life.

Freezers might benefit from some of the mindfulness strategies mentioned in the other stress personality chapters…particularly in a moment of numbing or shutting down.

Body scan: Take a quick body scan and locate the source of tension. Is it in your shoulders? Chest? Neck? Imagine releasing that tension, one body part at a time. Maybe you're feeling very heavy? Try imagining yourself light as a feather.

Grounding: Notice how your feet are connected to the ground. Better yet, remove your shoes (if possible) and feel your feet on the floor (or in the grass), or your body in the chair. Notice the weight of your body melting into the earth.

Journaling: As with other stress personalities, journaling your emotions is a great way to reconnect with them. If it helps, use a sentence stem, or thought prompt.

Complete the following sentence: I refuse to feel _____. Then ask: What is the next step I can bravely take?

Visualization.

Visualization has long been known to improve performance and the way we show up for ourselves and others. We'll talk about this more in a later chapter but know this: visualizing who we want to be and how we want to show up can be a powerful motivator for action and reconnection.

My newly Freezer superintendent successfully navigated the pandemic by choosing Stress Resets to help her reconnect with her emotions and better manage her energy during the workday. She took more frequent, smaller self-care breaks and asked for her husband's help holding her boundaries on the weekends to fully disconnect from work. When she had the time, she chose to journal daily and list her emotions, then worked to communicate those feelings with others in small moments.

An interesting twist to her story: A year after the pandemic when we thought she was through the hardest few years of her career, she experienced a life-altering injury that took her literally off her feet for more than two months. Despite the extremely high stress and total disruption of her life, she processed and worked through the experience with grace and high emotional literacy. She expressed her feelings better than she had before the pandemic began. She and her husband grew closer than ever; I was thrilled with how she handled the entire experience...bye bye, Freezer personality.

And Amber, my alternative school leader? Her Freezer stress personality was a bit tougher to navigate than her Fighter, but as you may remember, she chose to connect with a licensed therapist to work through it. For Amber, the underlying triggers were deeper than what a Stress Reset alone could manage, but that didn't mean she didn't benefit from a few: in combination with therapy, she practiced regular meditation and practiced small moments of connection, and she's thriving today because of her brave step to get professional support.

FINAL THOUGHTS

Freezers, I know this is a tough personality to identify and to manage. This is mostly because it's hard to recognize but also because what makes you so good at what you do is likely the same reason you struggle to connect when stressed. *Learn to recognize when you're disconnecting* and find a Stress Reset to reconnect. You've got this—you're amazing.

TL:DR

+ Freezers might feel emotionless, drained, sluggish, indifferent, apathetic, or disengaged.

+ They might struggle to feel empathy and compassion when stressed and connection feels difficult.

+ Freezers often don't think through their stress and often intentionally block negative thoughts. They may have thoughts such as, *I'm not cut out for this, so I'm going to give up* or *I'm not going to deal with this right now.*

+ They might seem like they don't care, or seem disconnected, curt, callous, or as if they aren't paying attention, forgetful or spacey. They might seem stuck or checked out.

+ Freezers can be both highly productive and action-focused but emotionally "frozen" (powering through but emotionally disconnected) and/or mentally and physically "frozen" (collapsing on the couch/unable to be productive).

+ Freezers can become Freezers because of past negative experiences or even traumatic experiences that create complex and powerful memory traces.

+ Freezers can also become Freezers simply because they have been conditioned this way through training, their work, upbringing, etc.

+ Over time, Freezers might struggle to produce dopamine the same way as the rest of us due to repeated "blocking" of this pathway.

+ If not careful, Freezers can create disconnection with themselves and others, and find themselves out of alignment with what matters most to them. They can also risk burnout, or worse.

+ Freezers can leverage Stress Resets to help reconnect to themselves and others:

  » Connection and Capital F friends

  » Purpose and values work

  » Grounding, body scans, and other mindfulness strategies

  » Emotions journaling

  » Visualization

You are rockstars, Freezers, keep connecting.

9

THE PLEASER

Alice was only in her late 20s when she found herself in the hospital after collapsing from burnout. She wasn't a likely candidate for such a poor physical state: she was young, engaged to her soulmate, physically healthy, a former elite collegiate athlete, and working in a high pressure, high expectations recruiting position. And she was *really* good at her job; so good, in fact, that she was leading her team in closings and fast-tracked for a leadership position. The problem was, every time Alice met a new deliverable, they increased her reach goal (as they should; it's incumbent upon organizations to give you more work the better you perform, right?). Every time they moved the needle, Alice stretched again and rose to the occasion.

Alice was, from the moment she could walk, a serious high performer. A former elite collegiate swimmer, she came from a family of high performers. Her mother was an Olympic swimmer, and both of her parents held prestigious positions within their respective jobs. Alice's sister, her best friend, was also an incredibly brilliant and talented entrepreneur.

Alice had *always* been surrounded by high achievers. Because of this, Alice had a specific idea of what it meant to be "successful"— which was nothing short of perfection in all areas of life.

So, she pushed and pushed some more, and took on more and more demands at work. Alice was (and is) an incredibly deep thinker with a beautiful soul and a heart for others. She didn't want to sacrifice her strong bonds with her fiancé, friends, and family, so she gave and gave and gave some more. Alice placed the world on her shoulders, and then some.

The problem is, Alice eventually found herself pouring from an empty cup and wasn't willing to drop any frantically spinning plates: professional, friend, fiancé, sister, daughter, dog mom, athlete. Her big heart, her drive for perfection in everything she did, and her high expectations of herself were exactly what landed her in the hospital.

Alice was a card-carrying Pleaser. Her superpower is (still today) her larger than life ambition, her talent, and her heart; but this was also her kryptonite. Ending up in the hospital due to burnout, hooked up to all sorts of machines telling her *you overtrained, you pushed your body to collapse…STOP!*, was the rock-bottom moment which motivated her to start working with a therapist and also a performance coach (me).

Before I go any further, let's get this one straight: *Pleasers are _really_ good people.* They usually have a natural desire to put others before themselves; they are innately *other-centered*. They're often pretty darn great at reading people, tend to be highly empathetic, and they're great communicators and listeners. They're incredibly ambitious and driven to succeed but care about others (and often the way others see them) in a way the rest of us often can't imagine.

When they're stressed, though, they don't tend to back up and consider how to best manage their energy and time—they lean *toward* demands, often at the expense of their well-being.

EMOTIONS OF A PLEASER

The predominant emotions of a Pleaser under stress are kind of funky and contradictory. Here's what I mean: Let's say, for example, a Pleaser is asked to take something on when their plate is already full. Initially, they may feel *overwhelmed, stressed, hesitant, fearful, exhausted, nervous, etc.* But their *eagerness to please or measure up* usually leads to taking it on anyway. The reaction from the person asking for their time and energy (*Wow, thank you so much! You're so helpful! How do you do it all? We can't live without you! You're irreplaceable!*) creates a surge of dopamine (that feel-good reward-based neurotransmitter), so then they may feel positive emotions of *satisfaction, value, warmth, compassion, ambition, validation,* etc.

Pleasers feel *enormous* pressure to help others and meet obligations and expectations set by themselves or others. They could go days, weeks, months, or even years doing a job they don't want to do, putting up with a person they don't care for, taking care of other people's work, without saying a word. They might do so with high energy and ambition, or low energy, lethargy and hesitation—but they do it. Regardless of the energy they bring, they always defer to others' needs and expectations over their own and measure their success by others' praise and affirmation.

Because of their thin-to-no boundaries and drive for perfection and pleasing others, Pleasers can also *at the same time* feel equally *resentful, anxious, stressed, exhausted, overwhelmed, worried,* or *physically/mentally/emotionally depleted.*

Pleasers are the "appease" in fight-flight-freeze-appease. They don't just please when they're pressed to take on others' to-dos or asks; they can also take on the *emotional* stress of others. Because they're such great listeners, sounding boards, and compassionate empaths, Pleasers tend to find themselves the dumping grounds for others' stress, worries, baggage, etc.

Sometimes, their stress is *internally* created by the drive for perfection or urge to overextend and help others. Even if no one asks them to do anything, they still must get things *just right,* so they wear themselves out addressing every minor detail or take on what they shouldn't.

For example, Alice would have a terribly long and hard day at work, yet still make a big meal for her fiancé, get in an intense workout, check in with a few friends and family (because she's thoughtful like that), and check back in with work several times between—then she'd feel guilty because she didn't feel she really gave enough of herself to *any* of those things. No one asked her to do all that—she created the stress simply by not meeting the big, impossible expectations she set for herself. Some days she felt she could take on the world; others she felt depressed, unsure, and like a failure. Lots of highs and lows.

And that's just it. Pleasers often find themselves on a rollercoaster of highs and lows. Stressful situations can either be a result of people-pleasing and perfectionism driving unhealthy behaviors *or* they turn to fixing, pleasing, helping others, taking on more demands, all in an effort to scratch that insatiable itch to measure up and avoid confrontation. *Doing*, not *being*, is a critically important measure of success for Pleasers.

THOUGHTS OF A PLEASER

Success and confidence are often measured by the validation of others for a Pleaser. Like a Negative Self-Talker or Worrier, the Pleaser might become *overly focused on the details, outcomes, productivity*, and likely *obsess over the tiniest of mistakes or setbacks* or *fixate on what others are thinking*. They might focus on what others are thinking over their own thoughts.

They often measure their worth on others' opinions, validation, and feedback—even thrive off of it. They might also struggle to receive constructive feedback for fear of letting others down. Like a Negative Self-Talker, they take the opinions of others very seriously, likely over their own opinion of themselves. The small difference is that a Pleaser's critical inner voice tells them they're only enough when others see them a certain way or get things *just right*, whereas the Negative Self-Talker usually has an inherent core identity that they will never measure up or simply aren't enough no matter what they do (both can overextend themselves, though, I think). In other words, where a Negative Self-Talker might have a *fixed mindset* that they are inherently flawed, a Pleaser might have more a *conditional mindset* (*If I do this/get this right/take this on*, **then** *I will measure up*)—a conditional self-worth.

Side note: The lines between a Pleaser and Negative Self-Talker are quite blurred. In fact, I see the Negative Self-Talker as a root culprit in many of the stress personalities. If you keep seeing yourself in another stress personality even though you identify as a Negative Self-Talker, this might be why. Your thoughts and behaviors might be the biggest differentiator.

BEHAVIORS OF A PLEASER

Like the Negative Self-Talkers, Pleasers often find themselves watering down their own needs, ignoring their core values (or don't apply them to themselves), and measuring their success and self-worth by the praise, feedback, and validation of others, or their status, or their achievements, or their title, and so on.

Pleasers are almost always perfectionists by nature and love to set unreasonable goals. They are often careful and calculating in conversations, seek perfection not progress (in themselves), and tend to accommodate others *no matter what and at all costs*. Their behaviors and decisions are driven by others.

The following are some other parallels to a Negative Self-Talker:

+ A Pleaser might struggle to *speak up when it's important*, especially to advocate for themselves but sometimes to advocate for others.

- A Pleaser might *avoid confrontation* or play the *peacemaker,* not siding with anyone or not having an opinion. They're not doing this because they're cowards or lack an opinion on something, but because in a fight or flight situation their instinct is to fix and appease, not disappoint—their way of squashing the "threat."

- A Pleaser might *lack clarity of their* inner *voice and intuition.* Listening to that inner voice and gut is so difficult because they are focused on what others think and feel (more on how to combat this in the Stress Reset section).

If you're not a Pleaser, you might find it odd and ironic that anyone would take on *more* stress in the face of, well, more stress. But it's just the way a Pleaser was wired (or has wired themselves) over time. Jenny Blake, author of the book *Free Time,* calls this "Superhero Syndrome"—an addiction to swooping in and helping others, at the expense of our own needs.[1]

Pleasers are often earlier in their careers or lives in my experience, as a by-product of being driven, eager to climb the ladder, prove themselves, hustle for their worth. The problem is, burnout is a real risk for a Pleaser.

Just recently I spoke about stress personalities at an event for Human Resources professionals and one of the members approached me afterward. He was on his *third job* in two years—he left the other two because of feeling overworked, underappreciated, and burned out. But while listening to this keynote on stress personalities, he saw himself in the Pleaser personality and wondered, *Could I be the issue?* I suggested he do some reflection and journaling on how much work he allowed into his personal life, how clearly and directly he communicated his needs to his team and his boss, and how he approached the interview process. Did he ask during the interviews, for example, about the company's culture and work/life integration? Did he have autonomy to sometimes adjust his hours based on, say, attending important family events? How did they handle vacation days, weekends, and off-hour communications? How regularly would he meet one to one with his boss?

It was like a lightbulb went off. He left feeling hopeful and more self-aware, for which I was very thankful.

If we don't stop to really think about our own role in the stress in our lives, how can we ever move through it?

THE PLEASER PERSONALITY: UNDER THE HOOD

Where does a Pleaser personality come from?

Pleasers by upbringing.

As mentioned previously, some are Pleasers by nature in our everyday life outside of stress, which could explain the stress personality. My guess is, if you are a Pleaser in everyday life, you're likely a Pleaser under stress as well. But it could come from so many places:

+ Like Alice, it often comes from the way we were raised: maybe in a home of high achievers and high expectations (like the parent who focuses more on grades than effort, or that sports parent we all know who constantly yells at their kid from the sidelines). Perhaps this stress personality originated as a vie for attention and approval from these highly demanding parents.

+ Perhaps you were raised under high pressure to perform (for example, you were a competitive athlete with a high bar for performance from coaches, parents, etc., which bled into other areas of life).

+ Maybe it was the opposite—it originated as a grasp for order and control in a chaotic, dysfunctional home environment, or emotionally distant or unavailable parents and caregivers.

+ Maybe you had a great, safe, positive upbringing and you simply bought into the illusion that you must die to self in all areas of life to be considered a good person, or to get ahead and be successful.

+ Or, you could have been raised in a "them-first" home with amazing, well-intentioned, servant-hearted parents who regularly volunteered their time and whose family mantras were "Serve others before yourself." Heck, I have this as part of my own little family's manifesto on our wall! *Yes*, this is a great sentiment and value to imprint into your children; *but*, without the right communication or modeling, this might create some unintentional conditioning that you *never* put yourself first.

The opposite is also true, by the way. Too much focus on self-care and getting ahead at all costs, and not enough focus on serving others and impacting the world can create a generation of self-centered, narrow-minded, values-starved humans. For what it's worth, we're healthier and happier when our purpose for life involves some sort of service to others; but that must be balanced with taking care of ourselves first.

Pleasers are *trained* to be Pleasers.

Like the rest of the stress personalities, Pleasers can emerge through sheer conditioning. Think about the nature and training of social workers, military personnel, nonprofit workers, special education teachers: these are inherently other-centered human beings whose lives are dedicated to serving others.

This group has quite literally trained in their daily vocations to put their needs aside. Inevitably, their default in all areas of life is to focus on others before themselves. It should be no surprise to anyone that these wonderful humans respond to stress by continuing to help others at the expense of their own health and well-being. But beware: compassion fatigue is a *real thing*. My company worked with hundreds of educators and educational leaders during the pandemic and the impact of compassion fatigue was staggering. I'm thankful to my team of amazing coaches for supporting this group who supported our children.[2]

So yes, it could be our upbringing or our conditioning, but there is also a bit of brain science to Pleasers being Pleasers. This takes us back to dopamine, discussed in the Freezer chapter.

More about dopamine and the Pleaser.

I've introduced dopamine as the "feel good" neurotransmitter and hormone, but it's much more than that. Dopamine influences many regions of the brain, regulating the way we think, feel, act, learn, and stay motivated. You've probably heard of Pavlov's work with dogs and how they salivated when food was in front of them; as a reminder, they salivated *before* food was even delivered in anticipation of their food (reward). The dogs' brains released dopamine when they even *thought* of food.

We all have a similar "Pavlov's dogs response" when learning something new. Dopamine creates a powerful connection between an experience and the brain's ability to store new information and alter behavior because of it. All of us, regardless of stress personality, are addicted to the rewards and pleasures of life, and this influences our behavior.

What does this teach us about dopamine and its role when it comes to stress? Dopamine plays two key roles in how we manage our stress: it keeps us alive by constantly *maximizing* reward and *minimizing* danger.

Consequently, we seek rewards all the time—pleasurable foods, comfortable water temperatures in the shower, getting an A on a test or a good report card, scrolling social media and taking note of the "likes" on our photos, pleasing others (Alice). However, out of a drive for survival, our brain is also constantly trying to maximize our dopamine by minimizing danger at every turn (avoiding constructive feedback, for example). So, we avoid stress (by saying yes to everything, for example) because we don't want to give up our dopamine stores—see, and you thought you were addicted to your coffee. Our dopamine needs are next level!

Even more interesting, and sort of paradoxical, is that acute stress like a cold shower, a high intensity workout, or taking on a new, exciting challenge at work can actually *increase* the dopamine response of the brain. So, a little high stress (controlled, predictable, etc.) boosts dopamine; but consistent or chronic negative stress can dysregulate our dopamine system, and we actually start to *decrease* or impair dopamine release.[3] So, the dose makes the poison.

Why take this dopamine conversation so deep? Because this is at the heart of a Pleaser personality: they've learned to get their "dopamine hit" from pleasing others rather than through self-satisfaction, learning from mistakes (aka, embracing imperfection), or protecting their own energy. Pleasers don't often get the same "high" from fighting, running, freezing, or self-care, boundaries, etc.

Over time, the "reward" of pleasing others can dampen, so they might start to take on more, and more, and more and it never feels like enough. They have trained this way for quite some time and this behavior becomes stored deep in the memory banks (with the help of, ironically, the same dopaminergic reward system of the brain). And then one day? Crash and burn.

Let's face it, Pleasers: you're dopamine addicts!

EXERCISES TO UNDERSTAND THE PLEASER PERSONALITY

Here are a few questions to consider if you think this might be your default stress personality:

Reflective Questions

+ Does your ambition ever cause you to overextend or have trouble saying no?

+ How important are others' opinions versus how you feel about yourself?

+ How was success and "enough" defined for you as a child? How do you define it now?

+ Do you have a fear of rejection, conflict, criticism, or abandonment?

+ When you put your needs first or you express your opinion, does it make you uncomfortable?

+ Do you have trouble saying no?

+ On a scale of 1-10, how assertive are you? Does this often get in the way of holding your boundaries, asking for what you need, or saying no?

+ Do you feel like you *need* to help others or take things off their plate, or simply *want* to?

+ Is getting things just right important to you? Would you self-describe as a perfectionist?

+ On a scale of 1-10 how strong are your boundaries?

Boundary Mining

Pleasers often have weak to no boundaries under stress. There's an exercise I use with clients (Pleasers or not) where we self-assess and clarify our boundaries. Let's use this as a litmus test to assess where you might need to do some work.

Directions: Fill out the table, thinking about boundaries you have in place in different areas of your life (work, home, emotional boundaries, etc.).

Then think about the boundaries you allow others to violate (your coworkers or manager think they can call you at any hour, for example) *and* the boundaries you violate yourself (you say you're not available to work on weekends but work anyway, but then complain that you don't have any work-life balance). How do you feel, think, or behave?

Current Boundaries (circle the absolutely non-negotiable ones)	Weak/ Limited/ Non-existent Boundaries	Signs/ Symptoms/ Red Flags (how do you show up when this boundary is violated by you or others?)	

Two quick things: one, non-negotiable boundaries are the ones you would *never, ever give up*, no matter what. So choose wisely. And two, draw the fourth column but leave it blank for now: we'll get to it.

When you're finished, look at the results of your exercise; pay attention to the third column and answer the following questions:

+ *How often do I give up my boundaries? (Even the non-negotiable ones, let's be honest.)*

+ *What's at stake if I continue this path?*

If you're anything like Alice, it's not going to end well.

WATCHOUTS

Burnout and Overtraining Syndrome

Of course, Pleasers are susceptible to burnout in the way they expend their energy with very little renewal. They'll quickly justify this though:

+ *They're counting on me.*

+ *Serving others is more important than serving myself.*

+ *We're in this together. It takes a village. Teamwork makes the dreamwork.*

+ *I only need to do this for a little while…*

Nonetheless, they're headed for overtraining.

Remember the story of Simone Manuel from Chapter 2 about her training for the Tokyo games and overtraining? This is the statement we took from her story:

Stress without recovery = Overtraining

Stress with recovery = *Growth*

This was Dr. Jim Loehr and Dr. Jack Groppel's concept of stress and recovery; a lesson we can learn from the world of sport that easily translates to our world of business and the sport of life.

Don't forget this, ever—our minds are *no different from our bodies* when it comes to stress, demand, pushing ourselves, reaching new heights—without proper recovery in place, there is a law of diminishing returns no matter what challenge we face (physical, mental, emotional, spiritual).

Freezers put themselves at risk here, too. All of us do, really.

We simply *need* recovery to thrive in life and at work. When we're careful with how we use and spend our energy and have clear, consistent boundaries in place to protect that energy, we can reach new heights of performance even during moments of stress and give our best to *every* area of our life, without all the guilt and exhaustion.

In other words, watch out for a lack of recovery. Focus less on the many things you're doing and more on how you're recovering from the many things you're doing—is there relative equity?

Boundaries: What Are Those?

Boundaries are a critical key to managing this stress personality. Weak or nonexistent boundaries increase the likelihood of chronic stress and burnout, which impair focus, creativity, innovation, problem-solving, and so on. When our boundaries are not in place, not communicated, or not enforced, we can quickly go off course of our values, sacrifice our energy, and our well-being. This is one of the major watchouts for this stress personality.

Pleasers Risk Close Relationships

Pleasers also need to pay attention to their relationships with themselves and others. When left unchecked, this stress personality can quickly erode relationships. One of my clients, Bill, is the CEO of his company. Bill has a big heart and is a wonderful leader whose life purpose is to develop people to their full potential. The problem is, he's also a Pleaser (kind of rare for a CEO). The result is that he really struggles to set clear expectations, boundaries, make decisions and stick with them, and hold his team accountable. The impact:

+ Consistent miscommunication and lack of clear lines of communication; people going over their superior's heads to come directly to Bill when there are issues.

+ An erosion of his relationship with the immediate senior leadership team who cannot get direct answers or feedback from him and feel slighted by their direct reports going over their heads to come to Bill with issues.

+ His personal life was rife with friction. He was so very available that he allowed texts at all hours, emails or calls on vacation; his wife and children reported that he was rarely fully present at dinners, sports events, in conversations. He was missing out on life.

+ His inner voice was elusive. He rarely stopped to listen to his own thoughts, trust his gut and intuition, and rely on his very deep knowledge and experience. He always sought answers from others, not within. Along the way of being helpful and focused on others, he lost the ability to listen to the most important voice in his life—his own.

Pleasers can quickly build resentment toward others by overextending, and they can also create situations where others unintentionally (or intentionally) start to take advantage of them. In some situations (like with Bill), others might even start to feel unsympathetic toward their self-sabotaging behaviors (like Bill's wife). For example:

+ *Why don't you stop saying yes? Why don't you stop agreeing to do things you don't want to do?*

+ *Why don't you gently tell that manager to speak with her immediate supervisor rather than burning an hour of your time?*

+ *Don't complain to me about it if you don't plan to do something about it.*

We had to work a lot on boundaries and effective communication of boundaries, procedures, and policies. It was a "yes, and" for Bill. He could be available, empathetic, and develop people, and he could also hold boundaries for himself and his senior team.

PLEASER SUPERPOWERS

I said it before, and I'll say it again: Pleasers are incredible humans.

Pleasers Are Responsive Team Players

Pleasers are great at taking orders and running. They are responsive and helpful: the ones who always go the extra mile. If you need them, they'll be there; no questions asked.

Pleasers Are Ambitious

There's a high probability that if you're a Pleaser, high performance is in your blood. Ambition, drive, and a high bar are your love language. My guess is you don't settle, you dream big, and you know what it means to perform at a high potential and work hard for your goals, and you don't crush others on your climb. Am I right?

Pleasers Are Selfless

Remember Jocko Willink, the SEAL Team 3 commander mentioned in the previous chapter? He says that a SEAL's mentality is to look out for the guy to your left and right...that *they matter more than you*. He calls this mentality "50/50 security." Valuing your neighbor's life more than your own is what keeps you all alive.

I love that thought and I resonate with it. In my life, my boys and my husband come first, and everything else comes second; as a practicing Christian, I'm supposed to live by these standards. *It is a good thing to put others before ourselves.*

Pleasers have this incredible inherently selfless worldview. The world needs people like you! Just don't lose sight of how to advocate for yourself along the way; you're a pro at *not* putting yourself first and making decisions based on others. If you're not careful, eventually, "dying to self" starts to become, well, literal.

Pleasers are Compassionate Empaths

As mentioned before, Pleasers are often incredibly empathic, compassionate, and great at reading others and addressing others' needs. Empathy and compassion come naturally to them, even under stress, which makes them a diamond in the rough...especially because these qualities are often the first thing to go under stress for the rest of us.

The Latin root for the word compassion is *pati* which means "to suffer," and the prefix "com" means "with." So being compassionate toward someone means to *suffer with* them; and to suffer with someone means to deeply connect with them. What a power skill!

I'm ashamed to tell you this story. But I'll share it anyway because hey, we're all human. My family and I were on a spring break trip recently in London and walking through a beautiful park near Buckingham Palace on our way to a museum. My older son Jake, 13 at the time, was bouncing off the walls and driving my husband and I crazy (nothing new). He was getting in people's way, poking and punching his brother, and generally being a teenager. At one point while walking, he hopped off the path and tried to hop on one foot to look at the bottom of his shoe—only to slip and fall right into a big, thick, black mud puddle. Wet, dark black mud covered his *entire* body, literally from head to toe.

Dozens of people stopped to gasp, laugh, and stare. Someone even took a picture of him.

Because we were already at our patience limit, my husband and I both handled it terribly. I wanted to just walk away and give up on our happy little family vacation (Runner much?), not so much out of embarrassment from the crowd gathering but from the fact that we had no change of clothes, no towel or napkins to clean up, no bathrooms nearby, were two Tube rides from the hotel, and would surely miss our tour.

Instead of walking away I just stood there staring at Jake, my eyes sending the message that I didn't feel bad for him, and that it served him right. My husband just kept on walking. I can't blame him, really. Jake had been jumping off benches, skidding through fallen leaves, and darting through crowds of people with all his boundless teenager energy. My husband's reaction said it all—this was bound to happen at one point or another and walking away was his way of saying "serves you right."

Like I said, we didn't handle it well.

If you're a parent, you probably get it (or, you're judging the heck out of us right now), but it doesn't make it any less of a certified Parent Fail. My poor son was mortified, his eyes welling up with tears. Feeling his embarassment, my energy immediately shifted, and I felt tremendous guilt for my initial reaction.

It was right at that moment a homeless man who was feeding some geese nearby walked over and handed Jake a package of tissues without a word. Jake looked at him with a deer-in-headlights expression—*What do I do now?*—and tried to take just one. But the man told him to take the whole pack. The man wasn't laughing, he wasn't sneering, and he wasn't judging—his eyes were full of compassion and the genuine desire to help. I was instantly convicted by the compassion of a stranger for a stranger; not to mention it was likely the only tissues he had on him, let alone other hygienic items we take for granted.

Nonetheless, he gave.

Jake thanked him, and we tried our best to clean at least his hands and face. It wasn't but a few seconds that passed when we turned around to thank the man again and try to offer him something for his generosity. But he was gone, absorbed into the busy crowd. He didn't expect a thing in return.

Our boys learned a lesson about compassion that day we could never teach them. We learned a lesson on compassion, too. I apologized to Jake for not showing up the way I should have, and he talked about the man the entire rest of the trip. I truly believe he was sent to teach my family many lessons in that one fleeting, high-stress moment.

The point? Being a Pleaser is a true superpower.

Pleasers, you have some serious superpowers. I am in awe of your compassion and grace. You're always there just at the right time, no questions asked.

STRESS RESETS FOR THE PLEASER

If you're a Pleaser, knowing your kryptonite and being protective of your energy, your time, and space to recover is so very important. If you struggle with this, spend time on the earlier reflective questions to really get to the root of what drives your need to please others. When you're done, use the exercises to find the right balance between that beautiful side of you, and protecting what's important in the process.

Boundary Mining: Part II

Return to the boundary mining exercise from earlier. Remember that fourth column? Let's fill it out.

Current Boundaries (circle the absolutely non-negotiable ones)	Weak/ Limited/ Non-existent Boundaries	Signs/ Symptoms/ Red Flags (how do you show up when this boundary is violated by you or others?)	Strategies to Protect and Reinforce your Non-negotiable Boundaries

In this last column, brainstorm ways to better protect your non-ne-gotiable boundaries—the boundaries you would never give up, no matter what. Here are a few suggestions:

- Create an exhaustive list of *all* situations where you believe violating a boundary is warranted. For example, if you said, "I won't work nights or weekends," is that always and forever true, or are there any exceptions when you would violate that boundary? My husband, working in finance, has times of the year when work is just plain busier. We, as a couple, know that he must work weekends sometimes, or later at night, during budget season. We communicate, we plan, and there are no surprises (he also makes sure to build in more time on the back end for a few work-from-home or PTO days to recover). That's how we navigate and plan for a negotiable boundary that has a bit of an outlier to it. Where are those areas for you? And how often do you or others slip? Is this a pattern or truly an outlier?

- You might need a boundary around when it's warranted to say *yes* or *no* to things and when it's not. Perhaps you can create some questions to help guide your thinking:

  » *What is my intention for saying yes to this?*

  » *What is the opportunity here for me?*

  » *Is this in alignment with my values and my purpose?*

  » *What does my gut say about this?*

  » *Would I say yes if no one would care or be disappointed in me?*

- Speaking of knowing when to say yes or no to something, take a page from the Runner's superpower book and build the muscle of "creating space" between the ask and your response to give you more time to process. Are there a few phrases you can memorize to use before responding to a request for your time or energy? Maybe some phrases that are simple, direct, and clear no's? Here are some suggestions:

» *No. (Yes. That's it, you don't need to always apologize for saying no).*

» *I don't feel comfortable talking about this. Can we change subjects?*

» *Thanks, but I'm not drinking right now (or: going out right now; gossiping about others; willing to talk about XYZ person or issue with you).*

» *I don't have the time for this due to XYZ expectations. What would you like me to put aside or delay to get this completed on time for you?*

» *Can I give you a response in 24 hours (or however much time you need) so I can make sure I'm giving you the right answer?*

» *I can do that, but I'm going to need XYZ resources/support.*

» *I'm struggling to get XYZ done in a timely manner within my working hours; would you mind supporting me with XYZ (delegation is a power skill.)?*

» *Can you help me understand the process and specifically what success would look like for this ask, so I can determine if I can take it on?*

For Pleasers, saying no is hard. It might be worth pausing to feel what it feels like in your body and heart to say No, Yes, or I'm not sure in smaller moments. Sit with how it feels to hold a small boundary before holding a bigger one.

+ Build in your boundaries. There is great power in blocking your calendar for what you need: exercise, work-free lunch, focus or creative time, personal time, etc. One of the absolute greatest life hacks I ever put into place was restructuring my calendar with better boundaries around calls, meetings, heads down time, reflection time, and so on. This is a Thriver Accelerator that we'll unpack further later. For example, Tuesdays are for heads down time, and Fridays are no calls or meetings after 12 p.m. Now my clients, coaches, and team members can clearly see when I'm available and I can also hold myself accountable to my morning workouts, which are the lifeline for my energy and resilience. I have "flexi-firm" boundaries around meeting with my international coaches and partners when needed, but those are outliers and not regular occurrences.

Remember, boundaries are kind and helpful for everyone—but, *they're only as strong as your ability to communicate them.* Melissa Urban has a great new book on boundaries titled, you guessed it, *The Book of Boundaries*[4] which is packed with tips and strategies if this is a struggle for you.

Recover Well and Often

Back to the idea of stress and recovery for a moment: for a Pleaser, the idea of recovery is so important. Recovery was integral to Alice's coaching plan—I didn't ask her to give less of herself, take on less demands at work, or work less hard in the gym, etc.; instead, I challenged her to find opportunities to recover and hold those boundaries.

This didn't come without discomfort for Alice. Protecting time for herself, not taking calls during lunch, not checking emails during workouts, and shutting down her laptop a few nights a week for full focus on her fiancé and dog was *hard* for her. But my former elite athlete leveraged her competitive superpower, and she kept her eyes on the mission until, eventually, recovery felt natural. With regular recovery through her day and stronger boundaries, she felt more rested, connected to her fiancé, and her work team appreciated her boundaries and even encouraged them. By the way, her work performance *improved*. I was thankful Alice tackled this earlier in her career—she'll likely experience more balance and joy for the rest of her life.

Here's a suggestion: make a list of strategies (Stress Resets!) you already have in place, or wish to have in place, to practice during protected boundary times. Try this:

What would you do to recover if you had:

+ *60 seconds or less?*

+ *2-5 minutes?*

+ *10+ minutes?*

Think about: nutrition, movement, mindfulness, breathing exercises and meditation, exercise, massage, music, phone-a-friend, etc. It can be the same list as your Stress Reset strategies. Just keep it on hand to integrate recovery into your day. You are so much more like Simone, the Olympic athlete, and Alice, my dream-big, full-hearted high achiever, than you might think. We *all* need recovery, but particularly those who consistently give of themselves.

Then, set calendar or phone reminders, use Post-it notes, ask friends to check in on you—find ways to hold yourself accountable.

Clarity of Values

Like the other stress personalities, having clarity of your values is an important part of your ability to determine what's worth taking on—literally and emotionally. See the Fighter chapter for a great exercise on clarifying values (Exercise 3: Values Mining).

Make it very clear *why* your non-negotiable boundaries are what they are. More than likely, they are non-negotiable because they are directly related to parts of your life or people who are most important to you—your values, your purpose, your reason for being. Like an anchor, values prevent us from drifting when life gets busy or asks more of us than we're willing to give.

Make a Stop-Doing List

In his book *Good to Great*,[5] author Jim Collins shares the great idea of creating a "stop-doing" list. We're so used to making long to-do lists (Pleasers, you'll even add other people's to-dos onto your list). Collins suggests questioning activities, processes, and to-dos that don't directly contribute to your missions and goals, and work to stop doing them. This might look like letting go of outdated processes, or saying no to groups, clubs, boards, events, meetings, calls with people who drain you, etc.

You can do this occasionally, or you can grab a Post-it note when you're feeling stressed and make one in the moment. Whatever it looks like to you, see if this shift in thinking works for you.

Inner Voice

Get to know your inner voice more intimately; reference the Negative Self-Talker chapter for a great exercise on how to get to know the beautiful champion inside you, who is often the same one who takes you into taking on more than you should.

Triage Your Time and Energy with the Eisenhower Matrix

See the Distracted stress personality chapter for more info, but sometimes triaging your day and deciding what's most urgent will help you learn to say no more often, delegate more, and narrow your focus on what's most important.

FINAL THOUGHTS

Pleasers, you are the compassionate, grace-filled, empathetic, driven high achievers of our world. Imagine the world without you! Just keep protecting your energy so you can continue to shine and be the light in our lives.

TL:DR

+ Pleasers are often driven to please others, measure up, and measure their worth and success based on the feedback and validation of others. A Pleaser might have a conditional mindset about measuring up or lack intuition and an intimate knowing of their inner voice.

+ Pleasers are often perfectionists and trained to be other-focused.

+ Pleasers often feel overwhelmed, stressed, nervous, etc., and take on more to feel valued, worthy, and scratch their high performance itch.

+ Pleasers are often highly empathetic and compassionate.

+ They often have thin-to-no boundaries leading to feeling resentful, anxious, stressed, exhausted, overwhelmed, worried, or experience physical, mental, emotional depletion.

+ Pleasers take on others' stress but also create stress by taking on more and more. They can be overly focused on the details, outcomes, productivity, and likely obsess over the tiniest of mistakes or setbacks or fixate on what others are thinking.

+ A Pleaser is often brought up in an environment that is high achieving, high expectation, or is trained to be other-centered. They can also be "dopamine" addicts, seeking the reward of helping others. Unintentionally, they can often stifle dopamine production through chronic stress.

+ Boundaries, recovery time, and space before taking on something else are all important strategies to managing this stress personality and really letting its superpowers shine.

10

THE NEGATIVE
SELF-TALKER

If you've never seen the movie *Little Miss Sunshine*, you're missing out. The movie follows Olive, a sweet and ordinary young girl on
her way to compete in a beauty pageant with her dysfunctional quirky
family, including a father who battles negative self-talk and is his own
worst enemy. Olive's ever-supportive (and extremely brash and inap-
propriate) grandfather is her biggest fan. He challenges the superficial
reputation of the beauty pageant culture by instilling in her that self-
love, not fabricated beauty, is the most important thing to strive for.

In one sweet but sad scene, Olive is gazing at her body and face
in a mirror and asks her grandfather if she's pretty. He responds that
she is the most beautiful girl in the world, jokingly adding, "and it's
not because of your brains or your personality." If you haven't seen the
movie, I'm spoiling things a bit here, but the confidence he gives Olive
ends up inspiring the family to find each other, and themselves, again.
The movie is so much more than this lesson but it's a central theme of
the movie, which each character must learn for themselves along the
journey.

I wish we all had a grandpa like Olive's growing up; maybe there
wouldn't be as many of us Negative Self-Talkers out there.

EMOTIONS OF A NEGATIVE SELF-TALKER

The Negative Self-Talker stress personality is pretty self-explanatory. It probably isn't a surprise that their predominant emotions are persistent *insecurity, worry, uncertainty, helplessness, fear, guilt, shame,* and so on.

THOUGHTS OF A NEGATIVE SELF-TALKER

Under stress, Negative Self-Talkers immediately *self-attack* and can quickly find themselves *stuck in self-directed negative thought loops.* They don't lean into stress, but rather *push away and then retreat inward,* appointing themselves the offender in most stressful situations.

Often their thoughts are *self-deprecating, second-guessing, self-blaming, disappointment, embarrassment, frustration,* and they feel *unsure* and *insecure.* They tend to *take things personally* and often *assume the worst* about what others think of them (*I know they're talking about me; I know he doesn't think I can do this; she didn't give me the project because she doesn't believe in me*).

Their *inner voice is their own worst enemy: unsupportive* and rife with *hyperbole* (*I'm such an idiot; what was I thinking? I **always** do this; I will **never** get this job*).

Unlike the other stress personalities who might fixate on their behaviors, Negative Self-Talkers have fixed inherent beliefs about themselves and the world around them (*Ugh, I'm a **total** failure! I'll never reach that goal. I'm unimportant/unlovable/unteachable.*).

Under stress, things feel impossible rather than possible, and the world happens *to* them, not the other way around. They might stop believing in themselves, or filter information to rule out anything that could serve or work in their favor, like what they're doing right, or what's going right.

BEHAVIORS OF A NEGATIVE SELF-TALKER

Negative Self-Talkers can magnify situations; they can make every-thing about them; they can fade away in the hopes of not being seen; they can give up, push away, or avoid like a Runner; they can deny themselves pleasure; they can polarize themselves; they can catastro-phize like a Worrier.

The primary thing to remember is that their inherent, fixed beliefs about themselves propel them away from confident action, dreams, goals, connection with others, and so on.

Often, Negative Self-Talkers create the situation. Sometimes they're negative self-talkers in normal, non-stressful home, work, or social situations, so their general sense of self-worth can trigger the stress response and keep them on high alert. Think about the person who is headed to an after-work event and before they even walk in, beat themselves down to the point where they leave before entering the room. Despite being a kind, funny, successful, totally normal per-son, they convince themselves they're not worthy of taking up space on the team. This is a great example of how our stress personalities can create the stress.

Like a Pleaser, Negative Self-Talkers often *won't speak up when it's important*, especially to advocate for themselves.

Or sometimes, they speak up and up and up...*a broken record of complaints, woe-is-me, or an "Eeyore mentality"* (*Winnie the Pooh's gloomy donkey friend*), which can drain their energy and that of others around them (I think here about the *Saturday Night Live* skit with Debbie Downer played by comedian Rachel Dratch.) Of course, this isn't their intent, but it's often an outcome.

They have a *strong fear of failure and rejection* and often behave as if they don't deserve success or happiness. Even if they inherently believe they're worthy in most normal situations, when stressed it's like they flip a switch and turn on themselves.

Like the Pleaser, *confidence is often measured by validation of others,* so seeking to please can take hold but never quite squelches the insecurity. Taking and delivering feedback is tough because in the moment they can be so hard on themselves, any outside critics amplify their sense of low worth. Or, they water down their own needs to meet others' perceived expectations.

Also like a Pleaser, *perfectionism* could be a persistent red thread; they might obsess over productivity and output or freak out over the tiniest of mistakes or setbacks, and overwork to measure up. And sometimes the opposite. They can cut corners or give up, or be unproductive because what's the point? The difference between a Negative Self-Talker and a Pleaser is that a Negative Self-Talker's behaviors are driven by inherently low self-worth where the Pleaser has more conditional self-worth.

As I mentioned in an earlier chapter, this sneaky little stress personality often shows up in all the stress personalities in one way or another. I'm a Runner and Negative Self-Talker, which shows up for me as an urge to remove myself from a situation—usually followed by (or sometimes driven by) negative self-talk and a harsh inner critic.

Curious which stress personality is in the driver's seat? To help define which is your dominant stress personality, ask: Do I *lead* with Negative Self-Talk as the first and most persistent experience under stress? The thing about Negative Self-Talkers is that it often goes deeper than surface behaviors and emotions: all the way down to their core beliefs.

THE NEGATIVE SELF-TALKER:
UNDER THE HOOD

What's the origin story of a Negative Self-Talker? Negative self-talkers, like the other stress personalities, are products of their environment—how they were raised, conditioned, partners, etc.—but there are also a few areas of psychology and brain science important to this stress personality.

Negativity Bias

Our brains have an inherent *"negativity bias,"*[1] which means we tend to react more strongly to negative input than positive as part of a deeper survival mechanism. This negative bias is normal and shows up in many areas of life:

- We dwell on bad weather days and forget the many days of sunshine.

- We fixate on one annoying coworker, forgetting the dozens of pleasant, wonderful people on our team.

- We think back on the bad times more than the good (this is also due in part to emotional tagging and memory traces—from the Freezer and Worrier chapters).

- We tend to focus more on what our kids, partners, and/or employees do wrong than what they do right—discipline and criticism over gratitude and positive reinforcement.

- We are afraid to take chances, make decisions, connect with others, or make commitments out of fear of failure, rejection, and so on.

It's not that you're a bad person for this; you're simply wired this way…which isn't always a bad thing. We need this bias to help us balance risk-averse behaviors with growing from the "good" stress we take on in the chances we take.

When we achieve the right ratio of positive to negative experiences (it's suggested to be 5:1 by the way[2]), we can live a relatively positive and happy life and existence. But if that scale tips, we start to see the world and ourselves through a more negative lens. This is in spite of our brain's *other* drive to seek pleasure and positive experiences and avoid pain and displeasure (remember the Under the Hood section for the Pleaser). For a Negative Self-Talker, the negativity bias is a very persistent pathway and a driving force of their behavior when feeling threatened or stressed.

Scarcity versus abundance mindset.

Like our negative bias, all human beings struggle to balance a perspective of *abundance versus scarcity*. Abundant thinking is the ability to see opportunities and maintain optimism in uncertain times. But this isn't our default setting from an evolutionary perspective: we are wired to see the world through a lens of scarcity to prioritize survival. The most resilient and skilled of us (Thrivers!) can experience a threat and quickly reperceive it as an opportunity, maintaining a perspective that we have everything we need to get through our challenges… abundance.

Self-blame keeps us safe.

To add to the category of "brain science working against Negative Self-Talkers," we are also wired to self-blame. This propensity comes from a desire to fit in and conform because we are social creatures, forever looking to assimilate into a community or tribe. This would keep us safe from harm because of our collective strength in numbers.

Funny part is, shame and self-demeaning language and blame often only create more disconnection from our tribe.

So, we have that going for us.

When things get hard, suddenly the confidence in your everyday life that makes it easy to give yourself a pep talk wanes: the world gets small, and your normal assuredness is out the window. This can drive behaviors that are out of alignment with your values: *quitting, giving up, fighting others, talking badly about someone* to lift yourself up, *cheating* or *cutting corners*, sacrificing *productivity*, losing *focus*, or even simply *feeling down about yourself.*

Nancy the Negative Self-Talker's Journey

Do you remember Nancy, the first female president of that national healthcare facility I mentioned in Chapter 1? Nancy's stress personality was the Negative Self-Talker.

Remember that when she and I started working together in 2018, she wasn't exercising, wasn't eating well, and slept maybe four hours a night. She was hustling for her worth and way out of alignment with her values and what was most important, including spending time with her husband.

Nancy's identity as a CEO and leader was her identity as a human being. When a mistake was made at work or a challenge surfaced, her sense of *worth* was attached to the outcome: a Negative Self-Talker, through and through.

Nancy and I spent several months gaining clarity of her purpose and values, identifying her stress patterns and her inner voice, and learning how to retell the story of her worth. She was a great client—incredibly ambitious and so driven by her purpose. She created stronger boundaries, found her confidence, and reprioritized her physical health. She really did an incredible job of leveraging the strengths of her stress personality and facing the opportunities head-on.

When the pandemic hit, Nancy was sleeping eight hours a night, exercising regularly, eating better than she had in years, and spending more time with her husband than ever. She was the epitome of health. Her primary Stress Reset strategy was prayer—she started her day in prayer which reminded her that her worth wasn't based on feedback from board members on organizational performance or the latest quarterly financial report, but instead in the belief that she was inherently worthy in the eyes of God.

It's challenging to lead others, be happy and resilient, have thriving relationships, or grow in your career when your most important and trusted advisor—your inner, private voice—is working against you.

If you're looking at the literature on the subject, consider this: people who believe they have the internal resources to deal with any unexpected changes are more resilient, respond better to stress, and better prepare for and deal with a crisis. We aren't always lucky enough to have picked those skills up in our upbringing—sometimes, quite the opposite: we are shaped by our parents and caregivers, our environments, and cultures, and so on; but that doesn't mean we can't shift those beliefs.

EXERCISES TO UNDERSTAND THE NEGATIVE SELF-TALKER PERSONALITY

Let's try three different exercises to get to know this side of you better.

Exercise 1: What's Your Inner Voice Under Stress?

The way you speak to yourself—particularly when feeling threatened or stressed—can really help you get to know your stress personality. The tone, the words you choose, the outlook and perspective you take, all influence what you believe and how you behave (in her beautiful book *Untamed,* writer Glennon Doyle calls it "the Knowing").

Here are a few types of inner voices:

1. Harsh Critic

2. Total Cynic

3. Fearful Coward

4. Personal Champion

First, answer this: which of these characters shows up most often for you in everyday life?

Now, answer the following. Does that change:

+ *When things go right?*
+ *When things go wrong?*
+ *When you accomplish something?*
+ *When you are at your worst or lowest?*
+ *When you're at your best?*

Who shows up when the road isn't smooth?

If you really want to unpack this, spend a week on it. Meditate, reflect, and journal over it daily. Really, truly get to the root of your inner voice and how you speak to yourself. More on tapping into it, and intuition, in the Stress Reset section.

Exercise 2: Checklist

Still a bit unsure if this is your stress personality? Read the following statements and check off the ones that ring true.

When you're stressed:

+ Is your inner voice suddenly harsher and more critical?
+ Are you the first person you point the finger at when looking to blame someone?
+ Do you doubt yourself more than believe in yourself?
+ Do things feel more impossible than possible?
+ Do you avoid asking for help because you feel like a burden?
+ Do you close yourself off from others to avoid rejection?
+ Do you avoid pursuing goals or dreams because you don't want to fail?
+ Do you use hyperboles like *always* or *never* to evaluate your behavior (*I always do this*)?
+ Do you use "I am" statements, more than "I'm acting" type statements? (*I am such an idiot!* versus *I acted like such an idiot!*)
+ Do you rationalize? (*I should feel this way,* or *I'm wrong to feel this way.*)
+ Do you attack your own emotions rather than acknowledge and embrace them? (*Why are you so worried? Get over it.* Versus, *I feel unsure, which makes sense given the circumstances; it's okay to feel this way.*)
+ Do you believe (again, when you're stressed) that you don't deserve success, happiness, connection, or joy?
+ Is it much easier to fight/advocate for others than for yourself?

Exercise 3: What Are Your Core Beliefs?

What core beliefs or identities might be present beneath how you're showing up under stress? Read the following statements. Do any of these resonate with you or feel like a persistent theme of your thoughts?

+ I'm inherently flawed.

+ The world is inherently out to get me/not in my favor.

+ I'm not enough/never will be enough.

+ If people knew the real me, they wouldn't accept me.

+ I'm not worthy.

+ I don't deserve success, happiness, love, acceptance.

+ Any of these core beliefs but add a condition (*I'm not worthy...unless I achieve XYZ.*)

Were these beliefs part of your family dynamic or a past relationship? Are they pervasive undertones of your work culture? Did an awful former partner or parent instill this belief in you?

Remember that stress personalities can be contextual. See if you can get to the root of why, when, where, with whom, and how these core beliefs might surface for you. This can be an emotional process, but facing what's lurking beneath the behaviors is a huge step toward shifting them.

WATCHOUTS

Of course, persistent negative self-talk comes with risk. If the Negative Self-Talk stress personality came with a warning label, it would read:

Caution! Negative Self-Talk may cause:

- *Reduced immune function and poor physical health.* Scientists have reported higher stress-related immune function issues in pessimists as compared to optimists.[3] Chronic stress comes with serious health implications; chronic negativity adds to that.

- *A negative outlook begets a negative life.* Energy is contagious. Negative thoughts will not inherently lead to a negative life, but *persistent,* subconscious negative thoughts will surely lead to behaviors, decisions, and actions that manifest a negative life. When we learn to recognize them, that's the moment we stop being driven by them.

- *You may miss out on what's going right.* Dwelling on what *could* go wrong almost always leads to missing what is going right. Sound familiar? Worriers have the same risk.[4]

- *Disintegrated relationships.* It should be no surprise that persistent negativity isn't exactly what attracts people to one another (unless you're in the "misery loves company" relationship category). We all know that one person in our world who seems to have a perpetual rain cloud above their head—they could win the lotto but complain about the amount, right? As much as you love them, people like this drain your energy. So, it's important to consider what energy you want to attract and how you want people to feel when they're around you. If you're not struggling with a mental health issue like depression or anxiety (this is beyond your singular control and not your fault—you know you need the support of a professional in this case), may I challenge you for a moment? *Controlling your negativity is within your control—the first step is facing it head-on.*

SUPERPOWERS

You may be thinking, What could possibly be a Negative Self-Talker's superpower?

I get that question a lot. What good could possibly come from this? Surprisingly, lots of good! Let's go back to the science of stress for a moment. Negative Self-Talkers are inherently self-protective; their insecurity, questioning, doubt, and so on often keep them on high alert and in a threat response in totally "normal" situations, which comes with some unexpected perks.

Negative Self-Talkers tend to communicate better, are more introspective and self-aware of their actions, think more clearly, tend to make fewer mistakes (because they're constantly worried about making them!). They tend to be less gullible and don't take everything at face value (critics like the best of us), are better critical thinkers, and are often better at decision-making than the rest of us. This is because Negative Self-Talkers are hard on themselves and hold themselves to a higher standard (maybe not as much as the Pleaser, but I'll let them argue that—unless you're a blend of both in which case I imagine your self-standards are sky high).

Negative Self-Talkers are also far from unaware and they tend to read others well...in most situations. Like a Pleaser, however, Negative Self-Talkers aren't always good at accurately discerning what people think of *them*.

They also tend to see themselves in others. They have a great knack for identifying other Negative Self-Talkers and lifting them up. How ironic, isn't it? So, most Negative Self-Talkers are empathetic, compassionate, kind, and sensitive to others' self-esteem and sense of worth. They know how to let others shine and grow, and they tend to be givers, not takers—it's just that they struggle to see the worth in lifting themselves up, too.

Negative Self-Talkers are beautiful people with a skewed sense of self. We don't want to squash the intuitive, empathetic, self-aware side of them. Remember, superpower-kryptonite—we can be both.

STRESS RESETS FOR THE NEGATIVE SELF-TALKER

An important reminder: the goal is not to remove all negativity and negative self-talk. We need both, remember? Sometimes, our inner voice isn't trying to hurt our feelings; sometimes it's alerting us to real danger or risk. For example, occasionally my inner voice whispers (or yells), *This person isn't to be fully trusted, be careful!* Or, *Don't take on this client*, and I'm rarely wrong in the long run. This doesn't make my inner voice harsh or critical, it makes it practical.

But how can we learn to know the difference? Get to know your inner voice. The ability to become really intimate with our inner voice—knowing when it's serving us well and when it's not—is a skill that can be trained.

Here are a few training strategies for this skill:

Make Your Inner Voice Your Biggest Champion

A few years ago, I was invited to speak before a large group in Chicago. It was a great opportunity, but there was a catch—it was on my son's birthday. I had made a promise to myself *never* to miss one of my boys' birthdays because of work. But this opportunity paid incredibly well, so my husband and I decided I would take it.

The day of the event, I woke up in Chicago feeling sick with guilt. My inner voice was *so* critical. *You're a terrible mother. You chose money over moments. You're not worthy of his love.*

I let these thoughts eat me up all day; I even seriously considered selling the business and simplifying our life so that I didn't have to work. But after the event, at least twenty people approached me to share how impactful the conversations were and how they planned to make some major changes in their life (even a year after this Chicago event, I was getting emails from participants sharing incredible success stories). And you know what? I spoke to my son a few times that day and flew back to celebrate with him the next day, just us.

So, was it worth going? Yes. I was reminded that I *love* what I do, and I don't want to stop.

Would I make it a habit to miss his birthday? Never.

My inner voice sometimes goes on a rampage. But I can't lock it up and stuff it away; and I can't let it take over, either.

Listening to your inner voice can help you observe your emotions and thoughts more objectively, and really learn to hear what they're saying and why. For example, in my case, the reality is I was feeling shame, not guilt. Brené Brown says of guilt: "Guilt says 'I made a mistake.' Shame says, 'I *am* this mistake.'" Shame speaks in absolutes. In Chicago, I was feeling shame.

Was I truly a bad mother? Was my son harboring resentment toward me? Had I ever done this before; was this my pattern?

No—no to all.

It was my *opinion* that I was a bad mom for missing my son's birthday, but I had no evidence for that to be true. And, I am *more than a parent*; I have more than one calling. I put my family first 99 percent of the time, but a large part of my life's purpose is serving others outside of my family.

Remember that you have thoughts, but *you are not your thoughts*. Our inner voice can sometimes be a wolf at the door. If we can detach our identity and sense of self-worth from our thoughts and emotions, and just simply observe and learn, we can retrain that inner voice in powerful ways.

Make time to listen to your inner voice—maybe in meditation, a conversation with a trusted friend, through journaling, or simply close your eyes when you're feeling stressed or anxious or overwhelmed (the "Ask" part of our Gift of Pause process).

Ask yourself:

+ What's the tone? What's she/he trying to tell me?
+ What's the emotion I'm feeling?
+ What's influencing these thoughts (context, beliefs, identities, opinions, etc.)?

Then, challenge the voice:

+ What's the opposite of this limited perspective?
+ Where might I feel misaligned to my values?
+ What is true? What are the facts? (Go back to the Worrier chapter for this one.) (As in, *No one likes me* to *I have a great small circle of family and friends who support my success*).
+ Can I change the direction of my voice with one word? What is that word?
+ What "I am" statement can I replace with an "I feel" statement?
+ Can I add a "yet" to this thought? (As in, *I'm not good enough* to *I haven't mastered this yet*, or *I don't belong here* to *I haven't found my footing here yet*.)

When you're kind to yourself, research shows you're far more likely to move forward and not stay stuck or stagnant.[5]

Another client of mine, an HR executive of a large nonprofit, received feedback from his CEO that he needed more confidence. He questioned himself whenever things got stressful—despite a deep resume, two decades of experience, and a team who would follow him anywhere. With a little journaling and training and getting to know his inner voice better, this client learned to catch his negative self-talk in the moment and redirect it with an affirmation acknowledging the emotion, then retelling its story.

He'd say, *I feel unsure, but I am capable.* Then, he'd ask himself, *Is what I'm saying about myself true and accurate?*

He learned that it was okay to pause to process his emotions and thoughts without judgment; his cautious, careful, practical nature is what his team likes best about him. Through a regular guided meditation practice, he learned to quickly redirect negative thinking to more confidence and focus. His next feedback session with the CEO was shining, and so was his smile when he shared it with me.

When you do the work of noticing and shifting that inner voice, it's like breaking up with a toxic partner and then meeting your soulmate. One day you hear a different kind of voice within—one that feels spacious and light, still, steady, unforced, and loud enough to hear when you need it but also peaceful, unobtrusive, and encouraging. It is *deeply connected to her values and sense of purpose.* By the way, that voice is a big part of *intuition,* and it's powerful.

So, use your inner voice to your advantage—listen, observe, learn, and use it to turn those limiting thoughts into empowering ones with just a word or two.

Widen Your Aperture

In his book *Wise Decisions*, Dr. Jim Loehr and coauthor Sheila Ohlsson talk about the concept of "narrowing the aperture." He says that when stress is high, we tend to fall back on old habits and stories, and narrow our focus, or "aperture," which limits what we perceive to be our choices in the situation (similar to a Fighter). For decision-making specifically, he says (Worriers, we know this) we need to both narrow *and widen* our aperture to look at a situation from differing perspectives to see the broader reality of all situations.

I love the metaphor for aperture and our perspective on a situation, particularly when we're hyper-negatively focused.

Here's your Stress Reset: when you feel that critical inner voice surfacing, stop and imagine your aperture *widening* on the situation. What positives can you see? What can you imagine in that moment? What choices and control? What aren't you seeing that you should see?

Again, this isn't about ignoring the negative and forcing the positive, it's about allowing *both to be true at the same time*. If you don't train to see the good, you'll continue to push off your happiness while forever looking for something better in the future.

Bring this aperture visual to your next stressful moment and see what changes.

Doubting Thomas Deserves a Reframe

What about doubt? What can we do about persistent doubt in ourselves? One Easter Sunday our pastor brought up one of the disciples from the Bible, Thomas. He was given the nickname "Doubting Thomas" by Christians over the years for his doubt in Jesus after He died on the cross. Our pastor challenged the unfair nickname, asking us to think about what was behind Thomas's doubt. The truth is, he felt fear and hurt. Was he doubtful? Or just afraid and saddened by an unmet promise?

You don't need to be a Christian to see the metaphor here. So often we doubt ourselves out of fear of the unknown, or a past hurt or unmet promise. *If I was hurt then, I'll be hurt again. If I was let go from this job, I will never get another. What if I'm not good enough? What if I fail?* Scratch the surface of doubt, and you'll find layers of past pain and uncertainty.

Whether you feel doubt in yourself, others, or a situation (Worriers, are you still listening?), peel back the layers and get to the root of what's underneath. What are you afraid of? What or who hurt you enough to question yourself this time around?

And then, address whatever is underneath. Go back to the inner voice exercise. Try to widen your aperture. What positive truths lie untapped?

Intervene. Reframe the inner voice. Reset.

Abundance Versus Scarcity Mindset

How can we move through stress with more of an abundance mindset so that we are well-equipped mentally and emotionally to manage anything?

Let me give you an example of when I did this right. Recently I woke up at 4 a.m. to catch a flight to Little Rock, Arkansas, from Orlando, Florida, to see a client and train one of my facilitators to deliver a two-day program. I woke to an alert that the flight was canceled and immediately checked the flights out of another nearby airport. There was a 6:30 a.m. flight, so I raced to the airport, bought a ticket, and got on the plane just in time. We connected in Charlotte, North Carolina, and *just* after I sat down in my seat on the connection flight, the pilot announced this flight was also canceled; there were tornadoes in the Little Rock area that morning.

I was now stuck in Charlotte with no other flights out that day. I would surely miss the start of our program.

For a moment, of course, I did my Runner thing—*Just let me go home and hide under my bedsheets, I don't want to adult anymore.*

I stood among 150 stranded, angry passengers circling the American Airlines counter and *for once* I leaned into the stressful situation and started to look at the options I *had* (abundance) rather than the ones I didn't. I could: 1) take a morning flight out the next day and we could start the program half a day late; 2) go home and trust my facilitator to do a great job; or 3) reschedule the program, which would be a logistical nightmare.

Ultimately, we decided my co-facilitator in training would move forward alone. In the airport, I kept my thoughts on what was going right and my literal life of abundance: I have work and the company is doing well; I get to travel and see the world while doing what I love; I have a front row seat to incredible moments of life transformation on a daily basis; I am healthy and able to walk the airport with ease; I have the money to buy a ticket home if needed rather than accept whatever the airline needs me to do.

My house was not on fire and my children were safe. My go-to reframe (from the Runner chapter) *is* an abundance-focused Stress Reset, and I get better at it every day.

Turns out, this was the *opportunity* my facilitator and I both needed. I had two unexpected days of no travel and book writing time after nearly a month of constant airport travels and flights and programs; and my facilitator, who chose confidence over fear in his own stressful situation, had a chance to rise to the occasion and deliver a homerun experience for our clients. By *choosing* an abundance mindset, we both thrived.

Next time something like this happens, ask the question: Am I looking at the situation from a scarcity or abundance mindset, and what would change if I switched?

Like the narrowing and widening of the aperture, this reframe is a game changer if you can implement it in the moment. If it's hard to think abundantly in a moment of stress, practice in smaller moments to build the muscle.

Own Your Space (in Small Spaces)

Sometimes Negative Self-Talkers struggle to take up space, feeling guilty or unworthy. This can be a huge silent stressor; sometimes, without even realizing it, we make ourselves small in moments of stress or anxiety. One of my good friends found herself in a situation where a male coworker continued to talk over her in meetings. At first, she made herself small (as she was raised to do), but it ate at her confidence and sense of right and wrong. Part of what made her amazing at her job was knowing when it was important to let others shine. *This* wasn't *that* situation.

Do you know when you deserve to take up space? (Hint: the answer is *always*). How do you do it? Through small moments of discomfort. If this is a real struggle for you, try this:

- Be the first to share your opinion in the next meeting.
- Speak up and tell your partner what you'd like for dinner.
- Stand in the middle of a room or restaurant or sit at the front of a classroom rather than being a wallflower.
- Volunteer to lead a small group at work or lead a project.
- Drop from your vocabulary the words "sorry" and "just," unless you're genuinely apologizing for a wrongdoing and seeking forgiveness.
- Share how you feel even if you're worried you'll hurt or offend someone—be clear and direct, and stay compassionate.
- Accept a compliment with no strings attached.
- Be proud and don't be sorry for it.
- Remember, "no" is a sentence.

Embrace the discomfort—that's just fear trying to hold you back.

Try this reframe: *fear and discomfort are your brain's way of trying to keep you safe.* They're on your side, just not in every situation. Lean into the discomfort of taking up space, being confident, feeling joyful and courageous. As Susan David says, *"Courage is fear walking."*[6]

Retrain Your Negative Bias

Yes, it's possible to retrain that negative bias a bit and build some stronger positive perspective neural pathways.

Try this: *Every day, spend one minute before bed recalling the many things you did right or that went right that day.* Doing so will slowly start to redirect your focus on those ways in which you are capable, worthy, and already shining.

Choose to Believe in Belief

This might be another parenting fail given the sheer volume of curse words in the show, but our family watches Ted Lasso together (if you haven't watched it, I highly, highly recommend). The show is about an American college football coach (Ted Lasso) who is hired to coach a struggling English Premier League football (soccer for us Americans) club in London. Ted is relentlessly positive with an incredible superpower to make anyone feel special.

(Spoiler alert: if you plan to watch the show, skip the next paragraph.)

Throughout the show you watch hilariously positive Ted also learn to process and deal with painful trauma, memories, his divorce, and the negative emotions he pushes away (a Toxically Positive Freezer, maybe?). Along the way, he wins the hearts of his players, his boss, and even his adversaries.

At one point in the show, his team is losing match after match and sits defeated in the locker room. He tapes a sign above his office door for all his players to see that simply says "Believe" and wins their hearts with this speech:

> *"So I've been hearing this phrase y'all got over here that I ain't too crazy about: 'It's the hope that kills you.' Y'all know that? I disagree, you know? I think it's the **lack** of hope that comes and gets you. See, I believe in hope. I believe in **belief**...."*

At the end of the day, we have a choice to believe in ourselves. And it will take *making that choice over and over again* in moments of stress to see a shift for the long haul. I know I'm a broken record here, but that doesn't mean ignoring, suppressing, or stuffing the negative emotions, the self-doubt, the insecurities, and so on. It also doesn't mean toxic positivity at all times. (See Ted Lasso end of Season 1 for the negative impacts on that one.)

No; it means making the choice to observe and acknowledge tough feelings and thoughts and choosing to visualize a different version of you—one who believes in yourself, who believes in belief.

Yes, And

It's easy to reduce our thinking under stress to binary "either-or" options or throw in lots of "buts" and "shoulds" into our vocabulary. This is also why we often try to force ourselves to "just focus on the positive." What if instead you practice *saying "yes, and" when you're feeling a negative feeling?*

Examples:

+ *Yes,* **everything feels hard right now,** *and* **I have lots of people around me who care and can help.**

- *Yes*, I yelled at my son for not putting his dishes away after breakfast and feel guilty about it, *and* I'm helping him learn to be independent and take care of his home.

- *Yes*, this situation is chaotic and I feel like I can't handle it all, *and* I can choose a few small things to focus on, including taking a few minutes to find calm and connect with my breath and inner voice and my next smallest step.

Or the other way:

- *Yes*, everything is fine, *and* a lot isn't going my way right now and I am struggling with that.

- *Yes*, I have a lot to be grateful for, *and* I'm scared, lonely, hurt, struggling.

- *Yes*, I'm great at my job, *and* I lost that proposal and I'm struggling to get over it.

When you notice binary thinking, how can you work to hold two truths in one thought, and find peace there?

Note: Sometimes everything is *not fine* and we need more than a simple reframe (like professional help), and that's okay, too.

Visualization

I mentioned this exercise for a Freezer as well. We can grow confidence, shift our inner voice, and build our efficacy and internal control all through the power of visualization. Visualization is the powerful practice of bringing to life through imagination your goals, who you want to be, and how you want to show up. Neuroscientist Dr. Tara Swart, author of *The Source*, calls this "your Mind's Eye."[7]

How can you use visualization?

- Start small: perhaps a few minutes two days a week. Set a timer and decide what you want to focus on (refer to the Thriver chapter for more visualization suggestions).

- Choose a positive affirmation: a confirming or empowering word or phrase (the best phrases directly address your limiting core identity or negative inner voice). Then imagine yourself embodying that word—really bring this to life in your mind's eye. Here are some suggestions:

  » *I am safe.*
  » *I am calm.*
  » *I am enough.*
  » *I am powerful.*
  » *I am capable.*

Affirmations can help combat negative thinking loops and create a more positive inner voice. Give them a try.

- You can also make *one* decision about what you plan to do to stretch your growth potential the next day and then visualize your success doing it. Grow your belief in yourself and sense of control by one minute each day and see how far you can take it.

Don't underestimate the power of "others"

As the Worrier and Freezer know well, connection with others is a powerful antidote to stress and negative self-talk. How can you leverage your network—family, friends, partners, trusted advisors, community, and so on—to lift you up and challenge your negative thinking?

Try this: Journal about a recent stressful moment when you experienced negative self-talk, then share with a friend (or speak to a therapist or third party who will listen without judgment). Lean *into* the stress and discomfort by sharing it with someone else.

One final reminder as you choose your Stress Resets as a Negative Self-Talker—this pattern of negativity is *not your fault*. It's a product of wiring, encoding past experiences, genetics. We were pre-wired to *walk* toward positive experiences but *run* away from negative ones. Visualize that for a moment: it takes longer to build the muscle of positive perspective amid stress. This is a matter of biology working against logic. So be patient with yourself—you've got this.

FINAL THOUGHTS

In her book *Braving the Wilderness*, Brené Brown says something that really struck me and changed my perspective on the idea of self-worth, belonging, and feeling like I was enough:

"Don't walk through the world looking for evidence that you don't belong or that you're not enough, because you will always find it."[8]

Isn't that a truth among truths? Why do we do this? We seek validation of our story that we're not enough; and each time we find a clue, the story sinks its claws just a bit more into our deepest sense of self. Remember, we're *rewarded* with dopamine for affirming a story, regardless of whether that story is true. It's called "certainty bias,"[9] and it creates disconnection and wreaks havoc on your life.

But in that same paragraph, Brené goes on to quote Maya Angelou who said,

"You are only free when you realize you belong no place—you belong every place—no place at all. The price is high. The reward is great...*I belong to myself.*"

Angelou wasn't saying we don't belong anywhere; she meant that when you start to negotiate your values and who you are with others to fit in and belong, you no longer belong to yourself.

Back to *Little Miss Sunshine*. Another spoiler alert: Olive does make it to the beauty pageant and looks *nothing* like the other girls. When she walks on stage for her talent routine, dancing, the audience stares in disbelief. Her dance was...well, you just need to watch the movie to find out.

But the important part is, Olive kept dancing. I won't spoil the ending for you, but thanks to her grandpa's humor and wisdom, her family came together, for once, and they all learned a powerful lesson that day...one that Dr. Angelou and Brené Brown and many others have been trying to teach us for decades: *Our worth, our belonging, our values are* **not negotiable**. We are already whole. We are already enough. We already belong.

Never forget that.

TL:DR

+ Negative self-talkers often feel insecurity, worry, uncertainty, helplessness, fear, guilt, and shame.

+ They can self-attack, get stuck in negative thought loops, push away and retreat inward, and can be self-deprecating, second-guess, self-blame, feel disappointment, embarrassment, frustration, and tend to take things personally.

+ They often assume the worst in what others see of them.

- Their inner voice is their own worst enemy: it's unsupportive and tends to speak in hyperbole.
- Their inherent beliefs and identity are limiting and unsupportive.
- Negative Self-Talkers have a strong negative bias, a tendency to see the things working against them and not for them. They have a Scarcity versus Abundance mindset and tend to have low self-efficacy and higher focus of external control.
- Their superpowers are abundant: they tend to communicate better, are more introspective and self-aware of their actions, think more clearly, tend to make fewer mistakes (because they're constantly worried about making them!), tend to be less gullible and don't take everything at face value (critics like the best of them), are better critical thinkers, and are better at decision-making than the rest of us. They're other-aware and tend to read others well. They're compassionate, kind, and sensitive; givers, not takers.
- Negative Self-Talkers can try a few Stress Reset strategies to better manage their stress personality including:

  » Working on getting to know and shifting their inner voice.
  » Widening their aperture to see more than what's wrong.
  » Adopting an abundance perspective.
  » Practicing visualization and using positive affirmations.
  » Seeking power in their connections.

11

THE DISTRACTED

In an ironic turn of events, I had the worst writer's block when starting this chapter. It was a rainy Monday morning after a very busy youth-sports-parent weekend. The house was gray and cold, rain-drops steadily pattering the roof—one of those mornings you need a sweater inside the house and a little extra caffeine. My mind kept drifting to my overflowing inbox, text messages, and my long to-do list for the business. I stared at a blinking cursor; I was really struggling to organize my thoughts and my head hurt.

My Distracted people, did I get it right? My guess is you find your-self in a similar spot when stressed.

Candidly, I struggled with what to name this stress personality. Is Distracted really the right fit? Or is it The Foggy-Brained? The Men-tal Clutterers…Team Brain Farts? One of my dear friends and fellow coaches calls it "Mental Spaghetti," which I love. Regardless of the name, I think we can agree that the predominant experience of a Distracted personality is pretty straightforward: cognitively, you're a *chaotic, unfo-cused, easily distracted, fuzzy-headed, mentally exhausted hot mess.*

It might be helpful to leaf back to Chapter 2 for a moment if you think this is your stress personality to really understand how this one comes to be, because truly it goes back to the mechanics of the stress response itself. Remember that when *any* of us experience arousal or a "threat," our New Brain—responsible for most higher-order thinking, ability to focus and remain lucid, stay attentive, control our thoughts, respond with clarity, make decisions, problem-solve, and so on—is negatively impacted. Our Reptile Brain assumes control of the wheel so that we can fight, flee, run, appease, and so on without having to think. We're cognitively impaired for as long as we're in fight or flight.

The Distracted might be tricky to self-identify because if I polled the readers of this book, 100 percent of us would agree that at the end of a busy or stressful day, we feel this way *every. single. time.* For most of us, being distracted is a by-product of another, more dominant experience (driven by powerful emotions like exhaustion, fear, insecurity, anger, and so on). *But that doesn't make you a Distracted stress personality.* Nor does feeling unfocused and distracted here and there during your day. For the Distracted, this is *the* persistent way stress shows up.

The Distracted stress personality is an *intensified* version of the mental fatigue any of us would experience at the end of a long day. This is their experience *every time* things get difficult *and it's really difficult to come down from it*, whether it's an argument with a loved one, a new project or deadline assigned at work, an unexpected bill in the mail, a traffic jam, a sudden request to perform under pressure, being asked an unexpected question in a business meeting and feeling the glaring proverbial spotlight of those waiting for a response (a Distracted might feel like they cannot come up with an answer on the spot, which sends their fight or flight response into high gear...or vice versa).

EMOTIONS AND THOUGHTS
OF THE DISTRACTED

The Distracted stress personality is an interesting one, because the experience is *mostly mental*. I wouldn't say that a strong emotional tug doesn't come with a Distracted's experience; it's just more cerebral in origin.

And I mean that quite literally; many stress personalities are iden-tified and *driven* by the intense emotions we feel, but a Distracted personality might have a more cognitive or mental manifestation of stress:

+ *Full or overfull brain* to the point where they can't take in any more input.

+ *Forgetful*

+ *Spacey*

+ *Foggy-headed;* the opposite of sharp and lucid

+ *Trouble thinking straight and focusing*

+ *Decision fatigue* (if I even have to choose what flavor creamer I want in my coffee right now I might lose it…)

+ *Mentally/emotionally exhausted. Thinking* feels like running a marathon.

+ Subsequently *irritated, short-tempered, overwhelmed, drained, distraught, demoralized* or *disengaged, insecure, anxious,* etc. Aka, secondary stress personalities emerge from this cerebral overload.

The best analogy I ever heard was that a Distracted stress personal-ity feels like they have *100 windows open on their computers, and they're trying to focus on each one at the same time,* leading to an inevitable crash.

BEHAVIORS OF A DISTRACTED STRESS PERSONALITY

Here's how the Distracted might look on the outside:

- They might *struggle to execute decisions or tasks* (indecisive, am I right?).

- Likely *overwhelmed* or *irritated* by questions or someone asking their opinion.

- Might *stumble over their words.*

- May appear *unorganized, spacey,* or not "with it."

As a result, they might also feel:

- *Apathetic* or *indifferent,* like a Freezer.

- Possibly *irritated* or *short-tempered,* like a Fighter.

- Totally *exhausted, anxious,* or *overwhelmed,* like a Runner.

- Possibly *insecure,* or *uncertain* like a Negative Self-Talker.

- Possibly *indecisive,* like a Worrier.

A Distracted stress personality is the opposite of "clarity under pressure."

And by the way, none of this has to do with their intelligence, problem-solving capabilities, ambition, or intellect. Rather, I'd venture to guess that a Distracted stress personality is one of the higher achieving type individuals in everyday life, like a Pleaser. Maybe they're the cerebral/deep thinker types who typically make decisions using time, intellect, intelligence, and the cold, hard facts.

Perhaps, like a Pleaser, they're very busy, ambitious people who hold themselves to high standards and have multiple competing priorities—with no plan to offload any one of those priorities, of course.

If my Distracted friend was missing and I was putting together a description for police, I'd tell them, "You're looking for a driven, capable person with a lot on their plate and lots of high priorities in life, but she might look like she's losing it." Or, look for the, *cerebral, deep thinkers* of the group (I think they challenge the Worriers on this one).

One of my clients, Tammy, is a superintendent of schools in California (I work with a few). She's highly intellectual, a deep thinker, a tremendous leader, zeroed in on her purpose for life and her life's work, always with her head in a book or academic study, lots of short and long-term growth goals, and she's highly focused, organized, and capable—she can handle a lot but when things get really, really hard, she is suddenly easily distracted and mentally exhausted to the point where work and home life are affected. She starts to take things personally, has trouble sleeping, and her husband mistakes her "mental spaghetti" for disconnection.

ORIGINS OF A DISTRACTED STRESS PERSONALITY

The origin story of a Distracted stress personality likely varies quite a bit from person to person. Of all the stress personalities, though, this might be one that doesn't necessarily stem from childhood, difficult past experiences, or modeling, but may be a result of more current or more recent patterns and environment.

Possible Explanations in Your *Current* Life

Environment:

- ◆ Chaotic home or work environment (remember, stress personalities are context dependent). If your home, calendar, office, and/or work culture are a chaotic, unorganized mess or you believe staying busy is staying productive, it's not a stretch to assume your stress personality is going to follow suit.

- Current work environment or home environment rewards *doing*—busy, always something you can be doing, don't stop, at-all-costs type of behavior so you're frantically on the bandwagon and racing to keep up because that is what "success" and "productive" look like.

- You're addicted to your devices, plain and simple: information overload.

- High achiever with a head full of musings, reflections, theories, observations, and your entire to-do list for the next 30 years front and center *at all times*.

- You have a natural desire to seek change, excitement, variety, and constantly need new stimulation so you hop from task to task, commitment to commitment, job to job, say yes to everything, and so on. This is exciting, but you rarely feel peaceful or grounded.

- This is an inevitable challenge due to a neurodiversity like ADHD or OCD; so it would be a no-brainer (pun *not* intended) that you struggle with "ordinary" cognitive tasks under stress or your capacity for input is limited or challenged. (Fun fact: neurodiversity is an absolute *superpower*. Neurodiverse people with ADD or ADHD, Autism, OCD, processing disorders, dyslexia, and so on actually have *hyper-abilities* in certain parts of the brain like creativity, problem-solving, pattern matching, etc., but that doesn't mean the conditions come without challenge; a Distracted stress personality is certainly one possibility.)

If we dug a little deeper, there *could* be more psychological stress underneath:

- Being busy, cluttered, and overcommitted is a way for you to avoid uncomfortable memories or anxiety—a form of self-nurturing.

- Being busy, cluttered, overcommitted is your way of building a life that looks exciting, successful, and adventurous (*YOLO! FOMO! Burn the candle at both ends!* And all that) but the truth is, you don't like discomfort so you stay too busy to address it.

Possible Explanations From Your *Past*

- Dysfunctional family dynamic and/or home environment growing up.

- Unreachable expectations set for you as a child, leading to overachieving and overreaching on goals.

- Overly busy or emotionally unavailable parents or caregivers who didn't model what it looked like (and felt like) to recover well or give full energy and attention to others.

- Being busy is or was a badge of honor growing up. Sitting still too long was considered lazy and unproductive. Distracted *was* the perpetual state of your caregivers so you knew, and know, nothing else.

Regardless of the origin story, the Distracted stress personality can be *exhausting*. But good news: it's also one of the "easiest" (all things considered) to manage because we can often leverage brain science to solve this one—rather than needing deeper emotional or spiritual work or wrestling with your past, like some of the others.

Of all the personalities, this Under the Hood section *should be read by everyone* to better understand why and how our attention, focus, creativity, problem-solving ability, and clarity under pressure operate, and how we can improve our brain performance through a few small hacks to our daily schedule. Bottom line: no matter your stress personality, this next section is a handy one.

THE DISTRACTED: UNDER THE HOOD

On a healthy day when you're eating well, getting good sleep, moving often, exercising, feeling confident and positive, and you're stress-free—you know, those impossibly rare days—you have about an hour and a half to two hours *max* at a time to push your brain's high performance center (Central Executive Network—remember that from the Runner chapter?) to its peak performance potential. In fact, you can even *stress* your brain on purpose (*eustress*, remember?). In this situation we can take on new challenges, push ourselves to our highest potential, stretch our capabilities...*grow*.

But we can't push ourselves this hard all day long without stopping. Why? Because we have a built-in ceiling on our peak brain performance potential. It's called our BRAC, or Basic Rest Activity Cycle. Our BRAC is the brain's natural rhythm of high cognitive activity followed by reduced cognitive activity. In other words, *our brain puts itself into a forced recovery* every 90 minutes or so.[1] During this dip in activity, we're meant to pause and let our mental battery recharge for a bit. Guess where we're meant to go? That Default Mode Network: the mind-wandering state (remember that from our Worrier chapter?).

We are quite literally *wired* to recover.

Here's an analogy: During the Tour de France, or any professional cycling race, teams in the larger peloton, or main group of cyclists, will often work together and leverage each other's speed and strength to work harder, go faster, or to catch up to a breakaway group. One team's best rider will "pull" in the very front of the main field for a bit, taking the brunt of the headwinds, then fall to the back of the peloton and settle in to draft others and recover while a new person takes the lead. From above, the peloton takes the shape of a continually shifting funnel, the pointed end being the various front riders. If the whole peloton didn't work together, everyone would be gassed before the finish.

Your brain is no different: allowing one part of the brain to rest while the other works helps your entire operating system function at peak performance potential. This comes in handy when you need your brain at its best: a big presentation, an important conversation, an intense, focused work session.

If we're being honest, most of us, even us non-Distracted people, work against it, don't we? We operate at a full-blown sprint throughout the day, trying to stay "on" and barely coming up for air (if you're looking for a way to *not* succeed, this is it).

We constantly try to push through and get by on less; in fact, in westernized culture, it's celebrated to do more with less: less sleep, less food, less rest. And you know what? If you think you can get by on less than what you really need, you're exactly right—your body will adapt. But it will have to make concessions; there will *always* be consequences.

Pushing against your BRAC rhythm too far may cause:

1. **Increased negative stress** (duh). Ordinary manageable tasks, to-dos, comments, or responses from others, etc. can suddenly be experienced as threats (less emotionally resilient, more susceptible to stress—enter your stress personality into the room).

2. **Unintentional, unwanted mind-wandering.** We slip into a mind-wandering state at *precisely* the time we don't want to (like when you're trying hard to listen to someone). My

guess is your BRAC is sending you a little red alert. *Unintentional* mind wandering is not good for our health; in fact, some studies suggest it can lead to ADD and/or anxiety.[2]

3. **Cognitive overload.** Suddenly, we hit max capacity for what we can take in mentally and experience cognitive overload (shows up as distraction, irritation, overwhelm, headache, cluttered mind, anxiousness, a foggy brain... sound familiar, Distracted folks?).

How do we get here? How do we set ourselves up for this?

Multitasking

Outside of simply not taking time to mentally reset, one of our biggest culprits is that we try to do too much at one time. Our brains were not designed to focus on two *cognitively challenging* tasks at the same time. If you don't believe me, try to recite your 7-multiplication table, and write the lyrics to "Twinkle Twinkle Little Star" at the same time.

However, when one or two of the tasks are *automatic* and operated by our basal ganglia (Reptile, unthinking brain), we have enough mental energy to focus intently on the cognitively challenging task at hand (now try to recite your 7-multiplication table while walking...piece of cake, right? Unless you're not good at math).

My point: *when we find ourselves behaving in inefficient ways with our mental energy, our brain cannot physiologically give its best* and we burn through our energy at lightning speed, leading to *cognitive fatigue, or cognitive overload.*

The solution? When we make time for *both* high performing, sustained focus *and* mental rest and mind wandering, and start to design our workday to align with this natural rhythm of the brain, there are some incredible outcomes:

- We're better able to handle our high workloads including people, tasks, and demands…aka, less stress personality showing up in our day-to-day.

- When stress *does* show up, we have the mental/emotional reserves to better manage it.

- We experience less cognitive fatigue and perform at a higher cognitive potential (aka, you're smarter, more focused, better at your job).

- We become highly creative.[3]

I would venture to guess that a Distracted stress personality doesn't have great management of their BRAC. Would you?

Bottom Line

Why is all this brain science around BRAC so important? When we consistently try to manage too many demands at once, overcommit, and never stop, distractedness is an inevitable outcome—and often, a preventable one.

It would really benefit you, Distracted friend (and the rest of us), to start examining the way you structure your day—you might find your solution right there in your calendar.

EXERCISES

Think you might be a Distracted stress personality? Here are a few exercises to consider:

What's Your Rhythm?

Remembering the BRAC principle, it's time to assess your own daily rhythms. I want you to take out a sheet of drawing paper.

1. Draw a graph like the following, labeling the x-axis as the time of your day (moment you wake up to moment you go to sleep), and the y-axis as the quality/performance/degree of mental energy used (aka, how hard you're working your mind).

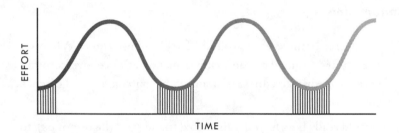

Your line should reflect your mental rhythms during a typical, non-stressful day. Indicate the times you're mentally "on" with upward little hills that "peak" when you're really pushing yourself mentally. Indicate breaks from that mental effort with dips or valleys. These are the *real* breaks—not working lunches, or switching from a meeting immediately to check your social media—but actual disengagement from mental effort *on purpose*.

Now examine your patterns—what do you see? What do you *really* see?

So often we think we're taking a mental break, but the reality is these aren't breaks at all. We take lunch but answer emails from our phone; check social media; read news headlines; and so on. Hence, we're not giving our mind the rest it needs. Sometimes we barely even come up for air during the day (I know people who don't drink water during the day, so they don't need to use the bathroom and even people who take their phones to the bathroom—now that's a problem.).

Through this exercise I hope you can see an accurate reflection of how hard your brain is actually working throughout your average day...now imagine how hard it works on a stressful day. Is that BRAC rhythm even further devolved into peaks and valleys? Or maybe one continuous rising peak?

How well do you balance your own BRAC? If you don't manage it well, could this be a key contributor to your feelings of clutter, distractedness, and cognitive overwhelm—your Distracted stress personality?

Distractions Reflection

The following are some questions to add to your journal for reflection. Answer the following:

+ Where and when do you face the *most* distractions?
  How do you normally handle them (physically, mentally, emotionally)?

+ What is your current strategy when your brain feels full, you need to make a difficult decision, you're stuck on a problem, or you need to be creative and think outside the box? How or where did you learn these strategies? Is it helpful?

+ What was your upbringing like? Your past and current work and home environments? How do they help with your ability to manage distractions and demands...or not?

Pie Chart Your Distracted Symptoms

Let's get to the bottom of your predominant experience when you face this stress personality so we can determine the right solutions for you.

You're going to draw some more. This time, you're going to make a pie chart. (I adapted this from an exercise in the book *Burnout* by Emily and Amelia Nagoski, by the way. I loved the insights I gleaned about my own life and where my energy was going.)

Make a list of the *symptoms* you experience *most* when your Distracted stress personality shows up, and then assign them the correct piece of your pie. For example, you might mostly feel foggy-brained, but also overwhelmed and fatigued. So, your pie chart might be 80% foggy-brained, 10% overwhelmed, and 10% fatigued. What are those slices you need to include? Mentally overfull, unorganized and cluttered, slow thinking, exhausted and fatigued, anxious, indecisive? Create your own unique pie.

(Side note: if you are struggling to figure out your stress personality in general, this is a great exercise to do using emotions, behaviors, and persistent thoughts.).

Why is this exercise important? Because it will help us choose the best Stress Resets to tackle it. Like I said in Chapter 3, the symptoms must match the cure.

WATCHOUTS

This full, distracted, overworked brain of yours comes with red flags, and many of them are the same for all chronic stress: poor physical health, burnout, fatigue, sleeplessness/restlessness, ADD/ADHD, depression, anxiety, and so on. But let's also consider the unseen costs of perpetual cognitive overload and failing to *intentionally seek* that restful, mind-wandering place on a regular basis. Pay attention to these (pun *intended* on this one):

- *Energy.* Being "on" all the time is an energy sap. Imagine what you could do with just a little more energy? How could you use that energy? What would be possible?

- *Brain performance.* You think you're smart, focused, creative, and productive now? Imagine the potential you haven't tapped yet.

- *Relationships.* Social connection, intimacy, and beautiful, meaningful moments. What, or who, do we miss because we're overworked, distracted, and disengaged?

- *Moments of awe and wonder.* If you never stop to notice and smell the flowers, the sound of rain, a beautiful sunset, the sweet sound of a child laughing, or the beauty of a brief interaction with a stranger, what is being lost? Life is lived in these small, precious moments.

Remember my superintendent client? There was a cost to her Distracted personality. When stress was persistent and chronic, she became *exhausted*...the kind of exhausted that often left her unable to function. She lost sleep, she struggled to connect at home with her family, her productivity plummeted, she cried more often; and despite being typically confident and optimistic, she felt defeated and unsure. She wasn't willing to give up her performance at work, at great cost to her physical and mental health.

Let me ask this another way: *What are you missing out on because of all the noise? How much of your life are you rushing by?*

SUPERPOWERS OF THE DISTRACTED

The Distracted stress personality has a few superpowers that might surprise you; and some that might not. You already know now that this person is likely a *high achiever, high performer, loves adventure* and *challenge*, and likely loves a *packed, exciting schedule.*

This will likely be the person who will say yes to any new challenge or opportunity, not unlike a Pleaser; but in this case they aren't aiming to please, they simply like the chance to grow and reach new heights of potential.

Here's an interesting superpower: the Distracted is also likely to be more *creative, inquisitive,* and *curious.* Their constant need for challenge or change, and their head full of "mental spaghetti" is, in the literature, usually associated with more creative thinking, abstract thought, innovation, and natural curiosity about the world. This means they are also often excellent *problem-solvers* and sometimes even paradoxically have great *attention to detail* (yes, detail-focused—new research is emerging that people who are easily distracted and have less cognitive control are sometimes more detailed-focused in the long term because their brain opens its "aperture" to allow more stimuli in... aka, more possibilities to solve a problem).

In a weird twist of fate, sometimes having *less* control of their attention causes these types of thinkers to find themselves in a mind-wandering space more often...like it or not. Though it can be an Achilles' heel when they need to focus or stay productive, frequent "mind wanderers" are often the ones with better memory and problem-solving ability, and are more open to creative solutions. This is why researchers consider this ability a double-edged sword.[4]

If you want a creative solutions person, choose a Distracted.

The lesson here is that when we make time for it, letting our mind wander often helps set it free—but it's much easier when you're the one in control of when your mind wanders.

One more "potential superpower" for a Distracted person. *When managed right*, they grow to be more *emotionally regulated*; the Distracted can be the one who *adapts to change, thinks well under pressure*, and can emotionally roll with the punches, particularly when a sudden stressor or challenge comes their way. Get lost on the streets of London? No problem! There's an issue with the back-end server and clients are complaining of a lapse in service? No worries, let's dive in and find out what's going on!

The *challenge* doesn't scare them, so they are rarely the ones in the corner of the room biting their nails and questioning their self-worth when the proverbial poop hits the fan.

If you can rein in your Distracted tendencies (see "training under pressure" in the following Stress Resets), and better manage your energy, you're the one we look to when we need something done or we need creative solutions.

STRESS RESETS FOR THE DISTRACTED

As you can imagine, the Stress Resets for a Distracted stress personality are more focused (lots of puns in this chapter!) on mental or cognitive strategies that play around with activating different areas of the brain while allowing other areas to rest. In other words, Distracted friends, we're going to literally hack your neurobiology!

Here are a few pressure-tested Stress Resets that work well for a Distracted stress personality:

Oscillation

Oscillation is building *strategic* and *intentional* moments of recovery (Stress Resets) into your day to maximize your energy and help *distress* as *eustress*. It's a term coined by Drs. Loehr and Groppel of the

Human Performance Institute. A Pleaser would consider oscillation a boundary setting strategy, and oscillation creates better alignment between your daily work rhythm and your BRAC rhythm.

We already learned that when we *seek* moments of recovery (and not just reactively grab for them), we are more productive, we're higher performers, and we can often even reframe what would normally be stressful moments as opportunities to stretch ourselves and build resilience.[5]

But we need to consider *what kinds* of breaks are best, and that depends on you, how you're feeling, and so on. Time to break out both the pie chart and BRAC rhythm exercise again and put them together.

Try this: Let's build on the BRAC chart you drew earlier. How can you break up the "peaks" using your insights from the pie chart as guides to seek the right type of break? For example, if you're foggy-headed more than anything, what would help you most? Here are a few general ideas:

+ *Find a healthy snack, or drink a glass of water.*

+ *Listen to music.*

+ *If at home, snuggle your pet, fold a few pieces of laundry, or water a plant.*

+ Get *moving* (moving the body through light exercise, stretches, a walk, a plank, arm rolls—anything— improves energy, cognition, and helps you better manage cognitive load, particularly under stress).[6]

+ *Take a walk/get out in nature.* As mentioned previously, spending time in nature reduces anxiety and rumination. (Worriers, remember this?)

+ *Get social.* Take a social break. Talk to coworkers about something other than work. Not only does social connection improve mood and reduce anxiety and stress, but it's also good for the brain.

+ *Mindfulness and meditation.* Meditation and mindfulness are so important, they get their own section in the Thriver Accelerators chapter. For now, consider this: if both the Worrier and the Distracted get stuck in a mind wandering place, and guided meditation helps the Worrier return to the present moment, would it also help the Distracted? Likely, quite the opposite. There's enough mental noise going on up there and we'd just be adding to it with a request for more mental resources to be used; we need something different.

Try one of these two strategies:

+ *Open-monitoring meditation.* Open-monitoring meditation is the practice of not focusing on anything at all, allowing the mind to wander where it may go. At first, this is tough: the mind wanders back to our daily noise. But over time, it works amazingly. What does it look like in practice? I might set a timer for 10 minutes and lay on the floor in a comfortable position and close my eyes, letting the mind drift. Or, I might take a walk outside with no intention, goal, or structure. Staring out the window can be a form of open-monitoring meditation. For the same reason that *focused* meditation draws a person back to the present moment and to a focused state, *open-monitoring* meditation achieves the opposite: it allows us to tap into the mind-wandering state, helping us refocus, re-energize, and find calm when feeling overwhelmed or mentally overworked.

+ *Panoramic meditation.* Like open-monitoring meditation, panoramic meditation is the practice of widening our

view (our aperture!) and taking in a wider field of
vision of our environment, allowing *every part* of our
surrounding environment in. Some people even allow
their vision to blur a bit and sort of zone out. This is a
great practice for a cluttered mind, mental fatigue, racing
thoughts, anxiety before a meeting or event, and so on.
(I recommend this to my clients who have ADHD or
struggle with focus before an important call, meeting,
test, etc., including my son who struggles with attention.)

Did you notice that none of these recovery breaks were mentally
taxing, like journaling for example? That's the point: we don't want to
work an overworked brain.

Need more ideas? Return to Chapter 3's Stress Reset exercise and
look at the list you made. Hopefully by now you've added to it. It's a
great place to start looking for ways to integrate recovery into your
day; they're not just useful for when you're feeling stressed.

Please don't miss this: *a rested brain is a less-stressed brain.*

DISTRACTIONS REFLECTION:
SOLUTIONS MINING

It might help you to reflect a bit more on where you are facing the most
distractions and mental exhaustion in your day. Though this isn't a
Stress Reset per se, it's a great exercise to assess some possible broader
pain points.

Go back to the Distractions Reflection questions, and let's unpack
them even more. Let's think of some possible new solutions to minimize distractions, be more creative, and create more opportunities to
recover mentally through your day.

The original questions:

+ Where and when do you face the *most* distractions? How do you normally handle them?

+ What is your current strategy when your brain feels full, you need to make a difficult decision, you're stuck on a problem, or you need to be creative and think outside the box? How or where did you learn these strategies? Is it helpful?

The follow-up question:

If these strategies aren't working, what's a better strategy to put in place to minimize distractions and create an environment that doesn't trigger your Distracted side?

Can you:

+ Make priority lists each morning?

+ Test out singular focus on one task at a time rather than multitasking?

+ Close windows on your computer/turn off pings and dings, etc.?

+ Delegate more?

+ Block time for focus in your calendar (like the Pleaser boundary exercise?)

+ Create harder rules around putting devices down during meetings, mealtimes, after work, etc.?

One thing about multitasking: sometimes, our jobs *require* it (teachers, nurses, doctors, etc.). If that's you, don't stress about it. Your brain wasn't technically optimized for multitasking, but thanks to neuroplasticity you're likely getting pretty darn efficient at it...for short periods. If multitasking is an inevitable part of your day, keep this in mind: *your recovery time should match the intensity of your multitasking.* Where possible, take a little extra time on breaks or really disconnect at the end of the day to mentally unwind—or take a day off here and there and truly do nothing. Be creative and find ways to quiet the mind during your workday wherever possible. I promise, this will help.

Eisenhower Matrix

Another one of my favorite strategies is the Eisenhower Matrix. First responders usually prioritize patient treatment needs by addressing the most critical needs first (airway, breathing, circulation, etc.), then working outward on the less life-critical issues. They'd do the same with multiple patients on one scene.

You could easily apply this same mentality to the way you tackle the day and your stressors by asking yourself, *What is the most urgent thing I need to address first?*

Former US President Dwight Eisenhower developed a model (which he called the "Urgent-Important Principle" and came to be known as the Eisenhower Matrix) to help him prioritize and manage the many high-stakes issues he faced as a US Army general, Supreme Allied Commander of NATO Forces, and eventually as President of the United States. Essentially, the model helps you decide what is most urgent to tackle, and what else you can decide on later, delegate, or remove altogether.

Here's what it looks like:

The Eisenhower decision matrix

Source: www.spica.com

Use this template to create your own. You'll: 1) determine what's most important for you to DO first; 2) DECIDE what needs to get done next and schedule that; 3) identify what you can DELEGATE to others and learn that most precious skill of asking for help and leaning on support resources; and 4) DELETE and eliminate what's left, what you can mentally or literally let go.

The hard part isn't filling this out—it's executing it. Try it out perhaps at the beginning of the week.

(Pleasers reading this, the delegating part will be your greatest challenge. My suggestion is to start with small asks; reframe delegation as not just a way to flex your "letting go" muscle, but also as a way to let others shine and support.)

Additional ways to improve focus and eliminate your "mental spaghetti":

+ Can you integrate the Eisenhower Matrix into your daily or weekly routine?

+ If that doesn't feel doable, can you create a list every morning of what items are most important and what your *one* priority is (there can only be one; "mutiple priorities" is an oxymoron). All other tasks should fall under that one.

+ Can you use the stop-doing list from the Pleaser chapter to eliminate the unnecessary tasks creating misalignment between you and your goals?

+ Consider when you should do your most mentally taxing work: Are you a morning person, or night owl? Research shows that it can vary from person to person. What's your most productive time of day? Try to do your most taxing work then.

+ Can you break down tasks into smaller, more manageable steps, like those baby steps from the Runner chapter?

+ Want to level up from the Eisenhower Matrix? Ask yourself, *What can I* automate *when it comes to my daily processes? Are there inefficiencies that need solving? A new system I need to put into place?* Examples:

  » I mentioned to you earlier in the book that I blocked my calendar for meetings and calls limited to certain hours in the week, then shared the new calendar with my team. This *automated* my team's ability to schedule time with me....or not. This led to So. Many. Less. Emails.

  » Two, I created a Standard Operating Procedures (SOP) folder and a Coaching + Facilitator Folder for the team. It includes links to everything the team needs from start to finish to facilitate a program or complete a process, including a FAQs section for where to go if there was an issue. This changed the game for me because I was no longer the go-to for all the questions, which then freed up mental space to be more productive with my time.

» My husband created "auto-buckets" on his work email by assigning certain recipients to automatically flow into different folders as their emails came in. Now, the more "urgent" emails are the first inbox he checks in the mornings. Genius!

Pomodoro Technique

Let's look at one more productivity strategy—the Pomodoro Technique, which is a well-tested time management, learning and focus tool based on 25-minute stretches of focused work broken up by five-minute breaks. Try it out for yourself: set a timer for a certain amount of time (doesn't have to be 25 minutes), remove all possible distractions, and deliberately focus on a problem or task until the timer goes off. If you honor your break times, this strategy is a great way to create oscillation in your day and reduce the chances your Distracted stress personality will surface.

Protect time for wandering, curiosity, and daydreaming.

Let's take a different perspective on the wandering mind: what if we thought about a wandering mind as wandering *toward* what it finds interesting and wonderful?

Of course, we need to get stuff done; but what if part of your day was dedicated to where you mind prefers to go? Let it wander, be creative, and be curious—just follow your brain's lead. What would that look like for you?

This could look like reading articles that interest you, taking a walk, coloring, journaling, browsing podcast titles and choosing one to bookmark, searching travel destinations, or wandering the office or house for a bit and just…noticing. I have a friend who has a stationary bike in her house and she gets on there for 10 minute stretches and just allows her mind to go where it needs to go. She keeps a notebook and pen near her bike in case anything wonderful comes up—it usually does.

(Remember my amazing Thriver client Bob who taught me to "be where my feet are?" Well, I jokingly shared with his group that I wished I had a pen and paper in the shower because that's where I get all my greatest ideas. And a few days later back at home, a waterproof pencil and writing slate used for scuba diving arrived at my house from Bob…I use it often! I've jotted down some great ideas in between the shampoo and conditioner.)

What would you do with more mind-wandering time? Give yourself space to daydream and wander and see what comes up. My guess is you find more moments of awe, joy, and creative solutions.

Thinking Clearly Under Pressure: Training Stress

We've identified a lot of strategies that work well if you struggle with cognitive overload, focus, attention, and so on. But what about our other Distracted friends who experience more cognitive fog and scattered thinking? Who struggle to act, or find the right words when stressed? Sometimes it's less about too much noise and clutter in the mind and more like a smoke bomb went off in there, especially under pressure.

Thinking clearly under pressure is a super skill. And great news—you can train this skill. Here are a few ways:

Cold Exposure. As wild as it sounds, cold exposure is the newest trend in mental performance training. Deliberate cold exposure includes things like cold showers, ice baths, and cryotherapy, where you intentionally put your body into a physical state of stress (extreme cold immediately activates the fight or flight response) and then force yourself to think and activate the New Brain, like when solving math equations or reciting lines from a song.

Why on earth would you do such a thing? Because recent studies show that deliberate cold exposure improves mental performance by helping you better regulate your thoughts, emotions, and internal state *in a state of stress.*

If you recall from Chapter 3, the Gift of Pause skill is designed to help you *acknowledge, ask,* and *act* more quickly. Cold exposure trains you to move through that process more quickly. It also increases your dopamine and endorphins, providing you a boost of temporary focus and improved mood.[7] It's also been found to help with chronic stress, recovery from tough workouts, depression, and general long-term health (the Polar Bear Club knew it all along, didn't they?).

Don't have an ice bath? Take 2 minutes at the end of your shower and turn the water as cold as possible; focus on a mental task like simple math, make your to-do list for the day, recite phone numbers, etc.

Other ways to trigger the stress response and think under pressure:

- ✦ **Perform those same mental tasks while doing sprints or intervals during a workout.**
- ✦ **Attend a Toastmasters class and speak in front of a large crowd (or any controlled fear that would trigger your stress response).**
- ✦ **Set timers and solve crossword puzzles under time pressure.**

Any of these strategies will have similar positive benefits.

Reframe stress as opportunity in the smaller moments as much as possible. This goes back to changing our story and challenging our inner voice, but what if you stopped perceiving certain stressors like a last-minute change of plans or an unexpected setback at work as "bad" and shifted your perspective to the positive? Could you turn anxiety and worry into excitement? Scarcity into abundance?

Tammy's journey through her Distracted stress personality.

What about my "super" superintendent? Through conversation and reflection, she made a few changes: she redesigned a few systems in her day to focus better and minimize distractions; she asked her assistant for support in honoring her break time; blocked time for deep work; and scheduled more prep time in advance of bigger, more important meetings. She also took up restorative yoga and swimming after work. She found peace and more control with these changes and her Distracted stress personality minimized significantly.

FINAL THOUGHTS

Whatever Stress Reset strategies you employ, remember that it truly is *in your head.* I mean that quite literally! Knowing this, how can you be as intentional as possible to build a day that supports your high-performing mind, body, and soul?

TL:DR

* The Distracted stress personality is an *intensified* version of the mental fatigue we often experience at the end of a long day. The Distracted may feel cognitively overwhelmed, unfocused, have a full brain, or think they can't come up with an answer on the spot, which sends their fight or flight response into high gear or vice versa.

* The experience is mostly mental with less of an initial strong emotional tug. The Distracted often have chaotic schedules or home/work environments, are overcommitted, over-deviced, avoiding self-reflection by keeping busy, overly ambitious, or perhaps balance a neurodiversity like ADHD.

* They could also be a by-product of a dysfunctional family dynamic or home environment growing up, with overly busy or emotionally unavailable parents or caregivers, or they were taught that busy is or was a badge of honor and idleness was lazy and unproductive.

* A Distracted stress personality can quickly find themselves unintentionally slipping into their mind-wandering state or overloading their cognitive potential. This causes them to be more susceptible to cognitive fatigue or cognitive overload. It's also because they are less intentional about allowing the brain to wander, drift, and rest from being "on."

* A Distracted should be mindful of their energy, brain performance, relationships, and missing out on moments of awe and wonder.

- The Distracted stress personality *can be* highly *emotionally regulated* and *adaptive to change* under pressure when trained right.

- They are more *creative, inquisitive,* and *curious.* They have great memories, are excellent *problem solvers* and can have great *attention to detail.*

- They benefit most from Stress Resets that help them mitigate the chances of cognitive fatigue or overload:

  » Calendarizing their mental breaks and getting to know their work rhythms.

  » Oscillating between being "on" and recovering (recover using any strategies that quiet the mind including open-monitoring meditation, panoramic meditation, taking a walk, being out in nature, finding time to mind wander, etc.).

  » Designing better systems to manage distractions and overload

  » Pomodoro Technique

  » Eisenhower Matrix

  » Minimizing multitasking where possible

  » Automate where possible

  » Where possible, train the brain to think under pressure (cold exposure or similar stress-inducing exercise): reframe the stress.

12

THE THRIVER

We all know one...and we love to hate them. Just kidding; we really do love them, don't we?

Stop for a moment and think about that person in your life who screams "Thriver." They are the ones who are content, collected, present, and somehow know exactly what to say and do in difficult times—the ones you look to for answers and guidance. They're not perfect, but they don't pretend to be. They're self-aware, thoughtful, reflective. They're laser-focused in the chaos—agile, resilient, and calm on even the most stressful days...darn right *joyful* even.

There are so many famous people I'd bet are Thrivers: Maya Angelou; Nelson Mandela; Mr. Rogers; Malala Yousafzai...too many to name.

Let's take a moment to appreciate the Thrivers in our lives for who they are and what they teach us.

Everyone has a Thriver inside—we just haven't fully tapped into it yet.

Because...

Thriving is a skill, not a trait. It can be trained.

The whole point of this book is to help us move toward a Thriver personality more of the time—every Stress Reset gets us closer to achieving that.

Nevertheless, Thrivers weren't just born resilient, and they aren't perfect people. Let's not put them on an unreachable pedestal: they make mistakes, lose their cool, fail and say things they don't mean.

Although they are agile, it doesn't mean they're devoid of stress, challenge, mistakes, fear or uncertainty. Sure, thriving might look like confidence, clarity, grace, self-awareness, and so on, but it also looks like giving up, letting go, getting angry, being scared or worried; Thrivers aren't Thrivers because they don't experience what we experience—it's just that they know what to do in those moments; they learn to move *forward* and take action more quickly.

Let's break down the great qualities of a Thriver and how they came to be. This chapter is structured a little differently from the others.

HOW DO THRIVERS BECOME THRIVERS?

Several reasons. Perhaps:

+ These skills were modeled for them as children.
+ They've been through tough times and came out the other side with hard, beautiful, meaningful wisdom and perspective.
+ They're intentional about training in these specific areas, as we're trying to do.
+ They're Thrivers in certain circumstances more than others and are still working at it (this might describe a good majority of us).

WHAT ARE THE QUALITIES OF A THRIVER?

Thrivers are **highly agile**. Resilience is often described as bouncing *back* from tough times, but I believe there's a level up to this. I call this *agility*: the ability to not just bounce *back* from stress but to learn how to *thrive through* it. This is an entirely different subject that could warrant its own chapter (or book), but agility is a whole other level of resilience. Thrivers are agile.

Thrivers have three key skills dialed in—awareness, mindset, and vision/values.

1. Awareness

Thrivers are highly *self-aware* under stress—they know what triggers it, how they're showing up, and how others see them. Thrivers are keenly aware of *their thought, emotion, and behavior patterns under stress*, but have a greater ability to catch these patterns nearly right when they experience them (strong Gift of Pause).

Their inner voice might say, *Looks like you're having a stressful moment here and that's why you're feeling the urge to turn and run; let's check in.*

Thrivers inherently understand that our emotions filter and often skew our experiences, so they're great at checking in with their emotions on a regular basis and especially when they're stressed (*Ask*, step 2).

They can also separate their emotions and thoughts from their behaviors and judgment, which helps them *Act* (step 3) with intention. They stay *present and connected* with themselves and others.

Thrivers have awareness of others, too—how others might see them and how others might be feeling. They're empathetic and recognize that their behaviors have an impact for better or worse. They can listen and stay present.

I know a wonderful man, Jon, who has a practice he calls his "Ministry of Availability." Jon is a senior executive of an insurance company in Florida and he builds open, unscheduled time into each week to simply be available to others. Whether it's a colleague who needs to chat, an employee wanting feedback, a college student looking for guidance, or a total stranger needing a hot meal and a conversation, Jon makes time, no questions asked. And when Jon makes time for you, he is fully there in the moment. He's not distracted or rushed, and he makes you feel like you're the most important person in the room. Jon is certainly a Thriver.

2. Mindset

Thrivers have the right *mindset* through challenges, changes, the unexpected, difficult times…stressful situations. When it comes to stress, *mindset is king*. Maybe it's their past challenges, their training, or maybe they were just brought up with these skills, but Thrivers *sustain great perspective through challenging times*.

This is difficult to do, by the way—perspective is easy until, say, our car breaks down, we're short-staffed on the team and picking up the slack, or someone spills coffee on us in a busy subway car.

Often, Thrivers have a different story about *stress itself*. Here's what I mean:

There was a longitudinal study conducted by researchers at the University of Michigan that tracked 30,000 people over eight years in the US. At the start, researchers asked study participants two questions: 1) How much stress have you experienced in the past year? And 2) Do you believe stress is harmful for your health? Then they used public death records to track who had died during the study.

The bad news first: people who experienced *a lot* of stress in the previous year had a 43 percent increased risk of dying—but this was only true for the people who *also believed that stress is harmful for your health*. By contrast, people who experienced *a lot* of stress in the past year, but did *not perceive stress as harmful*, were no more likely to die than any others in the study and they had the *lowest* risk of dying, *including those who reported little stress in their lives*. This study was a huge breakthrough in our understanding of the power of our *beliefs about stress*.[1]

Based on this study we might be able to assume that it's not the stress that kills us, but the *belief that stress is harmful*. It also helps explain how some of the hardest hit people we know, who were dealt the greatest blows in life, are also some of the gentlest, calm, longest living, and most agile and resilient. What do they have that we don't? The right story. The right *mindset*. A belief that, truly, what doesn't kill us makes us stronger—they believe this to their core and live their lives this way. If this sounds familiar, it's because we also learned in Chapter 3 that it's stress in the absence of recovery that gets us—not stress itself.

So, Thrivers tend to inherently believe that stress is an opportunity for growth, challenge, wisdom, and isn't always harmful; often they don't usually look at stressful situations, busyness, challenges, and so on as threats in the first place. Thrivers can quickly *reframe*. We'll focus on that in the Stress Resets section on training to be more like a Thriver below.

3. Thrivers have clear *vision* and *values*, and *train* for alignment in these areas.

Thrivers have a *vision* of who they are at their absolute best, where they want to go, and who they want to be in the process, no matter what happens. They are also clear on what's most important. They know what they stand for and stick to their values even when things aren't easy. We'll unpack purpose more in the Thriver Accelerator chapter, but Thrivers are generally highly *purpose-driven*. This is easy to do when sitting on a beach on vacation, or life is smooth sailing—it's another thing to stick to our values when life throws a curveball. When we're threatened, our world gets much smaller, our negative bias and survival instinct kicks in, and we fall back to our defaults. If we aren't clear on our values and they aren't an *active* part of our daily life, how can we automatically default to them?

So, Thrivers *define themselves by their values rather than their opinions or beliefs.* And they can use curiosity to be more *flexible in their thinking* and adjust back to grounding in their values, which is an essential ingredient to resilience.[2]

Want a tough exercise? Journal about this question, which is a sort of face-the-truth moment:

Are you the same person in the bad times as you are in the good times?

Meaning, do you sacrifice your values or lose that vision of who you are at your best when you're put in difficult situations? Which values are the first to go? Which parts of the best version of you are the first to go? And how long does it take you to realign and recalibrate with that best version of yourself?

Thrivers Fail Forward

Along those lines, Thrivers know how to *fail forward.* They might find themselves off course, but it doesn't take long to course correct. They know how to *acknowledge and learn from their mistakes* because *they build time for this kind of reflection and look for opportunities to be persistently curious and eager to learn.* They practice *grace* and *humility* and recognize the very *humanness* of the stress response. They're also more likely to extend these qualities to others.

As such, they're likely the ones to *seek feedback and forgiveness from others* and *own their actions and feelings.* Thriver parents, partners, and bosses are great at modeling this, and are more likely to own their role in an argument or misunderstanding—not the next day or a week after, but right then in the moment, without conditions—*I'm sorry I was a jerk but in my defense you were…*—just a genuine apology and acknowledgment of their behaviors.

Thrivers lean into tough conversations and are vulnerable to share their feelings. They have the courage to be who they are and don't feel pressured to hide, stuff, avoid, distract, appease you, play up, or inflate themselves. They boldly own their flaws, protect their boundaries, lean into discomfort, and practice humility.

Thrivers understand that mistakes are how we grow into the people we want to be. When people are afraid of imperfection or to mess up, they aren't willing to try new things, be brave, be innovative, and forget that mistakes are where learning is most potent—the very place where resilience and agility is built and forged.

Curiosity is a skill.

Curiosity is truly a skill—it helps us recognize that *our* beliefs or perspectives aren't the *only* way to see things and can even sometimes do us a disservice. Remember, our aperture gets narrower when stressed: the Fighter becomes so attached to his opinions, he's hostile at the thought of being challenged; the Negative Self-Talker's beliefs about themselves keep them in the shadows, unwilling to speak up or try something new. Thrivers keep their aperture wide under stress. Which is invaluable, becuase when we define ourselves solely by our critical inner voice or limiting beliefs, we stop being open to other perspectives or feedback (except that pineapple *does* belong on pizza and you can't convince me otherwise).

Thrivers are intrinsically motivated.

Whether a Thriver is fortunate enough to work and live in a supportive environment that fosters these qualities, or they work hard to create the conditions themselves, Thrivers can stay highly motivated even when stressed because they know they have *choice, control*, seek meaningful *connections* with others, and feel *capable* in the chaos.[3]

Thrivers can hold space for opposing emotions, beliefs, and thoughts at the same time.

Like their ability to stay curious and look at different perspectives, Thrivers know the value of accepting *opposing feelings* about things. Whether managing a stressful situation or discussing polarizing subjects that can easily trigger the stress response (politics, religion, sports, gun control…pineapple on pizza), a Thriver inherently understands the importance of being able to hold two often opposing emotions or thoughts about something at once and not feel the need to choose one sword to fall on, or at least not have to make everyone else agree with that decision.

In other words, they have high emotional literacy, particularly under stress. They recognize the nuanced, complex, diverse beings we are and are at peace with that.

Thrivers are tapped into their inner voice and it is generally supportive.

This should go without saying, but *Thrivers have a supportive inner voice.* They've been able to shift their inner critic to a coach and a champion and recognize the times when it isn't supportive.

This doesn't mean that a Thriver doesn't challenge themselves to grow and thrive—it's not positivity-at-the-expense-of-self-awareness. We all know that person; the one who is painfully confident to the point where they really believe they have no room for growth (such glaring blind spots you need sunglasses to look them in the eye, right?).

No, I'm referring to the curious, non-conditional, growth-minded, ambitious, champion inside that says, *You messed up, and you can learn from it…you could do better, and you're doing great…you are enough, and you can grow and rise even higher.*

They know their "best" looks different on different days. They can push themselves with the *full* acceptance of who they are, not an admonishment of someone they've yet to become. This inner voice has the *yes, and* concept completely dialed in. *Yes, I am enough. I am safe. I am capable. And, I can grow; I can mess up; I can be wrong; I'm not good at this thing...yet.*

Thrivers are intuitive and able to balance emotion, thought, and logic.

Daniel Siegel, an expert on mindful awareness and Clinical Professor of Psychiatry at the UCLA School of Medicine says that emotion is "the subjective experience of the body and brain's projection of *meaning* in response to our experiences of threat."[4] Thrivers inherently get this—that emotion is subjective and our interpretation of a threat, not reality. Though the gut isn't always right, neither are our emotions, nor our thoughts. We need to balance all three together simultaneously.

(Need more on this? Go back to the Worrier chapter.)

Thrivers are courageous and vulnerable.

One of the greatest qualities of a Thriver is that they are who they appear to be. How often do we spend precious energy focused on how we *seem to be* to others? We try too hard; we adjust our behavior or opinions based on the company we're around or what someone can do for us; our handshake might be a little too hard, or our laugh a little too loud. Cringy, right? The truth is, we've all been there. Social media is a great example of the inherently human need to look less like a mess than we really are.

But then you come across that warm, quiet, still soul here and there who simply *is* and isn't "appearing to be." You sense that you are seeing this person for who he or she really is...someone *be*-ing. These folks are as indispensable as oxygen—you can't put a price on a Thriver friend.

Thrivers are intentional about training under stress.

Thrivers can reperceive stressful experiences as opportunities for growth, but they also *seek* opportunities to train under pressure. Whether learning a new hobby, taking on a new project at work, choosing a challenging professional development course, facing a tough relationship challenge or conversation head-on, a Thriver leans *toward* perceived threats and demands, not away, with courage, authenticity, confidence, awareness of their patterns, and the right Stress Resets in place.

Things you might hear from a Thriver:

+ *I'm feeling frustrated right now because....*

+ *Gosh, I didn't handle that meeting well.*

+ *I'm sorry if I was snappy and short; I didn't eat lunch and I'm a bit hangry.*

+ *I could have been more patient and slower to respond to Sarah's ask. Do you have any suggestions for the future?*

+ *You seem to be hesitant to help with this project, which puts more of the workload and responsibility on me. I'd love more support with this lift—how can we better share the load? The writing part is most taxing to me. Do we have anyone on the team who can support us if you're unable? (Notice this isn't a Pleaser behavior...do you see the clear ask and the boundaries?)*

+ *I'm sorry I didn't stand up for you. I was too worried about what others would think. Can you forgive me? How can I make it right?*

- *I messed this up big time! I'd love to learn where I went wrong. Could we make time to unpack this?*

- *I feel overwhelmed and worried about how this project will go, but also a little excited—can I reach out here and there to process?*

- *Can we talk about what happened in the meeting earlier? I'd love to work through it together. Let's find some time.*

THE THRIVER: UNDER THE HOOD

We've tapped into a *lot* of different areas of the brain and psychology responsible for our stress personalities throughout the book. Here, I want to dive a bit deeper into two key qualities of a Thriver that are unique to them: emotional literacy and intuition.

Emotional literacy (or intelligence) is the ability to recognize our emotions (and others' emotions) in the moment, which we sort of know already at this point in the book.

We also learned that, despite their tendency to oppose each other under stress (emotions can smack up against logic like a whack-a-mole game under stress), our emotions work nicely along with our logic, reason, and values to help us make important decisions (Worrier chapter).

This is, in a nutshell, *intuition*.

Friendly reminder: research has found that emotionally intelligent, intuitive thinkers are those who can effectively balance their emotions, logic and reason, their values, and hears their inner voice well...and these intuitive thinkers outperform those who use effortful reasoning, control, or analysis alone to make decisions as well as those who act only on their emotions.[5]

Knowing how our emotions might filter our experience helps us be more flexible in our thinking, objectively weigh the facts, be better able to receive and incorporate other ways of thinking and weigh it all together equally to decide how to act.

Let's take it even further: are you tapped into your *physical* body during stress, too? Your gut? Thinking is far more than an above-the-neck operation. The more aware you are of bodily sensations—smell, touch, taste, sound, sight— especially when feeling stressed, the more self-aware and intuitive you become. This also means you're more likely to default to the right Stress Reset strategies.

Looking for a level up? Learn to *anticipate* imminent stress by noticing a bodily sensation like fatigue, anger, an anxious stomach, worry, hunger, lethargy, a scattering mind, etc., and act before it becomes an issue. (Side note: the way we *care* for our bodies matters *so much more* than previously realized when it comes to resilience and thriving—we cover this more in the Thriver Accelerators chapter.)

Exercise to Understand the Thriver Personality

Think you might be a Thriver? (Remember, it's a *yes, and*...you can be both another stress personality and this one too.) Let's reflect on what we know about a Thriver and evaluate yourself against that.

Evaluate yourself using the following sliding scale *when things are hard or you feel stressed*:

0 = Never   5 = Sometimes   10 = Always

_____ I trust my own wisdom and judgment when faced with tough situations or choices (including when I disagree with others).

_____ I believe in myself.

_____ I feel in control.

_____ I'm in tune with emotions without being driven by them.

_____ I'm in tune with my physical body.

_____ I can observe my thoughts without being driven by them.

_____ I seek others' advice in balance with my own inner voice.

_____ I can calm myself down *before* acting.

_____ I can listen to other people even if I'm in direct conflict with them.

_____ I can stay present and "be where my feet are."

_____ I can remain available to others.

_____ I see how my behaviors and words impact others.

_____ I stay with difficult emotions, rather than avoid them.

_____ I stay connected to my values, my purpose.

_____ I stay consistently in alignment to the best version of myself.

_____ I can fail forward and remain curious and courageous.

_____ I am adaptive in my thinking (growth versus fixed mindset).

_____ I see most stressful situations as opportunities for growth.

_____ I can stay connected to my goals and focused.

_____ My inner voice remains positive and supportive.

How'd you do? Where do you think you might need additional learning and practice? Anywhere you gave yourself a 5 or lower, highlight it as an opportunity for growth.

WATCHOUTS

Are you surprised that I included a Watchouts section for the Thriver? What could possibly go wrong if you have it all figured out?

You may be surprised.

Self-Care

For one, Thrivers are good people who care deeply. Because they are self-and-other aware, present, empathetic, connected to themselves and others, and intuitive—they tend to become sounding boards and support systems for others who haven't quite tapped into that Thriver self.

Can you understand where I'm going with this? When you're the one Thriving and others are attracted to that, consider that you might run the risk of exhausting your energy capacity on supporting others—with great Thriving comes great responsibility!

Watch out for exhaustion and compassion fatigue; always put the oxygen mask on yourself first. If you make self-care a priority and a regular practice, you can *sustain* that Thriver personality through anything.

False Positive

I have an acquaintance who took the stress personality quiz on my website and attended one of my virtual sessions and was *convinced* she was a Thriver through and through.

Except...between you and me...her outward behaviors are *not* Thriver behaviors. I gently suggested such, but she wasn't in a place to hear it. In fact, she comes across as more of a Freezer than a Thriver: consistently avoids confrontation but has conflict with others in most areas of life; is "right" all the time; visibly stressed by her job and always complaining about it; and stuffs negative emotions into little toxically positive sentences here and there like "too blessed to be stressed." She just can't see it (yet). Now, I'm not privy to her thoughts and emotions so that must be acknowledged, but I've been a performance coach for long enough to see through the cracks. She *wants* to be a Thriver—but she has some internal reflection work to do first.

The watchout is this: be careful about a "false positive." How can you tell the difference? The following are a few ideas:

* Check the balance between your positive and negative emotions through the course of a typical day. You *know* intuitively that you're not feeling positive, joyful, connected, peaceful, etc. Can you be honest with yourself about that?

* Gauge how quickly you recover from stressful moments.

* Ask others: check in with your VIPs (or your Capital F friends—you know they'll call you out). Find someone who can be real with you and ask how you're showing up. When this particular friend of mine is ready, I'll be there to share my perspective with love and compassion.

Autonomy + Connection must be balanced.

Just a quick thought: autonomy is a great quality and one a Thriver knows well. Their sense of control and choice is powerful (remember, that's how they stay so motivated). But often when we're moving fast and charging forward through a challenge, we can easily dismiss the importance of connection with others and develop the habit of not asking for help and support. The more you tell someone they're a Thriver and *sooooo resilient*, the greater the pressure to stay that way, right?

Don't let ego get in the way.

We're wired to need social connection and support from others, *and* we also thrive with consistent autonomy. We need *both*; they're not a contradiction. We are meant to move between both as part of an agile, resilient, thriving life.

THRIVER SUPERPOWERS

Our entire chapter is on the superpowers of a Thriver, so I'm going to leave this one alone. Congrats! You win at life, Thrivers!

STRESS RESETS FOR THE THRIVER

In this section, we're not asking how to better manage our stress personality; but rather, how can I as a Thriver *sustain* my stress personality? The following are a few ways:

A Thriver Knows Their Stress Resets

It's a bit of a "meta-Stress Reset," but Thrivers have their Stress Reset strategies locked in and ready to deploy; not just one but many depending on what they need. So here are some suggestions to sustain your skills:

Go Upstream.

We'll unpack this more deeply in the last chapter and have touched on it all along, but build an environment to support less stress and better management of stress through your daily habits and lifestyle (sleep, nutrition, exercise, and connection can all support more sustained resilience).

Consistently work to reframe your stress.

Remember the study mentioned earlier about beliefs about stress? In her TedTalk detailing the study, social psychologist Kelly McGonigal points out another Harvard study where participants were asked to perform some highly stressful tasks (speaking in front of a group unexpectedly; counting backward by 7's from 996 with a facilitator pressuring them to hurry up and start over if they mess up, etc.).

Naturally, participants would interpret the stress they felt as anxiety and inability to cope under pressure. But these participants were told to do something very different—they were encouraged to, when feeling signs of stress like a racing heart rate or pit in their stomach, consider these signs that their body was *energized* and preparing them to meet a wonderful challenge; their heart rate was preparing them for action; their increased breathing was just more oxygen to the brain; their stressful experience was helpful to their performance.

In other words, they were coached to rethink their stress response as *helpful*. And guess what? They were less stressed out, less anxious, more confident, and their physical response to stress was less intense.[6]

Point: reframing is powerful, and it works. So, look for any opportunities to practice reframing.

Let's go back to the examples we used earlier about a few typical stressful situations: our car breaks down, we're short-staffed on the team, or someone bumps into us on a busy commuter train and we spill coffee on ourselves. How can we practice reframing in these situations?

- ✦ My car broke down. Thankfully, I have roadside assistance and I wasn't in an accident on the side of the road. I'm safe and my daughter wasn't in the car.

- ✦ We're short-staffed. This is an opportunity to connect with my team on a deeper level—we're all experiencing the intense pressure of this additional responsibility; we'll get through this together and it will make us even stronger.

- ✦ Someone accidently bumps into me on a busy commuter train and I spill coffee on myself. This is a chance to extend grace to the person who bumped into me; of course, it wasn't intentional. I have the ability to change the trajectory of this person's day based on how I respond; who knows, maybe they'll extend that same compassion to someone else today.

The Gift of Pause

When we consistently train, we can learn to catch ourselves between our initial reaction to stress and our response to it, gaining more control over our next step. We know this is one of the most powerful skills we can hone, but how do we build this muscle and *train* for it?

Three suggestions to strengthen the Gift of Pause:

1. **Training through reflection and journaling.** Make it a habit to track how you're showing up: how you act, feel, and think.

   » When you mess up, work to reframe the failure.

   » When you reach an impasse, reframe quitting as knowing when to stop.

   » When you feel tired and want to quit but it's worthwhile and connected to your values, remind yourself that you can persist and find meaning in the mayhem.

This is how to train *after the fact*.

2. **Get ahead of it by anticipating what could happen and how you'll show up.** Think about how to future-proof your resilience. This is going upstream and applying some of the Thriver Accelerators we'll learn about soon.

This is how to train *ahead of time*.

3. **Train in the moment with intention.** We put ourselves in stressful situations and train through it. We seek "stress" and intentionally reframe it. This is how we train *in the moment*. Start small and build from there. Training stress, remember?

This is how to train *in the moment*.

The Enemy's Gate is Down

Here's another strategy to hone your reframing skills: remember the phrase "the enemy's gate is down." Let me explain:

My husband's favorite book of all time is *Ender's Game* by Orson Scott Card—if you're a sci-fi fan, you likely know it. In the book, a group of prodigy children are trained to win an outer space war waged against an alien lifeform that nearly destroyed Earth.

The children train in a simulation while preparing for war, and these simulation rooms make it extremely difficult for the groups to coordinate together and attack their enemy because the zero-gravity environment shifts perspective and orientation drastically from one moment to the next. One of the supporting characters, Bean, shares some advice with the main character and leader of the group, Ender, to help him reframe their environment. He says, "The enemy's gate is down."

He doesn't mean the gate is broken down; he's referring to the gate's literal direction. By creating a fixed focal point and imagining the enemy's gate in the "down" direction, Ender can use the gate now as a reference point in the room. Ender uses the new fixed focal point to ultimately lead the team to victory amid a chaotic, ever-changing, high stress environment (I won't spoil the rest, but the ending might surprise you).

There are many other metaphors and interpretations of the saying, but I like to think of the phrase as a reminder to *continuously look at your environment and situation from different perspectives.* Whenever you're faced with a high stress situation, remind yourself that "the enemy's gate is down." So, what's your new focal point? How are you going to navigate through and lead yourself, or your family, or your team, to victory?

Same moments; same stress; different energy brought to the table.

FINAL THOUGHTS

I briefly mentioned Viktor Frankl in the Fighter chapter, but here's a bit more about him. He was an Austrian psychiatrist and Holocaust survivor who wrote one of the most powerful books I've ever read, *Man's Search for Meaning.*[7] Frankl's entire family died in a concentration camp, but he remained a prisoner there. While imprisoned, he counseled other survivors through the unimaginable horrors. Frankl survived the Holocaust and went on to formulate the early theories on logotherapy, believing that human nature is motivated by the search for purpose in life—logotherapy is the pursuit of finding and rooting in that purpose even in the worst of circumstances. His book is life changing; in it, he shares two powerful quotes that radically shifted the way I think about stress and challenge:

> Between stimulus and response there is a space. In that space is our power to choose our response. In our response lies our growth and our freedom.

Everything can be taken from a man but one thing: the last of human freedoms—to choose one's attitude in any given set of circumstances, to choose one's own way.

What a great reminder that, even if we might be temporarily hijacked by our own biology, at the end of the day we have control and choice in how we respond to the stressors in our life—the small stressors and the life-changing ones, too.

Thrivers, you remind us of this choice daily. You're the type of human we strive to be! Thank you for giving us a vision of what to work toward.

TL:DR

+ Thrivers aren't perfect people.
+ Resilience (agility) is a skill, not a trait. *It can be trained.*
+ Thrivers are highly agile and thrive through stress. This means they have:

  » Awareness of their default patterns of negative thoughts, emotions, and behaviors under stress.
  » The right mindset through challenges, changes, unexpected, difficult times, stressful situations, even about stress itself.
  » They stay present and connected with themselves and others and the right vision and values to train for alignment in these areas.

+ Thrivers know how to fail forward, eager to learn from those mistakes.

- They exercise forgiveness, grace, humility, and curiosity.
- They're likely the one to seek feedback from others and own their actions and feelings.
- They are curious by nature. And, more importantly, they define themselves by their values rather than their opinions or beliefs. They can use that curiosity to be more flexible in their thinking.
- They're purpose-driven and highly internally motivated:

  » They believe they're in control.
  » They foster meaningful connection with others.
  » They believe in themselves.

- They are who they are, no matter what (radical self-acceptance).
- Thrivers have a supportive inner voice.
- They are intuitive and able to balance emotion, gut feeling, logic, and reason.
- Thrivers should pay attention to self-care as essential to sustaining their Thriver personality. They should be mindful about balancing their sense of control and autonomy with reaching out for help and connecting with others.
- Some of the key Stress Resets for a Thriver:

  » Know and have ready your best Stress Resets.
  » Build and maintain a lifestyle to support Thriving.
  » Actively and intentionally reframe stress.
  » Train for greater control over the Gift of Pause.

» Continually look for new perspectives and focal points. Remember, the enemy's gate is down.

FINAL FINAL THOUGHTS

Thrivers, no pressure but you are the standard upon which we all weigh ourselves. Thank you for that. For whatever path brought you here, you likely suffered, hurt, fought, scraped by, trained hard, lost precious people or things.

The road to becoming a Thriver isn't always smooth or easy. Nonetheless, you found yourself there. Which means, we can too. So, thank you for the inspiration. We see you, and we are so very thankful for you.

PART III

INSIGHT

TO

ACTION

13

THE INTERACTION

A Runner and a Worrier walk into a room...

Imagine you're on a subway in New York City, traveling across town to a sporting event. The train is chock-full of people: sports fans, tourists, and commuters heading home from work all packed like sardines as the train races along, bumping and lurching rhythmically around turns. Suddenly, the wheels screech and the train comes to an abrupt halt. The lights flicker and it becomes eerily silent. After a moment, the conductor shares the news across the intercom that the train has experienced a mechanical failure and it might be a bit before they can figure out what's going on and when you'll be on your way.

A collective groan rises from the grimy floor of the train car. The game starts in less than an hour. It's stuffy, crowded, hot, and the air is stale.

As you can imagine, the train car is bursting with a variety of stress personalities all stuck together in one very stressful experience.

Think of what a great case study this scene would be for what happens when different stress personalities experience stress together:

A fan in a sports jersey near the window angrily grumbles about the state of the public transportation system in this city to whoever will listen. A woman in a business suit looks concerned, tapping her foot like she has a nervous tic, checking her watch then staring at the floor, and checking her watch again. A man with a bag of groceries stares into the distance, exhausted and checked out. He closes his eyes and shakes his head as if this was the last straw of a long day. A woman sitting nearby with an open laptop and airpods in each ear pinches her nose as if she has a headache. Two passengers start to argue believing the other isn't giving them enough space. A third passenger tries to intervene and help but is shut down.

You? You're feeling trapped and eager to turn around and get home. Your inner voice reminds you that you should have taken an Uber like you originally had planned. Now, you have friends relying on you and you can't even text them the tickets because you don't have service—you've failed your whole friend group. You are a total failure and should have known better!

This is an example of an important concept I don't want you to miss—*not everyone has your stress personality*.

The thing is, despite the natural tendency to see the world through our own limited lens, we don't all react the same to stress. And when we forget this truth, it creates a significant amount of tension, doesn't it?

Let me give you a real-life example:

I have a former client, Charlotte. She is a Negative Self-Talker who works with a Fighter coworker. This Fighter is self-diagnosed, by the way (the whole team went through a virtual workshop on the subject with me, so we're not assuming here). This coworker was the type who doesn't fight with loud or aggressive yelling or backtalk: she prefers passive-aggressive emails, gossip, echo chambers, undermining, quiet murmurs, sour looks, or subtle eye rolls in meetings. She has quite toxic behavior and at this point was just starting to see it for herself.

Charlotte wasn't innocent, though. Her Negative Self-Talk prevented her from speaking up, owning her space, and sharing openly. Her fear and submission caused her to avoid confrontation, keep her mouth shut, and continue allowing this behavior to go on, at the expense of her health. She was getting sick more often, missing more days, totally disconnected from the team, and *hated* all-hands meetings. She had one ally in the workplace and resorted to dumping all her negative energy into this friend, who was, at this point, frustrated that Charlotte wasn't *doing* anything to change the situation.

Charlotte and her Fighter coworker couldn't be on a team together and their manager knew it—one would run the other over with passive-aggressiveness, and the tension grew. Through our coaching sessions, Charlotte worked hard to be more direct, honest, and address her coworker head-on. She first had a great conversation with her manager requesting more support, which turned into a great conversation between her manager and I about the team as a whole and how friction wasn't managed as effectively as it could have been. Things got better over time between them.

One strategy we employed was the power of empathy. As hard as it was for Charlotte, she faced the truth of what must have been a soft, fearful, self-questioning insecurity beneath her coworker's Fighter ways. When she tapped into empathy for her story, she softened a bit and sought connection, not just resolution. And whaddayaknow…it worked. This Fighter wasn't all that bad a person after all: she had a lot going on at home, and she was outspoken and brash because she lacked the skills to communicate her needs effectively.

Here's another example. My husband is a Worrier. He's a finance guy, and when he is stressed (particularly at home), he turns into a walking spreadsheet. He wants to *talk, talk, talk* it out: consider every detail, ask questions, and has this hilarious quirk where he attempts to quantify all his stressors in some way, such as saying, "Let's say Jake completes his chores 40 percent of the time…then he should get 40 percent of his allowance, right?" I sometimes feel like I need a calculator to have a conversation with him (or a strong margarita, I'm not picky).

Sometimes, he can compartmentalize and act more like a Freezer when things really need to get done, but more often than not, he's a

Worrier. And this makes sense, because it's: (a) the way he's wired; and (b) it's his literal job to worry—to anticipate, to assess risk, to prevent risk, to quantify...

As you know, I'm a Runner; and as you know, because of this the *last* thing I usually want to do is lean in and talk through things with him *in* a moment of stress. I prefer space to process. But what *he* needs is to process...*right now*. It drives him crazy when I wave him away, roll my eyes, groan, or walk away...and of course, I do all these things.

So, how do we possibly navigate this together when we're both stressed?

Well, first, sometimes we don't. Sometimes we fight, argue, bicker, or passive aggressively and immaturely navigate our way through.

But other times when we act like grownups, we *acknowledge* our patterns and *ask* each other what we need. Then, we *act*. Sometimes, very directly, he'll ask me to process with him; other times, I'll ask him for a minute to breathe.

Here's the second part of that critical message we need to drive home: *Not everyone has your stress personality, therefore,* **not everyone needs the same type of support.** Not your partner, your kids, your colleagues, your best friend, or a stranger on a train.

It's critically important to build empathy for *everyone's* experience of stress and learn what they need—this will help us forge and keep strong relationships in our life.

How can I best support others' stress personalities if I can't relate to them?

Ah, great question. Let's cover a few things that are important as both reminders and best practices:

1. **You can't help others without knowing your own stress personality.** It will be very hard to connect with others and support them if you don't know yourself. So, before you go

out to save the world, do the work of creating awareness for yourself. Get to know your patterns and your Stress Resets. Hone your Gift of Pause skills. Build that muscle so strong that it's automatic.

2. **You can't help others by diagnosing them.** Remember Rule 3 from Chapter 4? You can't diagnose other people from the outside in. So don't fall into the false belief that you can support others by assuming who they are and what they need.

Instead, *get curious about others' experiences of stress.* Rather than assume what they need, *ask.* Ask these types of questions:

How are you feeling? What can I do to help?

I know it sounds simple, but this is such a powerful strategy. As we just learned from the Thriver chapter, curiosity is a super-skill that often leads to deeper insights, stronger relationships, and clearer understanding of what support looks like for the people you care about.

Remember, your job is not to *fix* others.

The coolest part? Through this, you will learn more and more about what you need for yourself. And as you will learn in the next chapter, supporting others is a Stress Reset for yourself. So, it's a win-win.

Our stress personalities complement each other in wonderful ways, and so do our challenges. For example, remember that:

+ Fighters tend to be action-focused and quick on their feet, but they might need a moment to breathe.

+ Worriers are good communicators, detail-oriented, and risk-averse, but might need to process together or need help staying present and engaged.

+ Runners are careful and thoughtful but thrive with a little space and confidence and trust in themselves.

- Freezers can put their head down and get things done, but really need rest and connection, and a recalibration to what's most important.

- Pleasers are selfless, eager, and giving, but they can't overcommit themselves in the process so help them uphold the boundaries they set.

- Distracted types are highly creative and out of the box thinkers, but encourage them to take regular breaks.

- Negative Self-Talkers are kind and thoughtful, but might need some encouragement.

- Thrivers are an ace in the hole; help them stay that way.

When we are supported, we thrive. A great thing happens when people feel supported and when they feel like you're meeting them where they are—they start to thrive. When we support someone in discovering their own stress personality and what Stress Reset strategies work best for them, they build confidence (self-efficacy), a sense of control, and empathy toward others.

There's science to all of this, of course.

Have you ever watched the great TedTalk about superchickens? Entrepreneur Margaret Heffernan shared a famous study out of Purdue University by researcher William Muir who studied productivity. He put together two groups of chickens: the first were average chickens. The second were "superchickens"—the most productive (by way of egg production) which he bred and continued to breed for six generations, each time breeding the most productive of the most productive.

After six generations, the first group, the average chickens, continued to regularly produce as usual and even produced more. The second group? All but three were dead—they pecked the others to death. The chickens who were individually "super" only survived by suppressing the others.

In her TedTalk, Heffernan uses the study as a metaphor for creating work cultures where people can truly thrive. Often workplaces run their offices like superchickens—the way to "get ahead" is to climb, compete, be the best, have the most power. But the result is usually dysfunction, lack of trust, and disengaged employees—a "pecking order" (pun very much intended).

What does it take, then, to create thriving teams, families, sports teams, relationships?

Researchers have found that the *most* successful relationships are not those who have the best and brightest, the highest IQs, the one leader who is aggressively outspoken and decisive; rather, the most successful relationships have three characteristics:

1. They're *socially aware and sensitive* to one another's feelings.

2. *Everyone* has a chance to speak and share—not just the superchickens.

3. They are *more diverse*. All stress personalities welcome![1]

When we are connected to each other, support each other's well-being, embrace each other's stress personalities, and empower each other to build a life that works best for us, ideas start to flow and trust starts to grow. *Everyone* on our team or in our family or friend circles should feel heard and supported, and know they have value.[2]

The cool part is, we can also leverage each other's superpowers in an environment like this.

For example, when I need a moment to think or I'm unsure and hesitant, my husband comes to the rescue with his ability to process every detail and weigh options. I can depend on him when I don't have the energy or focus to move forward (thank goodness he puts up with me).

Other examples:

- We can lean on the Fighter to be decisive, loyal and protective, and remind us of what we're fighting for.

- We can lean on the Runner to seek and protect the space needed to process.

- We can lean on the Worrier to be thorough, detailed, and alert us to potential risks.

- We can lean on the Freezer to put their heads down and get work done, making tough decisions in a crisis.

- We can lean on the Pleaser to be supportive, helpful, and empathetic.

- We can lean on the Negative Self-Talker to be careful, cautious, self-reflective, and empathetic.

- We can lean on the Distracted to innovate, dream, and create.

- We can lean on the Thriver through it all.

No matter your people—your family, friends, community, teams—ask yourself:

- *How can I create connection in my circle and see their stress personalities and the superpowers therein?*

- *How can I help them generate positive emotions (or focus on generating our own, knowing that emotional energy is contagious).*

- *How can I build trust, knowing that trust wins over performance every time?*

How can you do this?

- Learn more about yourself.

- Practice and role model.

- Get vulnerable and share.
- Stay curious and ask.
- Seek to create an environment where everyone feels heard, valued, and belongs.
- No superchickens allowed.

You may be wondering: My partner/best friend/employee is an XYZ stress personality. How can I connect with this person specifically?

How can you support and connect with them, especially when you're *both* stressed?

Outside of knowing who *you* are (most importantly), here are a few suggestions for how to connect with each stress personality (not an exhaustive list).

CONNECTING WITH A FIGHTER

Has someone ever told you to calm down when you're mad? How did that work out for them? Are they still in one piece?

If you're in conflict with a Fighter or notice they're frustrated or irritated, approach with caution. In fight or flight mode, they might:

- Resist.
- Push back.
- Not respond well to criticism or being told what to do.

But if you handle it right, they might also:

- Be great delegators.
- Rise up to the challenge.

- Stand up for what's right and act right away.

Fighters usually place high importance on a sense of control, inde-
pendence, doing what's right, and seeking justice or defending others.
But first, they need a minute to come out of that fight or flight state.
If appropriate (you are in their inner circle and it's appropriate for you
to help):

- Remember, "physiology first." Try to help them close the
  stress response cycle. Suggest a quick walk; spend some
  time apart; suggest taking a few deep breaths together.
  Stay off the subject at hand.

- Then, try to get them to name the emotion. Anger?
  Frustration? Helplessness? Embarrassment? If you get a
  short answer (*I'm angry, obviously!*), see if you can help
  them gently peel back the layers. Remember: *I feel angry,
  but the truth is I also feel...*

- Matching their anger will get you nowhere, nor will
  logic or reason if they're in fight or flight. (Especially
  children...*especially* teenagers who *live* in their Emotional
  Brain. In fact, their New Brain is still developing. It's our
  job to model how to close the stress response cycle *in
  ourselves* before trying to get them to do so; I know, this is
  so much easier said than done. I live with two of them.)

CONNECTING WITH A RUNNER

Runners often feel overwhelmed, anxious, and need/think they need a
bit of space. So, leaning in and forcing a response from a Runner in a
moment of stress will get you *nowhere*.

Space can often *create* connection—give it to them. Better yet, ask what they need and then honor that request. If they're feeling anxious or overwhelmed and seek your support, help them regulate their nervous system like you would a Fighter. Take a walk, breathe together, run your feet through the soft grass outside, play a fun song and dance out the jitters together, or share a funny joke. Anything to quiet the mind and recenter to the present.

You can also try some perspective shifting: guide them to a 30,000-foot view of what's bringing them stress and observe, together, what the bigger fears, stressors, goals are. Brainstorm some small, manageable next steps. Sometimes even just staying quiet and holding space for your friend to get it all out works wonders. Just help them not to get stuck there.

CONNECTING WITH A WORRIER

Connecting with a Worrier is keeping in mind they aren't intentionally being distant or distracted or overly needy to process. *It's not that they don't care or value your opinion;* they're just stuck on that rollercoaster of rumination or catastrophizing and struggling to get off. How can you help a Worrier reconnect with the present moment?

One way is to be a sounding board. Worriers might just need an ear to listen (not necessarily for you to try and fix things, though, so fight the urge unless specifically asked). And sometimes, they want to keep their worries, fears, and uncertainties to themselves. If they turn away from your invitation to connect, don't stress it.

You could:

+ Ask what's on their mind and what they're stuck on.

+ Help them process a recent experience.

+ Ask what would help them *right now*, like a deep breath or a quick guided breathing exercise.

- Help them weigh pros and cons.
- Map out what success looks like.
- Help them reflect on what they know (the facts) and weigh those with their emotions.
- Simply listen.

Thought leader Stephanie Harrison, founder of NewHappyCo (she's a happiness expert who creates beautiful, thoughtful art on social media), suggests the following phrase when a friend is going through a tough time, "No matter what happens, I'll be right here next to you." It's a simple, and powerful message, and might be all they need to hear.

Quick reminder: Worriers might *unload* on you, so especially if you're not a Worrier yourself, find a way to decompress afterward. Oxygen mask on you first, right?

CONNECTING WITH A FREEZER

Connecting with a Freezer may be tough, mostly because Freezers often resist connection when stressed. Remember that Freezers usually take two forms: 1) they either shut out all worry, stress, fear, and they put their heads down and move through (but block out emotion and often, others...*I'm fine, stop asking!*); or 2) they're the type who physically, mentally, emotionally, and spiritually shut down in the face of high, persistent negative stress (*I'm done...I'll be under the covers if you need me...don't come looking*).

So how can we support either?

Freezers do need and benefit from connection—this is their greatest antidote to negative stress. Even if they resist it, perhaps consider brandishing these phrases from your toolbelt:

How are you feeling?

What can I do to help?

Remember they're not just compartmentalizing, they're *disconnecting*. Can you get them to tap into an emotion and help them move through it? Can you help them see the big picture and connect back to what's most important?

They might reject your request to connect, but don't take it personally. Don't forget that connection doesn't always look like conversation. There are many other ways you can connect:

- ✦ Offer them the afternoon off.
- ✦ Take the kids to the park so they can get some quiet time.
- ✦ Make dinner and clean it up even if it's not your night to do so.
- ✦ Take a task off their plate.
- ✦ Buy their favorite flower or candy.
- ✦ Send a funny meme with the message "just thinking about you."
- ✦ Just sit and *be* with them, rather than *do*. There is power in presence alone.

CONNECTING WITH A PLEASER

Pleasers are such wonderful people to be around, aren't they? They don't need compliments or too much thanks; they tirelessly seek to support, help, serve, and listen to others. But we know the risks, right?

So how can you support a Pleaser? The best gift you can give is a gentle reminder that their own well-being and energy matters, too. Try these:

- Help them hold (or even define) their boundaries.

- Volunteer to be their accountability partner (by the way, Pleasers love to help others; can you use this to your advantage and ask them to help hold your boundaries together?).

- Invite them to a screen-free lunch. (If they pull their phone out when they hear a notification, gently tease them about it. *Oh, so I'm not important enough to honor your screen-free lunch, huh? Who could be more important than me?*)

- Model delegation and encourage them to try it out, too.

- Look for opportunities to praise them when they're holding boundaries/practicing self-care.

- Give back to them—show them how great it feels to *receive* support as much as give it.

Any opportunity to show this Pleaser that they are *enough right now* and don't need to prove themselves, take it. Remind them of *yes, and*—yes, they can be servant-hearted, helpful, giving souls *and* protect their well-being at the same time. They don't have to choose one over the other.

CONNECTING WITH A NEGATIVE SELF-TALKER

When you're supporting a Negative Self-Talker, remember they often struggle to: (a) see what's going right; and (b) receive positive feedback. So, tread lightly: lip service is disingenuous, so compliment-vomiting all over a very perceptive and self-aware Negative Self-Talker is not going to work (in fact, it will likely backfire).

Here are a few suggestions on how to connect with a Negative Self-Talker.

- Recall that emotions are contagious and build upon each other, so keep your emotions positive and light around your Negative Self-Talker to take advantage of that wonderful law of attraction.

- Find ways to weave joy, awe, wonder, laughter, happiness, gratitude, and abundant light into your conversations. Hold space for their negative emotions, but also look for opportunities to point out what's right: the beautiful weather, a recent win, or gently offer a positive reframe of a situation they feel stuck on.

- Remind them that there is space to hold two opposing emotions at once—the good with the bad, together. If your Negative Self-Talker is fretting over having to speak in front of a group, you can hold space for their fear and uncertainty, but also observe the exciting opportunity to showcase their deep knowledge of the subject and talent for delivering that knowledge in a meaningful way.

- Negative Self-Talkers are kind, empathetic, and love to support others, so ask for help with your own positive self-talk and practice together.

- Find opportunities to give them genuine compliments (this works for everyone you know of course but would really help a Negative Self-Talker). For example:

  » *You have such a knack for being patient with kids. I've always admired that about you.*

  » *I'm proud of you for XYZ accomplishment.*

  » *Thank you for laying out our specific goals for this project; it really helps me see the big picture.*

> » *I'm so grateful for how you supported me through my move to the new company.*

> » *You inspire me to be a better person every time you bring our elderly neighbors banana bread; it makes me think about ways I can be a better person.*

Remember, we're talking about supporting someone who is *under stress*, not a generally negative or unconfident or even healthy, happy, thriving person. It's important to keep this in mind because they might not "snap out of it" right away or receive it well. But keep going: your words matter and are making a difference—you'll get through eventually.[3]

CONNECTING WITH A DISTRACTED

I imagine successfully connecting with a Distracted to be a little like herding cats. Or maybe the analogy is more like dumping a thousand marbles across a tile floor and trying to gather them up again into one neat and organized pile. (That's more like handling a Worrier or Runner, but heck, we've all been there.)

Either way, you're dealing with a card-carrying scatterbrain here. When they ask for your help or you notice a Distracted friend is feeling stressed, try to get them to get specific about how they're feeling: cluttered mind? Overwhelmed with things to do? Struggling to focus or get organized? Unsure how to prioritize? Head feel full? Having trouble gathering thoughts?

The more specific they will be about how they are feeling, the more specific your support can be when helping them relieve some of that cognitive pressure. Maybe they need help gathering their thoughts or making a list. Or perhaps you can encourage them to walk away for a bit and do something that doesn't require a lot of brain power like a load of dishes, decluttering their desk, pulling weeds, folding laundry, walking the dog, or any other activity to bring some mental calm during a cognitive hurricane.

You can also help them to "oscillate" more often. Invite them to lunch and look together at your calendars. Can you help them better manage their energy or organize their day? Maybe complete one of the exercises in the chapter together? Help them brainstorm small recovery rituals they can integrate to help prevent this overloaded brain from occurring in the first place.

CONNECTING WITH A THRIVER

Thrivers don't need your help! Move on (I'm kidding, of course).

If you think Thrivers don't need support, think again! Even Thrivers need support. And the way to do that is simple—help them stay a Thriver. Here are some ways to do that:

- Remind them of their need for regular self-care.

- Spend time expressing your appreciation of them: see above phrases in the Negative Self-Talker section.

- Protect regular 1 on 1 time together and continue to nurture your relationship.

- Encourage them to "level up" on seeking new ways to grow their capacity and find new challenges.

- If you're a leader of a Thriver (or any stress personality), ensure you're creating an environment that supports their well-being, not one that detracts from it.

- *Ask* what they might need to feel supported and valued.

Let's help our Thriver friends stay Thrivers!

Create an environment that supports other people's well-being.

Let's focus on this statement for a moment, because I get this question every time I speak on the topic. If you're in some way responsible for other people: a manager, a leader, a parent, a board member, a teacher, a fire lieutenant, a community club leader, etc., you have an obligation to create an environment for your team or group that supports their well-being. Here are ways you can support *all* stress personalities:

- Can't say it enough: put your oxygen mask on first. First figure out your own stress personality and Stress Reset strategies to then best support others.

- Share your stress personality and favorite Stress Reset strategies (as much as you feel comfortable sharing, of course) with others. Vulnerability often gives others the confidence and trust to speak up and share. It also helps build empathy in a team—sometimes we forget our teammates are human, too.

- When you mess up, own it, talk about it, share it.

- Spend time openly discussing work-home boundaries. This is a tough subject; but create a space for your team to share where they may feel the lines are too blurred and where things are working well or not. Have the same conversation at home, too.

- Co-create new rules for working together to support everyone's well-being. For example, you can:

  » At work, break down calendar management issues (people scheduling over others' downtime, for example).

» Discuss how to conduct meetings. (Does that meeting need to happen? Does it have to be exactly 30 minutes or can it be 25 to offer time between meetings for self-care? Who needs to be there?)

» Ensure people are respecting off-hours and time zones.

» Anticipate and plan for times of the year when the team is expected to go above and beyond (budget season, union negotiations, board meetings, etc.). Can you build in more flexibility of schedule before or after to get caught up and recover?

» Is everything urgent in your office? Those work environments can create unnecessary stress. Can you create better rules for what's considered urgent?

» Is delegation supported and encouraged?

» Can you ladder up all the recommended practices to senior leadership? Are they behaving the same way, or is your team receiving mixed messages?

» At home, can you call a family meeting and get to know what everyone needs in terms of favorite Stress Resets, how stress personalities might conflict, etc.?

Kick off the conversation with your team or family and start implementing this stress personality research now—you'll be amazed at how your work and home environments shift even when people know they have permission to talk about these things.

FINAL THOUGHTS

One final thought about connecting with other stress personalities. Sometimes it's not your place to approach someone with suggestions, especially if you're not in their inner circle or they didn't ask for help. Be mindful of if, when, where, and how you speak up. When they invite you in, go for it.

TL:DR

+ Not everyone has your stress personality.

+ When different stress personalities clash, friction can arise.

+ Stress personalities can also create deeper trust, engagement, stimulate new ideas and innovation, and help support problem-solving and productivity— especially when everyone feels valued, heard, and supported in the way they need to be supported.

+ When you want to support someone's stress personality rather than diagnose who you think they might be, ask two simple questions:

  » *How are you feeling?* and
  » *What can I do to help?*

+ Supporting and connecting with someone, regardless of their stress personality, requires meeting them where they are and trying specific strategies that work best for that person.

14

THRIVER ACCELERATORS FOR EVERY STRESS PERSONALITY

My father was an avid scuba diver his whole adult life, which meant my sisters and I spent many weekends on boats and underwater. When I was in elementary school he became a scuba instructor, which was an incredible accomplishment. After that, every family vacation was a diving destination—and still is today. Our boys are now certified, and I married a surfer, so really the entire family has gills.

I'll never forget my very first dive. When I slipped under the ocean surface, the lights and sounds of the above-surface world faded and gave way to the crackling, thriving life underneath. Underwater ocean blue is the most beautiful color you'll see in your life. The colors, the creatures, the weightlessness: it's like being in another world. It was love at first sight.

The certification process was, at 12 years old, intense. I learned the complex science of the human body under atmospheric pressure; how to put together and take apart equipment; all of the safety precautions and emergency protocols; how to safely enter and exit the water; how to help another person in distress; how to stay buoyant; the hand signals and signs for various communication with my buddy, or for fish and sea life; how to haul my equipment to and from the boat (the scuba tank nearly outweighed me). It was several months of practice, anticipation, and testing.

But all that training paid off in spades. When I got to my first dive and took a giant leap into the ocean, I knew exactly what to do without even thinking about it. Training until it felt natural and automatic (neuroplasticity!) afforded me the luxury of enjoying the underwater world around me without worry or fear.

Bottom line—training is *everything*.

So far, we've kept narrow focus on the best Stress Resets to support our individual stress personalities (even though many Stress Resets we explored benefit all stress personalities, they were placed with those on which they'd have the most impact).

Where Stress Reset strategies are more the tools you'll use in the moment or to more directly address your stress personality, this chapter is about going *upstream* to train: it's about building a life of resilience through daily habits and practices, no matter our stress personality.

These strategies aren't meant to *eliminate* stress (impossible) or hold the promise that our lives will suddenly be less busy or chaotic; it doesn't mean the storms of life will stop coming. Their purpose is to help us build thriving lives and strengthen our physical, mental, emotional, and spiritual muscles so we're better prepared for whatever comes our way.

HOW TO USE THIS CHAPTER

The following sections unpack key *Thriver Accelerators* to integrate into daily life, and a bit on the science of sustainable behavior change (how to make sure a habit *really* sticks…for good). There's no pressure to integrate them all *tomorrow*; you don't even need to read the whole chapter. You can:

- Read through the Thriver Accelerators that pique your interest or are known gaps you want to fill, or

- Read about the science of habit formation and creating sustainable behavior change, or

- Use the reflective questions at the end of the chapter to design small, realistic next steps that are *too small to fail.*

Or, read the whole thing—you're in control here.

THE FIRST AND MOST IMPORTANT THRIVER ACCELERATOR: *CALENDARIZE YOUR ENERGY*

Note: You might have done this exercise already: Return to the calendarizing energy/oscillation exercise in the Distracted chapter or boundaries exercise in the Pleaser chapter for ideas. The rest of this chapter is full of new ideas and Thriver Accelerators.

Back to scuba diving for a moment. One of the most important lessons in scuba diving, which you learn almost right away, is to descend very slowly while equalizing your ears every couple of feet. Why not just shoot to the bottom? As you descend, the water pressure increases above you, and the pressure differential between your inner ear and the water can cause pressure to build in the middle ear. If this happens and you can't equalize, your eardrum could rupture, which is *extremely painful* (trust me, I know—don't be stubborn and dive if you have a sinus infection).

The rule of thumb is to get ahead of it by equalizing both on your *descent* and *ascent*.

And I simply love this as a metaphor for how we should insert Thriver Accelerators into our day: *early* and *often*.

That's why the first Thriver Accelerator is to *calendarize your energy.* This idea was introduced in the Pleaser and Distracted chapters and describes the importance of fiercely protecting time on your calendar for boundaries, brain breaks, self-care, exercise, healthy snacks, etc. Individually, all the Thriver Accelerators in this chapter are great habits, but they're *impossible* to sustain long-term unless you're intentional about *protecting the time and space for them.*

Putting time on your calendar *automatizes the habit* so it's less effortful to plan and execute. Our brain learns that "with this cue (calendar reminder, ping, text, etc.), I stop and do (healthy habit)." Thanks to neuroplasticity, we create a nice, strong neural pathway that associates the two and—lo and behold—both motivation and chance of success increase.

Plain and simple: *The space you protect on your calendar for your favorite Thriver Accelerators should be non-negotiable.* Boundaries, in a nutshell.

Calendarizing your energy has three parts:

Step 1: Find the space and block the time on your calendar...right now.

Open your calendar and examine your day. Yes, right now. We can fill in what we do with our time later.

Where *could* you protect a few minutes here and there for some sort of growth or recovery practice? Can you find 15 minutes at lunch? Or 30-60 minutes twice a week for exercise? A few minutes on your commute? Even 1-3 minutes between meetings? Block the time like it's an important meeting.

Don't promise you'll honor every calendar reminder or commitment at first...you won't. And that's okay. If you have an "all or nothing" personality, it might be hard to swallow this reframe: success really looks like lots of little "failing forward" moments, not perfection. But with time and consistency, this new habit will be as natural as tying your shoes.

Step 2: Find the false rest and dump it.

Where is your energy currently going when you feel stressed? Is it a healthy place? Or is it places like mobile devices, TV, social media, games, gossip, complaining, or simply trying to power through? These are often (not always, but often) hidden energy suckers disguised as "self-care" that continue to fuel your stress personality. Which of these energy suckers can you eliminate?

Step 3: Equip your toolbelt.

Now look at your list of your favorite Stress Resets. Let's say that deep breathing is your primary strategy and works wonders for you in a moment of stress. Great! Now you're going to *calendar time for it* in the middle of the day and not just keep it in your back pocket for when you're already feeling stressed.

Imagine if, instead of quickly checking emails between midday calls, you heard a calendar reminder go off and spent a few minutes reenergizing with some screen-free deep breathing or stretching outside in the sunshine. What kind of energy would you bring to your next call? How might you respond differently to an unexpected traffic jam on the way home or a loud, rambunctious toddler wreaking havoc on your eardrums the moment you walk in the door? Imagine being able to show up as the best version of yourself in those moments that stretch and challenge us all—that's what oscillating and calendarizing your energy can do. And it's why I keep coming back to this practice over and over again in multiple chapters.

Make a list and keep it somewhere visible and accessible—not every day or moment or situation will warrant the same strategies, so keep a list handy so you don't have to think too hard when it's time.

Early and often—that's how we thrive.

SPIRITUAL ACCELERATORS

Thriver Accelerator: Purpose

Back to the scuba diving analogy for a moment. Recently my husband and I and our boys watched a documentary titled *The Trapped 13: How We Survived the Thai Cave*. It recounted the true story of the incredible rescue of a youth soccer team in Thailand who were trapped in a collapsed cave in 2018 after a torrential monsoon flooded the area. The rescue strategy was to put a scuba helmet on each child and, one by one, and return through the narrow, pitch-black underwater tunnels (devoid of light and sound) by holding onto a safety rope. If rescue divers let go of that rope in the darkness, they could quickly find themselves off course, disoriented, and out of air: the safety rope was their lifeline.

Purpose is a lot like that safety rope in the darkness: we can cling to it to orient us to the missions worth fighting for, who we want to be, how we want to show up, and how to find our way again when we're lost and off course in life. Purpose also provides us with clear boundaries, or guardrails, to help stay on course. (Pleasers, know the importance of boundaries; Freezers, the importance of reconnecting to our purpose.)

When we have a strong sense of purpose in life, we simply perform better across every area of life. We live longer, we're happier, more productive, more joyful, and more likely to thrive in the face of stress, no matter what comes our way. Think about all the famous stories of people triumphing through the most difficult of times—think of Viktor Frankl's experience. Purpose helps you find your way back from anything.

Try this:

Write a Purpose Statement for yourself. Some questions to think about:

- Who or what matters most in your life? (Family, a particular value, faith, your job…)
- What are your passions?
- What are your unique skills?
- What are your top core values? (List 2-3; see the Fighter Values Mining exercise for reference.)
- How do you want others to describe you?
- What does daily life look like when you are living out your purpose? (What adjectives you would use to describe yourself; see the Thriver exercise on visualization for reference.)
- What legacy do you want to leave behind when you're gone?

When you're finished, create a Purpose Statement that fully embodies this vision of yourself. Make sure whatever you create is so powerful, you feel emotional when you read it. Don't worry if it takes a while. This is your safety rope: make it a strong one. When I first got my purpose statement right, I teared up. It fully embodied who I aspire to be and what I felt called to do and to be.

My purpose statement: *To serve others in **any** capacity in **any** area of life and bring them **joy**, starting at home with my family.*

It's not flowery or poetic; it's simple and unspecific. But it's incredibly important to me. It embodies my two core values—service and relationships—a vision of what I want to bring others and embody (joy), and offers clear guidelines on how I want to run my business and personal life. And if you read closely, it reminds me of my priority— my family—so it also informs my boundaries.

The opposite of my stress personality is in there, too. I want to serve others in any capacity and lean *into* challenge, not run from it.

But my kryptonite is in there, too—serving others is so important to me, I can push too hard and set unrealistically high expectations, causing me to implode and run.

My purpose statement is a continual reminder of my need for boundaries and how to prioritize when I'm making big and small decisions. It is my safety rope for life. Now it's time to write yours:

My Purpose Statement:

_____

_____

_____

_____

_____

_____

_____

After you have written (or drafted) your purpose statement, how will you begin to apply it in your daily life?

I suggest that at first, you plaster this statement everywhere—on your phone background, on Post-it notes in your car, your bathroom mirror... Make it a reminder that pops up daily. Have Alexa remind you once a week. Pretty soon (thanks, neuroplasticity!) it will become second nature for you to think about it routinely (*early and often...*).

You'll learn to return to your purpose all the time—when making small decisions like whether to work out that day, what to order for dinner (fries or salad?) or bigger decisions like whether to take that new job or end a difficult friendship. It helps you listen to your inner voice and determine your next steps. *Is this in alignment with my purpose or not? Does it move me closer or farther away?*

One of Viktor Frankl's greatest lines from his book *Man's Search for Meaning* is a quote from Friedrich Nietzsche, who said in his book

Twilight of the Idols: "He who has a why to live can bear almost any how."

Think about that for a moment: no matter *what* you do in life, if you do it with purpose, it changes how you see that "what."

So, what matters the most to you in life? In what areas of life do you feel you're on track, and where do you need to be more purpose-full?

Thriver Accelerator: Social Connection

When you ask mental health experts for the single greatest intervention for mental illness outside of (and sometimes superseding) medication, do you know what they say? *Connection with others.*

Having a strong social circle and seeking ways to regularly connect with others is a superpower, and a Thriver Accelerator for all. It prevents us from disconnection, loneliness, and risking our mental health.[1] We covered this in our Freezer chapter.

How can you build in time *right now* to be more intentional about connecting with your VIPs (Capital F friends), coworkers, acquaintances, etc. on a more regular basis? Or maybe you spend time with them on a regular basis, but what about the energy and intention you bring to that time? Are you fully present and connected, or has that been harder to do lately?

Here are a few suggestions:

+ Put down your phone, look up, and really *see* your family and loved ones. We tend to fall into routines of social media, TV, and games around the house. Consider some no-tech nights with the family and seek ways to connect instead.

+ Schedule a coffee date with a coworker you'd like to get to know a bit better.

- Join a new club or committee at work.
- Find a meetup group who shares your hobby or interests (gardening, book club, pickleball, running, Mahjong, etc.).
- Schedule reminders to reach out to friends on a more regular basis to build and strengthen current connections.
- Go on an adventure with a group. (My mother, who is in her 70s, goes on cycling trips around the world every year and meets wonderful people along the way...she is way cooler than me).

Wherever you build and foster connection, be intentional about it—it will make managing stress so much easier.

Thriver Accelerator: Gratitude and Giving

Put the book down for a minute and do this exercise with me:

Think of one person in your life you're really grateful for: could be someone in your family, someone you work with, a long-time friend. You know that person: the one who's just a beautiful human who is always there to listen or brighten your day or has been through the darkest days alongside you. Close your eyes and picture the person's face: their smile, their expressions. Say their name out loud or write it down somewhere.

Now, pick up your phone, and if you're able to, send him or her a quick text message or email and express your gratitude. Be specific about *why* you're so appreciative.

When you're finished composing and reviewing the correspondence and have sent it, pause to take inventory of how you feel. Notice your body sensations and your emotions. Do you feel lighter? More peaceful? Energized?

Gratitude is a practice that infuses you with an immediate emotional and spiritual boost. It brings positive energy and joy, can calm us in moments of high negative stress, and can help us find perspective. Practicing regular gratitude is great for your long-term health and resilience.[2] It can also be a simple daily practice with some intentionality and planning.

Try making gratitude an *external* practice. Here are a few ways we can give and serve others:

- Set a weekly reminder to text/call/email someone and express your gratitude.
- Fill up a coworker's water bottle.
- Pack your partner's lunch.
- Leave your child a note to make them smile.
- Tell your regular barista/store clerk how much you appreciate them.
- Send your child's teacher a note thanking them for loving your child.
- Buy someone a coffee.
- Spend a few minutes chatting with someone eating alone at a restaurant.
- Give a little extra on your tip and leave a note to tell them why.
- Send regular handwritten thank you notes to your team at work.
- Volunteer at a local race or event.
- Buy a meal for someone on the street who looks hungry.
- Bring your neighbor's trash cans in.
- Send a treat to a friend who's having a bad day.

I know you have so many more ideas. What about gratitude as an *internal* practice?

For example, reflect on moments or people in life who shaped you for better or worse:

+ **Something hard that happened to you offered you the strength and wisdom you have today. Who showed up for you during that time? What did you learn after or despite this hard thing? How did you grow because of it?**

We can also express gratitude to *ourselves* in moments of compassion, forgiveness, or grace, or by protecting time for self-care, rest, recovery.

*Quick reminder about the idea of **yes, and**. We can be grateful for what we have and wish for things to be different; we can experience hard things and be grateful at the same time: one doesn't cancel out the other. You can hold space for both in your heart.*

We live in a high stress world today; an amazing source of control and peace is our ability to make things a little better in our small corner of the universe, one small act of gratitude and compassion at a time.

Thriver Accelerator: Play

Play is a big part of well-being, and one we often forget about when we get busy, distracted, or stressed. Play improves our cognitive function, resilience, relationships, and creativity, and helps relieve stress (this is likely why my dad still gets in trouble for flinging things off a spoon at restaurants…some kids never grow up).

Can you find ways to integrate play into your routine? Try these:

+ Add something fun to your workout routine.
+ Throw a frisbee at the beach.

- Attend a costume party.

- Play a lighthearted joke on a friend.

- Host a board game night.

- Try a new class (art class, dance, goat yoga, etc.).

- Attend a concert.

- Build a snowman or sandcastle.

- Play with your kids—on their terms! Enjoy the way their imaginations run.

- Play fetch with the dog.

- Go for a bike ride with no agenda or destination.

Thriver Accelerator: Navigating the BIG things

One thing we haven't talked much about in the book is how to navigate the big moments in life. Having a baby (or losing a baby), loss, trauma, death, divorce, chronic illness, new jobs, weddings, move—life can be beautiful, but also so, so hard. What do we do with life's major stressors…good or bad?

The answer is purpose. When life gets tough (like, *really* tough), find that safety rope and hold on tight through the darkness. Of course, purpose won't solve everything and it's not always an immediate reprieve, but when we go back to our *why*, it becomes a lifeline and a soft landing place from which we can make decisions on our next steps…even if that next step is to just keep holding on another day, hour, or minute.

Remember what Frankl said—we have control in the chaos over one very important thing, and that is the direction of our thoughts. This means we *can* control:

- How connected we stay to our purpose and values.

- Our perspective on the situation.

- The story we tell ourselves.

- Our next steps—even if it's just one foot in front of the other, or one deep breath after another.

If you need it, try filling in this sentence stem for those darker tunnels in life:

This is really hard because _____
_____ . I feel _____ _____
_____ right now. And, at the end of the day, there is nothing more important than
_____ _____ .

It might also help to focus on what you can and cannot control.

I feel like I can't control _____
_____ . One thing I can control is
_____ _____ .
This is important because (connect to your purpose here) _____
_____ . My next step forward is _____
_____ _____ .

When you're lost in that dark tunnel, grab hold of your safety rope, hang on tight, and look for the light.

Thriver Accelerators: Mental + Emotional

Thriver Accelerator: Mindset + Storytelling

I read the best analogy around mindset in the book *Free Time* by Jenny Blake. I paraphrase for you here:

> Imagine you arrive at a friend's house for a glass of wine and your friend answers the door with a frustrated, cold look on her face. She hurries you in and mumbles something about making you a cake. The place smells amazing, but you can hardly focus on that because she gestures for you to sit anywhere and goes on about how difficult and annoying the experience has been. She ran out of one ingredient, had to run to the store and still couldn't find it so had to find a substitute at home, spilled the flour...just a big headache. When the cake is done she lets it cool and cuts you a slice. She tosses the slice your way with a big sigh and a sarcastic "bon appetit."

Or.

> Imagine you arrive at a friend's house for a glass of wine and your friend answers the door with a beaming smile on her face. She gives you a big hug, hands you a glass of wine, and pulls you inside the house. The place smells amazing. Her eyes sparkle as she tells you she has a surprise for you. She lights a candle, puts on some fun music, and sits you down at the kitchen counter to excitedly share her cooking adventure with you. She was missing an ingredient and couldn't find it at the store so she started playing with new flavors and substitutes. She laughs when she shares that she spilled some flour and drew a smiley face in it— she points to the mess, which she left for you to see. When the cake is done she lets it cool and cuts you a slice. She dances her

way back to you with the plate and places it in front of you with a big smile and an enthusiastic "bon appetit!" Her eyes are like a child on Christmas morning, awaiting your reaction to the first bite.

The same cake was made in both scenarios. So tell me...which cake tastes better?

Of course, the second one. Why? Because sometimes, *how* we make the cake matters more than the cake itself.[3]

We've talked about this many times before, but it bears repeating forever and always—*the story we tell about what happens to us matters so much.* Our mindset is *everything.*

Whether it's your belief about stress, reframing a situation, or a major paradigm shift about your stress personality superpowers, *your mindset is everything.* Why? Because so much of our biology works against us when we're stressed:

+ The actual experience of what happens to us is vastly different from how we interpret it. Remember that we are quite literally wired to tell stories.

+ We also have that pesky inherent negative bias.

+ We tend to almost always be the victims in our own stories, think dualistically, and have limited focus when we are stressed (we narrow the aperture). So, we forge a story in which we are: (a) right, (b) wronged, and (c) there is no other explanation.

Don't miss this: When we are out of alignment with our purpose anywhere in life, it often comes with a powerful story to explain it away so it makes sense to us.

The stories we tell ourselves have powerful influence on our beliefs, behaviors, and even core identities. We know that Thrivers are good at seeing and reframing their stress, which is how they build resilience and agility and feel more in control of their circumstances. They're also less likely to think in absolutes and in fixed mindsets about who they are and what happens to them.

Ask yourself: *Am I seeing the whole picture? Am I losing sight of what really matters? Did I lose my safety rope?*

Try this quick exercise adapted from one of my favorite books by Dr. Jim Loehr, *The Power of Story*.[4] It's one of my most favorite Stress Resets:

Retell the story by asking yourself:

- Is my ego in the driver's seat here, or are my values?
- What's the story I'm telling myself? Is it true and accurate?
- How can I retell this story?

A word of caution: Healing hurts. This might open up old wounds. You won't always like the process of shifting your mindset, reframing, and taking a new perspective. It's uncomfortable. At times, it can be heavy. But that's growth in a nutshell—growth always comes with a little discomfort.

Thriver Accelerator: Journaling and Reflecting

I know, I know. If you're anything like me, someone asking me to add to my weekly to-do list feels like asking me to swim backstroke from New York to London. But, my friend, these two practices—journaling and reflecting—are powerful ways to be more intentional and self-aware, get to know your stress personality, and track your success. Journaling helps us process, problem-solve, action plan, and so much more.

Research backs up these claims and then some more: when you take the time to deliberately reflect in a journal, it comes with the following benefits:

1. You're more self-aware.

2. You're more empathetic.

3. You're more receptive to diverse thoughts, opinions, and new ideas.

4. You strengthen relationships in your life and connections with others.

5. It helps you better process complex problems and make hard decisions.

6. It helps you learn and remember better.

7. It improves emotional intelligence and cognitive function.

8. It can even boost our immune function and mood.[5]

What about stress itself? Does it help you tackle stress directly? *Yes.* Journaling increases your ability to regulate those tough emotions *in the moment*—meaning, journaling *then* helps me process *now*.

These are some seriously rockstar skills you can develop. How can we integrate journaling or reflection practices into our busy daily routine, so it doesn't feel obtrusive or demanding?

Try this:

+ Start small by writing just *one phrase or one sentence a day*. Just one.

+ Use journaling as a short practice to wind down your day. For some, journaling before bed improves sleep quality, though it might also generate some tough emotions and even create a little stress in the moment, so choose your timing wisely based on your stress personality.

+ Use journaling as a short practice to start your day. I work with leaders who use journaling to fall asleep and get out what's in their cluttered minds; leaders who start their day journaling, listing important tasks, writing their thoughts on a challenge from the day before, or processing long-term ideas and projects; and leaders who use journaling to plan for or debrief and process meetings.

+ One of my clients blocks time to journal after every one-on-one performance review or important meeting with her staff and board members, including her own reviews. She has made this such a structured and regular process that every month, she reflects on her journal entries and notices patterns, insights, growth and key learnings, and more.

+ Another client makes journaling a self-care act. She buys fun pens and journals, finds a beautiful spot outside her office once a week or so, and takes her lunch there, journaling about her day or week. She has years of journals she can reflect on to celebrate her growth.

- Jot down *one word* per day to describe your day or your predominant emotion for the day.

- Keep a notes section on your phone and use talk-to-text here and there.

- Alternatively, if journaling is a bit overwhelming to start, set a reminder once per week simply to reflect— no writing involved. At the very least, simply block five minutes of your week for reflection and/or journaling whether you use it or not. Use the space you block however you want. If it's protected time, you're more likely to honor the space for yourself.

Journaling can be what you need it to be: give yourself permission to skip the pages of prose and just start small. If you're looking for an easy way to level up your self-awareness, parenting, relationships, and leadership, trust the research—journaling is a power practice.

Thriver Accelerator: Mindfulness and Meditation

We've covered a lot of ground with mindfulness and meditation in many of the stress personality chapters, because these are such incredible practices. Let's spend a moment exploring all in one place.

Meditation is an intentional focusing of our mind. We can direct our attention to our thoughts, breathing, body sensations, emotions, environment, and so on. It's a space to recalibrate and reconnect to your inner voice. It's not as much about feeling *good* as it is simply feeling what you're feeling with awareness, which of course often makes you feel great.

Mindfulness and meditation parallel each other in almost every way. Mindfulness is considered a type of meditation by some, and others consider mindfulness the sporadic practice of connecting to the present moment, whereas meditation is more of a regular practice.

However you slice it, both practices leverage your mind and body to disconnect from the noise to connect with yourself.

There is so much variety to meditation in terms of the type, length, feelings you get, and intended outcomes that I want to be careful not to provide sweeping recommendations to simply "meditate often" or put the pressure on you to try to fit in yet another practice to your busy day.

Some of the power of meditation is simply to practice stillness; that Gift of Pause when we really need it. Stillness is our way to realign with ourselves by taking a step off the never-ending treadmill of daily life. Stillness can reframe *volume*. We have a lot of demand and activity in our life, but a few moments of stillness can help us see that demand as more manageable. When we integrate moments of stillness, we're less reactive, and can act informed by connection to our values and purpose. When we quiet the noise, we tap into our intuition and our hearts.

We've covered some ground on types of meditation and mindfulness already:

- ◆ Focus on your breath (Fighter chapter)
- ◆ Visualization and imagery (see next section; Fighter, Freezer, Thriver chapters)
- ◆ Body scan (Fighter chapter)
- ◆ Guided meditation (Worrier chapter)
- ◆ Productive meditation (Worrier chapter)
- ◆ Mindfulness cues like "Be where your feet are" or the "Three things" exercise (Worrier chapter)
- ◆ Take a walk in nature (Worrier, Distracted chapter)
- ◆ Grounding (Freezer chapter)

◆ Panoramic and open-monitoring meditation (Distracted chapter)

There are no hard and fast rules to meditation; these are only guidelines. What works one day might not work the next—likely, there are certain types of meditation that work best for you and your stress personality.

Keep one thing in mind: we don't meditate to *fix* stress; we meditate to *experience* stress and become aware of it. Meditation is an access point to connect with our thoughts and feelings, and to process, heal, and recalibrate.

Thriver Accelerator: Visualization

Visualization isn't conjuring up life dreams and wishes and *hoping* they come true; visualization truly changes our brain from the inside out. Professional athletes integrate visualization into their training regimens because it can significantly improve their performance. When a golfer for example creates a mental picture of success on a particular hole before a tournament, their brain begins to map out routes to get them there—the same areas of the brain responsible for motor control in those areas light up and start to repeat those motions…and even *grow stronger without even picking up a club.*[6]

If you want to feel a certain way—unshakable confidence, joy, hope, and focus—those regions of the brain will light up through visualization. This is a great way to find flow. Whatever you choose to visualize in your dedicated time—whether it's the best version of yourself, a dream or goal being fulfilled, a place you love, and so on—sit with this vision for a few minutes and check in with your emotions. Then, take notice of how you feel.

There are so many other ways to leverage visualization:

+ Take a few moments to visualize how you want to show up for a meeting or important conversation.

+ Take a few minutes each week to visualize how you plan to take on the week's expectations.

+ Use the last few minutes of a workout to visualize yourself growing stronger and faster and healthier.

+ Write down three words to describe yourself at your best. Keep those words on a Post-it note by your desk, bathroom mirror, etc. and read them daily.

+ Include visualization in your journaling, reflection, or meditation practice.

No matter where you integrate it, visualization can take you to the next level of awareness and resilience.

Thriver Accelerator: Seek "Training Stress" to Build Resilience

We talked about this in the Distracted chapter, but let's dive a bit deeper.

When I was younger, we'd go to the Florida Keys on weekends and find a reef to scuba dive and explore. On many occasions, I'd be hovering over a beautiful reef, darting in and out of little swim-throughs or playing with an anemone or Christmas tree worm…when out of nowhere my father would tap me on the shoulder and I'd spin around to see him, eyes dramatically wide, giving me the signal that he was out of air. Or he'd bump my mask and knock it off so that suddenly I couldn't see.

Of course, he was totally faking. Now before you judge my father's parenting, I promise he wasn't putting me in harm's way—he was training me for emergencies. He'd always warn me ahead of time that, at some point in the dive, we'd be practicing these emergencies. The cool part was that every time, I'd fall back on my training and know exactly what to do to help him or myself. Maybe it was because he had warned me, so I knew it wasn't a true emergency or because we'd gone over the safety protocols a hundred times before, so I didn't panic, and I knew exactly what to do. I know that because of his training, my sister and I are calmer, more confident divers today.

Remember I said Thrivers seek ways to train under stress? This is what I mean. What if you looked at stress like a Thriver—as opportunities to grow in our wisdom, experience, and resilience? Thrivers don't seek stress-free environments, but rather focus on being stress-prepared.

Like my father warning me ahead of time, we can only consider this "training" when certain conditions are in place; otherwise, it's just more negative stress. We must first learn to adapt to a "stressed state" by practicing in a controlled environment. Think of pilots who train for emergency landings in a simulation hundreds of times, so that when the real thing happens, they're better prepared.

Here are a few ways you can do this for yourself:

+ Protect a boundary by saying no or push back on an ask (see the Pleaser chapter).

+ Ask for help or delegate (if this is normally hard for you).

+ Take on a new challenge at work.

+ Learn a new skill or hobby.

+ Exercise with higher intensity intervals or try a new sport/type of movement.

+ Reach out to someone you had friction with or are uncomfortable around, and have a conversation (again, if it's manageable).

- Use visualization to actively let go of things you don't have control over but wish you did.

- Join a local meetup or take a solo trip.

- Attend a class that helps you think under pressure (brain training class, public speaking club, debate course, self-defense class).

- Try those cold showers or cold exposure (see the Distracted chapter).

Can you think of other ways to grow your resilience?

BODY THRIVER ACCELERATORS

How can you leverage your physical body to create a Thriving environment? The way we move, leverage nutrition, and the way we rest and recover from sleep all have a powerful influence over your ability to be resilient in the face of negative stress. Let's unpack each briefly.

Thriver Accelerator: Exercise and Movement

Try something for me right now. If you've been sitting or lying down for a bit, stand up and move around for thirty seconds. Move any way you'd like—stretch, shake out, do some jumping jacks, dance a little, anything.

Then take inventory of how you feel. What are the body sensations? How's your alertness and focus? Your energy?

My guess is you feel, at the very least, a little bit more alert and focused. Why? Because movement of any kind lights up your brain in almost every area: focus, attention, decision-making, emotional regulation, learning, memory—you name it. In fact, people who exercise regularly are more productive, they get along better with others at work, feel more able to handle their workloads and life-loads, manage their time better, have less sick days—I can go on. Exercise even helps the brain rewire itself. Movement and exercise are incredible thriver accelerators.

If you aren't exercising on a regular basis, remember it's still a *yes, and:* one small movement session will boost your mood! And, starting small is the ticket to long-term commitment. So, *try this:* commit to *one* small movement session per day. Just a few minutes at most: maybe between work meetings or calls you can take a quick walk; if you work from home, maybe do a few pushups, walk the dog, wash the dishes, etc.

And then, once per week, commit to one longer exercise session—30 minutes or so—just one! You can do anything one time. The goal is simply to protect the time; you can build and add from there.

Don't miss this: If you're just starting your exercise journey, begin by doing what you love and enjoy. Exercise is much easier to stick to when it's enjoyable and manageable.

Whatever you choose, protect the time for it and honor your appointment with yourself.

Thriver Accelerator: Nutrition

The choices we make in the kitchen have a significant impact on how we manage our stress personalities. In fact, food decisions have a powerful impact on our brains in general. What you eat influences your body and brain function in every way—from the New Brain down to the Reptile brain. Every food choice you make guides you closer to, or farther away from, your ability to thrive in body, mind, and spirit. How's that for pressure?

I'll make it clear early—the goal isn't to eat perfectly. Perfect is not realistic, nor sustainable (and it's incredibly boring). Perfect also means different things to different people (nutrition opinions are like religion and politics...everyone thinks their way is "the" way...and none of them are right).

Think about food as it relates to our ability to thrive from a stress and mental well-being perspective, and how you can *tweak* your food choices in small but powerful ways to influence this area of life. Here are a few ways:

Improve your mental well-being through diet.

Food isn't meant to be something we eat robotically for optimized function: we're not droids. Food is so many other things than fuel—it's memories and traditions; it's expression of culture; it's connection with others; it's creativity and personal expression; it's travel and adventure; it's celebration and joy; it's healing. Food is *life*, lived.

Rather than eliminate or significantly restrict certain foods, let's try a reframe. Why not *add a few of the right foods and beverages to your diet* instead? Like drinking one more *glass of water* than usual, or adding *an additional serving of wholesome fruits, grains, and vegetables* to your plate, or *adding more protein to your plate* (like cottage cheese, Greek yogurt, chicken, pork, fish, edamame, eggs). You'll feel a difference in fullness, energy, and mood right away.

Small tweaks can often lead to big changes when it comes to energy, mood, alertness, and physical health markers like body composition, inflammation, heart health, gut health, and so on.

Focus on eating often and lighter.

Your brain is like the CEO of your body: it runs the show and has the highest energy need of any other part of our body. With that in mind, eating often (every 3-4 hours) helps you regulate your energy levels. A starved brain is a stressed brain—don't forget that. So, feed it often.

Bonus? You'll notice you have more energy, focus, are less sporadically and frequently hungry, and can think more clearly.

Be mindful and listen to your body and inner voice.

Spend time being more present and mindful when it comes to eating. Often, we eat the way we stress—reactively. This is either because we're busy, hangry, stressed, or distracted, or perhaps sad, lonely, angry or overwhelmed. Either way, we can use food to squelch negative emotions without thinking about it. What if before a meal, or shopping, or ordering food you asked yourself, *How do I feel? What do I need? What's the impact of this next choice?* This isn't to make you feel guilty, it's to create a little bit of pause to let your inner voice—your New Brain—weigh in on your decision. In Chapter 2, I quoted Seth Godin who said, "Never let the lizard send an email." How about this—never let the Reptile Brain choose your meal!

Two Words of Caution

1. Consult with a medical doctor or registered dietitian before making any changes to your diet, especially if you have any medical conditions.

2. This advice is not meant to be prescriptive. Don't feel pressure to make any changes you don't want to. Nutrition is a touchy subject. Sometimes you need to go out and eat whatever the heck you want to eat and not worry. Your mental health matters when it comes to sustainable healthy eating habits. So, if you're constantly stressing over what to order and feeling guilty all the time, is it really helping you live a happy, thriving life? Or is it throwing you way off the trajectory of what really matters?

Weigh the emotional and mental aspects of making changes to your eating habits. This is another *yes, and* situation. Yes, you can make small changes to your food choices that yield healthy returns, *and* you can kick back with your friends every so often and not worry. Thinking in absolutes is harmful; don't let your stress personality invade your approach to food!

Thriver Accelerator: Sleep

One final incredibly important aspect of managing our stress personality is our sleep habits. Think about the last time you had 7-9 hours of blissful, uninterrupted sleep (new parents…I'm sorry to bring this up). How did you feel the next morning? My guess is, ready to conquer the world.

Sleep is an *essential* period of recovery, growth, and restoration for the body and mind. When we sleep well, we wake the next day feeling energized, focused, purposeful, and we have a much better time that day managing our emotions, our stress, our mood, and even our food choices.

Even *stages* of sleep affect certain areas of our brain and our ability to thrive. Consider:

- Stage 1. Healthy REM sleep is correlated with improved emotional regulation and working out complicated emotional/relationship problems.

- Stage 2. This stage of healthy sleep helps our brain reinforce the neural pathways for motor skills (especially important for any profession requiring working with your hands—surgeon, mechanic, learning how to play golf or ride a bike, etc.).

- Stage 3-4. In this stage we experience deep sleep, and our brain is busy problem solving and pattern recognizing (solving a math equation, discerning a pattern you're trying to uncover in any field, solving a Rubik's cube, etc.) and flushes neural trash.

Now think about the last time you had a poor night's sleep. How did you feel the next day? Did you struggle to think clearly? Could you find the energy to bring your best physically, mentally, and even emotionally to your work and your relationships? Yea, it's not pretty.

When we don't prioritize our sleep, it impacts our health, mood, focus, cognitive functioning, self-control, our ability to learn, and even our mental health. Our brain simply can't function at its optimal performance, leaving us much more susceptible to our stress personality.

Let's face a simple but important truth—we *need* sleep. Lots of it—*7-9 hours of quality sleep per night* to show up at our best.[7]

It's a two-way street: healthy sleep habits positively influence our ability to manage stress (Thriver Accelerator), but high negative stress in our life can negatively influence our ability to get good, quality sleep. On top of that, both anxiety and depression have a mutually causal relationship with sleep—one impacts the other.[8]

So, how can we improve our sleep habits...even when feeling stressed?

Try these sleep improvement strategies:

+ *First and foremost, stop feeling guilty if you have great sleep.* Why do some wear it as a badge of pride? You don't need to burn the midnight oil, and it's not lazy to retire at 9 p.m. (Pleasers...you reading this? Don't give up your sleep.) And remember, yes, you *can* get by on less sleep. Sometimes, you have to—new parents; raising a child with special needs or a chronic disease; night shift workers; first responders, healthcare workers, we see you. But know that just because you can get by with less sleep, doesn't mean you should. These are called *Thriver Accelerators* for a reason.

+ *Minimize alcohol.* Alcohol might help you unwind and fall asleep, but it comes with a cost. Alcohol prevents many people from staying asleep and moving through all their much-needed sleep cycles; rarely do you wake up after drinking the night before feeling refreshed and energized. Some are better than others at handling alcohol, so test this out if it's a struggle.

+ *Reduce or cut caffeine after 2 p.m..* Caffeine has a half-life of six hours, so your morning cup of coffee is still in your system at bedtime. Now compound that with your mid-morning, lunch, and afternoon coffees, and you won't wonder why you're struggling to fall asleep at night. Like alcohol, some of us are better than others at handling caffeine, so test this out if it's a struggle.

+ *Take naps* when possible and if needed.

+ *Meditate, journal,* or practice *deep breathing* before bed.

+ Create a *structured pre-bedtime routine*: silence and minimize screens and notifications; make the room dark and cool; get into your pjs; and start winding down mentally. Having a regular routine signals the brain that it's time to sleep.

+ Speaking of routine, it's best to *go to bed and wake up at the same time each day*. Our brain loves routine, remember? Create those strong neural pathways here.

+ Do some *light movement* before bed if it helps; yoga, stretch, etc.

+ Try a *white noise machine* to drown out noises in or near the bedroom (dogs, cats, snoring partners, we're looking at you!).

- Invest in a *good mattress and pillow* if you can—this can make all the difference.

FINAL THRIVER ACCELERATOR THOUGHTS

When I graduated with my doctorate, my father took me on a father-daughter trip to Bonaire, a Dutch island in the Leeward Antilles in the Caribbean Sea (scuba diving trip, what else?). Bonaire is a dream—it's a protected marine park with a beautiful, fringing reef surrounding the island which makes the island a diver's paradise and one of the world's best diving spots.

We spent the week with a few tanks in the back of the truck exploring the island and stopping for a shore dive wherever we felt compelled. On one of those dives I was exploring a wall of bright, thriving marine life. A few other divers were nearby as I gently kicked along the reef wall, moving only enough to maintain my buoyancy and stay in one place as I paused to look at this sea fan or that fish. Nearby were two clearly novice divers with an instructor. Not yet comfortable with buoyancy and the importance of calm, slow movements in the water, the two diving students frantically kicked against an invisible force (new environment, nerves, uncertainty, fear, anxiety, stress... totally normal). They were visibly uncomfortable and overweighted on their weight belts, kicking hard to stay off the ocean floor.

At one point I glanced around for my diving buddy, but Dad was nowhere to be found. I looked left and right down the reef wall and for a moment thought he was pulling another "Mike the Instructor" special on me and hiding because I took my eyes off him (you should know where your dive buddy is, always).

I turned my back to the reef and toward the deep, blue expanse of the open ocean behind me. And there he was, 20 feet or so off the reef.

He looked like he was suspended in midair, sitting cross-legged and perfectly buoyant—the exact opposite of the novice divers nearby. He looked amused, watching me enjoy the reef, looking about as peaceful as I've ever seen him. This was, is, and always will be, his happy place—diving is his own brand of meditation. This is where my father truly thrives.

How can we train with intention to be more at peace, balanced, and connected to our purpose and our values? How can we shift our mindset to show up the way we want to? How can we create and protect daily rituals and habits in different areas of life so that no matter the conditions, we can sit with stillness and observe, connect, and lean into both challenge but also joy, awe, and wonder?

That's where we move from Insight to Action, and conclude our journey together.

TL:DR

- There are a few key habits you can integrate into your daily life to help you be more resilient and agile in the face of stress.
- Making small but meaningful changes in the following areas of your life can even help to reduce the frequency or intensity of negative stress in your life:

  » Calendarizing your energy should be top priority.

Spiritual Thriver Accelerators:

- Purpose clarity and alignment
- Social connection

- Giving and gratitude
- Play
- Navigating the BIG things (return to purpose)

Mental/Emotional Thriver Accelerators:

- Mindset (storytelling and retelling stories)
- Journaling and reflection
- Mindfulness and meditation
- Visualization
- Training with intention for resilience

Body Thriver Accelerators:

- Exercise and Movement
- Nutrition
- Sleep

THE BOTTOM LINE

On January 15, 2009, US Airways captain Chelsey "Sully" Sullenberger (Captain Sully) successfully landed Flight 1539 safely on the Hudson River, saving hundreds of lives. How on earth did he do it? His courage certainly played a role (which he had in spades); his mindset I'm sure had much to do with it (failure was not an option for Sully); and likely, a little luck on his side was part of it. But there's one very important additional reason Sully saved all those lives that day—he had *trained* for this moment.

Captain Sully had trained thousands of hours in his life for an emergency just like this. And because of his training, his mind and body knew what to do without having to stop and think about it, or worry, or wonder, or even panic. In fact, in interviews afterward, Sully often said he felt in some ways his entire life leading up to that day was preparing him for that moment.[1]

I've said it many times in the book so far, and I'll say it one more time—mindset and training are *everything*.

Sully's story displays the incredible power of neuroplasticity in action—and now we're going to unleash it in our own lives.

So far, here's what we know about neuroplasticity:

+ **Our stress personalities are developed, in part, by this process.**

- Our brain is wired to return to what it knows, including our mindset. Often when things get hard or we feel threatened, we fall back on old habits and stories (old neural pathways).

- Neuroplasticity helps us design, implement, and automatize new habits to help us in moments of stress (Stress Resets, Gift of Pause), and even to get ahead of stress (Thriver Accelerators).

This entire book is about getting to know our current patterns (pathways) for what they are and deciding to forge new ones in service of better alignment with our best selves. Because at the end of the day, you are the owner and caretaker of your stress, your well-being, your resilience, and your happiness—*you hold the key.* What happened to you in the past is not your fault; what you do next is your responsibility. It won't come without discomfort, but the result is astoundingly beautiful growth in the process.

Now let's get to work on putting together everything you've learned so far and move from insight to action planning.

PREREQUISITE TO ACTION PLANNING: PURPOSE + VALUES CLARITY

It's important that we start making meaningful change in our life at the very beginning: our safety rope. Do you feel at this point you have a clear understanding of *what* is most important to you and *why?* This is crucial. If you don't have the GPS coordinates for your life:

- How do you map out the best route to your goals?

- How do you know where to even start?

- How do you make decisions or direct behavior?

*   How do you know where to protect your time and create your guardrails (boundaries, calendarizing your energy) to implement your next steps?

Before you begin, start with purpose. Go back to the previous chapter and answer those purpose questions and complete the values mining exercise from the Fighter chapter if you haven't yet.

EXERCISE 1: THRIVER PERFORMANCE REVIEW

Let's evaluate your *current state* when it comes to investing time and energy into your resilience and well-being. Here's a quick Thriver Performance Review.

Rate yourself according to the following chart.

Category	Level of Current Energy + Time Investment				
Rate yourself on a scale of 1-5: *1 = I'm not showing up at all,* *and* *5 = I'm fully invested and don't* *need to make changes.*	1	2	3	4	5
Work					
Social Connection with family, friends, community, etc.					

Purpose/Values Both clarity + alignment in day-to-day habits, decisions, etc. If you need to break this one up into two categories, go for it. You might have great *clarity* in your values for example, but your day-to-day decisions/actions aren't in alignment. There are no right or wrong answers here.					
Mindset What's your story about stress? Do you have a growth versus fixed mindset when stressed? Do you believe in yourself? Do you feel in control? Remember you're evaluating how you show up *when stressed or things are hectic*.					
Intentional stress to grow resilience Do you seek new hobbies, projects, challenges, etc. that challenge you to grow and stretch?					
Nutrition Do you feel your nutrition habits are supportive of a thriving, healthy, resilient life?					

Exercise/movement Do you exercise regularly in support of a thriving, healthy, resilient life?					
Sleep Is your sleep quality and quantity supportive of a thriving, healthy, resilient life?					
Boundaries/calendar management Are you clear on your boundaries and holding them?					
For the following questions, evaluate to what degree the statements are true on a scale of 1-5, where 1 = this is not true at all, and 5 = this is the most true.					
Stress Personality awareness *I am clear on my stress personality(ies) and when, how, and where they show up: I don't need more focus here.*					
In the moment: *In the moment, I have a strong Gift of Pause muscle: I catch my stress before it's an issue. I don't need more focus here.*					
Thriver Accelerators *I have strong habits around my well-being, and my lifestyle supports resilience and my ability to thrive. I don't need more focus here.*					

When you're finished, take a step back and evaluate your results:

+ **If you were your own boss, where would you put yourself on a "performance improvement plan"? Which rows had a 3 or less?**

+ **Asked another way—in which areas do you think some small tweaks might yield big returns on how you manage your stress?**

+ **This last question is very important to think about, as it directs your focus on taking action. Are there certain areas of life or even general insights you think are the best place to *start*? Prioritize and circle the rows you feel are most important to focus on *first*.**

Spend some time on this and really think about where the *opportunity* lies; there's no right answer, there's only the right answer for you *right now*.

For example, some of my clients choose to make small tweaks to their sleep habits first, which gives them more energy during the day, which then helps with more supportive nutrition choices and the motivation to exercise more often.

Other clients find that tackling excessive caffeine or eating more regularly helps them sleep better, which in turn gives them more energy throughout the day.

Others find that working on their mindset above all else puts them in the right mental and emotional place to tackle their stress personality, *then* their physical health. This is, to me, a strong place to start. Why? Because our emotions are in the driver's seat, right?

Whatever you choose, remember it's just a general area of focus for the moment.

There's no "right" place to start—it's highly individual. That said, *all* my clients are *clear about their purpose and values* before evaluating the areas of life in which they wanted to make meaningful change.

EXERCISE 2:
THRIVER ACCELERATOR ACTION PLANNING

When you have: 1) a general area you want to work on; and 2) clarity in your sense of purpose and values, select the Stress Resets or Thriver Accelerators you want to apply first. We've covered so many strategies in this book, so I know it can be quite overwhelming.

That's why I've developed the following training plan to help you identify some clear next steps. This training plan is rooted in current behavior change science, which helps us understand what it *really* takes to sustain meaningful change in our life. This is how we literally leverage neuroplasticity to rewire the brain and create new, more sustainable habits. There are four main steps to true behavior change (a rewiring of your brain):

1. A clear long-term goal.

2. A clear long-term goal connected to your sense of purpose and values.

3. A clear long-term goal connected to your sense of purpose and values, rooted in small, actionable, and realistic small micro-habits.

4. A clear long-term goal connected to your sense of purpose and values, rooted in small, actionable, and realistic small first steps, and protected by an environment set up for success.

Let's break these down. *Please do this exercise alongside me. Use the following worksheet in tandem with your reading.*

Step 1: Choose a clear long-term goal.

First, we need to decide on a clear long-term goal. The goal can be big and ambitious. Examples:

+ *I want to get to know and better control my stress personality.*
+ *I want to eat better to feel less stressed.*
+ *I want to meditate more.*
+ *I want to catch my Fighter personality more quickly.*
+ *I want to exercise more to improve my mental health.*

Step 2: Connect your clear long-term goal to your sense of purpose and values.

Then, tie your goal to your purpose, values, and what's most important.

Examples:

+ *My life is all about my nonprofit and serving those in need; how can I really stay focused if I can't manage the high stress that comes with the territory?*
+ *Knowing who I am under stress will help me show up as a business owner with more clarity and focus on the organization's vision.*
+ *I want to do this to feel more confident and in control, and ultimately to show up as a better friend, boss, spouse, and parent; my family matters more than anything.*
+ *I want to meditate more so that I have more clarity, focus, and sense of control over my stress. This will help me be more connected to my friends and more purposeful in my work.*

- *I want to catch my Fighter personality more quickly so I stop eroding my relationships with others and feel more in control of my emotions.*

Step 3: Connect your clear long-term goal to your sense of purpose and values, rooted in small, actionable, and realistic micro-habits.

Next, tie your big ambitious goal to small but meaningful next steps forward. Choose the Stress Resets or Thriver Accelerators that felt right and needed. Make them realistic, achievable—and most importantly—they must be *too small to fail*. Small steps in the right direction are much more likely to lead us to success rather than trying to make big, sweeping changes overnight.[2] Start small and stay consistent.

You can also try **habit stacking** to ensure your micro-habits are even stickier (easy to stick to). Stack one habit on top of another that you're already doing, such as brushing your teeth, commuting home, already blocked lunch hours, and workouts you're already doing. These are great places to start stacking habits.

Examples:

- *I'm going to set a reminder once per week to focus on my breath for one minute.*

- *I'm going to rewrite my purpose statement in a journal every day for three weeks.*

- *I'm going to add one vegetable to my daily intake.*

- *I'm going to spend 5 minutes visualizing myself at my best once per week.*

- *I'm going to put a Post-it note on my bathroom mirror with a positive affirmation that I can read every morning while brushing my teeth.*

- *I'm going to walk for 15 minutes before my morning shower, before work.*

- *I'm going to complete my worry journal once a week on Fridays at 2 p.m. because that's my best downtime and where I'm least likely to get interrupted.*

Step 4: Connect your clear long-term goal to your sense of purpose and values, rooted in small, actionable, and realistic small first steps, and protected by an environment set up for success.

And finally, we need some tweaks to our environment to set us up for success.

Calendar management. Your calendar is your greatest ally here. Take a long, hard look at your calendar to find opportunities to better protect energy and space for whatever micro-habits you create from your favorite Stress Resets or Thriver Accelerators. (Go back to the previous chapter on Calendarizing your Energy for more help with this one.)

Accountability partner. Find a VIP in your life who can hold you accountable to this goal. This person will be relentlessly positive and supportive. It's *your job*, not theirs, to determine how often this person will check in with you, and how (text, email, coffee time, etc.). How often do you need the person? What should the person ask you?

Literally tweak your environment. Look at ways to play with your surroundings to help you succeed. Do you need a quiet place to meditate? Should you pack your gym bag before work and bring it with you? Do you need to invest in a white noise machine? Invest in a grocery delivery service to avoid impulse-buying foods? Restructure your notification settings? Buy a cool new journal and fun pens? Anticipate what could steer you off course? Schedule connection time with others? Set reminders or calendar invites? This is how you set up your environment for success—it's the scaffolding that supports your goals.

Examples:

- *I'm going to check my purpose statement once each year and decide if it still resonates; I'll recalibrate if I'm off course.*

- *I'm going to enlist my best friend as my accountability partner to send me a text once a week to check on my progress.*

- *I'm going to set calendar reminders to alert me to take a minute to breathe.*

- *I'm going to block 2 hours of my week for unstructured thinking, daydreaming, creative time, and/or no-calls time.*

- *I'm going to place my workout shoes at the foot of my bed so I can step right into them when I wake up.*

- *I'm going to set aside two hours on Sundays to meal plan and prep.*

- *I'm going to block 5 minutes on my calendar each week to reflect on my progress and adjust as needed.*

- *I'm going to schedule regular meetings with my (therapist, mentor, counselor, whoever).*

INSIGHT TO ACTION PLANNING WORKSHEET

When you're ready, complete the following questions and calls to action:

1. My goal after reading this book is to:

_____

_____

_____

2. This change is important because:

_____

_____

_____

3. The Stress Reset/micro-habit (*one small step in the right direction that's too small to fail*) I'm going to make is:

_____

_____

_____

4. I'm going to set up my environment for success by:

_____

_____

_____

When you've completed this worksheet, and if you haven't already, get to work calendarizing reminders, setting up Post-it notes, texting your accountability partners, etc. *Do it right **now** before you forget.*

How long will it take to see results?

Well, obviously this depends on several factors: *consistency* is the most important factor, but mindset, level of support, cognitive flexibility (growth mindset), other life challenges you might be managing, and so on, play a significant role too.

Remember stress expert Robert M. Sapolsky, author of *Why Zebras Don't Get Ulcers? He* has a great theory on stress management success. He believes that 80 percent of your success will be accomplished within the first 20 percent of your efforts. On a certain level, no matter the Stress Reset, goal, or mindset behind it, the greatest progress you'll make is in that first 20 percent of effort, time, and energy. So...*get started!* Don't focus on the end just yet...baby steps, right?

SUSTAINABILITY, MONITORING PROGRESS, AND MANAGING SETBACKS

Monitoring Progress

Be sure to monitor your progress and set reminders to reevaluate every so often. My suggestion is every 30 days, make some time to check on your success.

Sometimes you'll need to adjust and tweak; other times you will be doing great and it might be time for a new "too small to fail" micro-habit. These micro-habits build on each other like stepstones leading to success. Do you know how to tell if a habit is sticky enough? My pulse check with clients is this:

Do you feel like you're still **pushing** *toward this micro-habit/goal, or being* **pulled** *toward it?*

One is an effortful feeling, and one is effort*less*. When your micro-habit becomes effortless and you don't even have to think about it anymore, it's time to level up and/or reflect on next steps (if any).

Keep your eyes focused on successes, not failures.

Let's close this book by *locking your sights on brilliantly succeeding at this new mission you're on to get to know and better manage your stress personality and build more thriving habits in your life.*

When you set your intentions for success and keep your vision on the finish line, you're much more likely to accomplish any goal you set. This method is rooted in science (I think at this point you realize I won't suggest anything that's not rooted in science). Our brain uses two processes called *value tagging* and *selective filtering* to assign value to a piece of input and then selectively filter what we should be focused on.[3]

When we *intentionally* direct our brain's attention to certain goals, images, visuals, and so on, and assign high importance and value to them, we're essentially telling our brain where to focus and why. If we're consistent, our brain eventually catches on and we start moving in that direction in our behaviors, thoughts, emotions—that's why intention setting is so powerful and effective. This is a visualization practice in and of itself—maybe a good micro-habit to bake into your routine?

Write down your goals. Speak them out loud to yourself or someone else. Find someone to hold you accountable. Accept the support. Shout it from the top of a mountain. This is how you reach your goals. Don't keep them in the dark—bring them out into the light and own them.

MANAGING "SETBACKS"

Friendly reminder: success is never, ever linear. So, how can we manage the inevitable "setbacks"?

Enjoy the detours.

Some of the best advice I have *ever* (and I mean *ever*) received when it comes to setbacks in life came from a friend and client, Dave. Dave was training for his first Ironman race about a year before my own first half Ironman. I was a personal trainer at a local YMCA at the time to help get through graduate school, and I was helping Dave here and there with the strength and flexibility parts of his training. Dave was also my pastor then, and a good friend of the family. He married me and my husband, my sister and brother-in-law, was there for my son's first birthday, and he baptized our children. Dave is an incredibly wise, kind, humble human—and a crazy-fast runner.

About halfway through his training, Dave injured his knee on a run. He shared the news in the gym one morning. Together we calculated how much this might set him back in his training and discussed how to integrate physical therapy into his routine.

The whole time we spoke, Dave looked a bit frustrated and disappointed, but had a surprisingly calm energy about him. It baffled me; personally, there are few things that mentally mess me up more than a sports injury. So I paused to ask him if he was okay.

Casually leaned up against the treadmill he was banned from using for six weeks or so, he looked at me, then down at his knee, and replied with a perspective that has stayed in my heart ever since:

"I'm disappointed, sure, but I'll just have to enjoy the detour as much as the route."

This small piece of advice he didn't even mean to give his own trainer? I felt it to my core. Dave wasn't referring to his knee as much as how he approaches everything in life—there is something to be learned and gained from the detours as much as the plans we lay for ourselves. His full trust in that truth changed my perspective on pretty much my entire life. These aren't setbacks—they're opportunities to fail forward and learn to enjoy whatever detour we find ourselves on.

I took that advice to heart when I faced my own shin splint detour when training for a half Ironman; I took it when I had a major career change that led me to my incredible calling today; I took it when our marriage was barely hanging on, and my husband and I had to choose each other—over and over for months—through the detours; I take it in the small moments when I simply set a new Thriver goal like meditating more often. It's an ever-present practice of grace and learning. I take Dave's advice through *every* detour in my life now, large or small, personal or professional; his words continue to inspire me today.

Dave has a growth mindset; in my eyes, he's a Thriver.

So, if you face a detour in your own training, no matter what area of life you choose to focus on, ask yourself:

- *What can I learn from this experience?*
- *How can I grow stronger and fail forward?*
- *How can I remember that this is a detour, and temporary; that there is no such thing as a setback?*

I hope this helps you move through the barriers of limited thinking and perspective.

Enjoy the detour: such incredible advice. I'll always be indebted to Pastor Dave for his wisdom. Oh, and by the way, he spent the next several weeks "running" in the pool and absolutely nailed his race.

Anchor in why.

No matter the goal, we must keep our sights on the main event—our why. Remember what Nietzsche said, "When we have a why, we can manage any how." When you feel yourself steering off course during your training—and you will take those detours, we all do—find your safety rope. Your micro-habits can't be built on an unstable surface, so always keep your why front and center.

Rehearse the detours.

To prepare for those detours and learn to thrive through them, it helps to anticipate and identify them in the first place, then brainstorm how to move through them.

My clients and I quite literally rehearse what could go wrong and how we'd manage it. This is part of the "setting up our environment for success" phase of the training plan. The more you plan and the more you train, the more likely you will fall back on your training. So, what setbacks can you anticipate on your journey, and what's your plan to manage them?

Know when to let it go.

Finally, there are times when your goals might need to be adjusted, reconfigured, and sometimes simply let go. Knowing when to let go of your goal or put it on pause is sometimes the most self-aware, self-loving action you can take.

A quick example: I was working with a client who set a big goal of losing 50 pounds while also trying to lead an organization, raise two teenage daughters, and navigate a difficult organizational change. She was losing weight with her "too small to fail" strategies, but her stress levels seemed to be climbing higher and higher—major red flag.

About six weeks into pushing through her micro-habits, during a check-in call she seemed weary and distant. I asked her to really think about how this goal was moving her toward her purpose—or not. She admitted that at this point, it wasn't. She was irritable, less focused at work, and feeling more insecure about her weight than ever. So, we decided to let it go for a bit. We took a month off of training so she could just *be*. During that time, I asked her to spend more time with her daughters and husband, do a few things each weekend that brought her joy, and work to *not* focus on food or weight.

After a month off, we connected again and the light had returned to her beautiful smile. She felt refreshed *and*, funny enough, had lost four pounds that month. By mentally and emotionally letting go of the expectations of her micro-habits, she found the freedom to reconnect with what mattered without thinking about it, and made better food choices because her confidence and energy were back. Happy to say that, today, she's kept to her goal weight.

When you check in on your goals every month or so, notice your energy and how you're feeling about things in general. Sometimes the best micro-habit is no micro-habit at all.

FINAL THOUGHTS

Remember when I said if stress personalities were like superheroes and they'd have to have an origin story, that mine would be the Great Donut Incident of 1993? And remember what I confessed to you? My family ate those donuts I spilled in a Miami back alley.

Here's the sequel to that story. In college I took a creative nonfiction writing class and wrote an essay where I fessed up to serving my family gravel-laden, alleyway donuts on a sunny, summer Sunday morning. I sent the essay to my mother, and then to my father.

My mother thought it was hilarious—we had a good laugh.

My father, after reading the essay, sent me a hilarious email in response. (We exchanged deep, funny, verbose emails about life back and forth while I was in college; I'm so glad I printed each one.) Anyway, his email set the record straight: *He knew I had spilled the donuts.*

Now, as a parent of two wild teenage boys, I should have known that my father took one look at those donuts and immediately pieced it together...but he ate them anyway.

That's the kind of parent I hope to be, forever.

Friend, I don't know your story, but I know you fought to get here. I know life gave you moments that brought you to your knees, where your heart was beating out of your chest and you were filled with fear, uncertainty, regret, worry, indecision, anger, eagerness to live up to others' expectations...

I know life was *so hard* in those moments. And I also know that, for all of us, those moments will continue. So will the daily stressors. And so will the moments you barely see coming but keep building and adding upon themselves until it all feels...like it's just too much. Darn that little pebble in the road I never saw coming; it caused my whole world to come crashing down in an instant.

But I also know there is no moment in life from which you can't pick yourself up and learn from the fall. There is no storm you can't get through. You *always* have a safety rope. Every bit of the awareness, peace, confidence, control, strength, resilience, spirit, and life you need is already there in your heart and between your ears. This science and these strategies are tools to make sure you're better prepared.

I hope this book brought new insights and ideas to your world, and I pray it yields abundant return.

Thanks for reading...I'm so grateful for you.

NOTES

PREFACE

1. Johnson & Johnson; https://jnjinstitute.com/en-us/additional
   -resources/human-performance-institute; accessed June 23, 2023.

2. Diane Herbst and David Walters, "People's 100 Companies that
   Care 2022," *People*; https://people.com/human-interest/people
   -100-companies-that-care-2022/; accessed June 23, 2023.

1 THE SCENE/THE SITUATION

1. "State of the Global Workplace: 2023 Report," *Gallup*; https://
   www.gallup.com/workplace/349484/state-of-the-global
   -workplace-2022-report.aspx#ite-393248; accessed June 25, 2023.

2. "Stress Level of Americans Is Rising Rapidly in 2022, New Study
   Finds," *The American Institute of Stress*, April 11, 2022; https://
   www.stress.org/stress-level-of-americans-is-rising-rapidly-in
   -2022-new-study-finds#%3A~%3Atext%3DBreaking%20it%20
   down%2C%20the%20Stress%2Cand%2058%25%20in%20
   June%202021; accessed April 25, 2023.

3. Jon Clifton, "The Global Rise of Unhappiness," *Gallup*, September
   15, 2022; https://www.stress.org/stress-level-of-americans-is
   -rising-rapidly-in-2022-new-study-finds#%3A~%3Atext%3

DBreaking%20it%20down%2C%20the%20Stress%2Cand%20
58%25%20in%20June%202021; accessed April 25, 2023.

Zachary M. Harvenek, et al., "Psychological and biological
resilience modulates the effects of stress on epigenetic aging,"
Translational Psychology 2021;11:601, NIH National Library of
Medicine, November 27, 2021; https://www.ncbi.nlm.nih.gov/
pmc/articles/PMC8627511/; accessed June 25, 2023.

5.   Jim Loehr and Tony Schwartz, *The Power of Full Engagement:
Managing Energy, Not Time, Is the Key to High Performance and
Personal Renewal* (New York: Free Press, 2003), 199-216.

6.   Tasha Eurich, *Insight: Why We're Not as Self-Aware as We Think,
and How Seeing Ourselves Clearly Helps Us Succeed at Work and in
Life* (New York: Currency, 2017).

2 THE SCIENCE

1.   Daniel J. Siegel, "Emotion as integration: A possible answer to the
question, what is emotion?" *APA PsycInfo*, 2009; https://psycnet
.apa.org/record/2009-20446-006; accessed June 25, 2023.

2.   Sydney Finkelstein, et.al, "Emotional Tagging: How Our Mental
Processes Increase the Likelihood of Making Flawed Decisions,"
Harvard Business Review, Volume 8(2), February 3, 2009, pages
60-66; https://hbsp.harvard.edu/product/3607BC-PDF-ENG;
accessed June 26, 2023.

3.   Seth Godin, "Linchpin: Are You Indispensable?" *ProQuest; Teacher
Librarian* Vol. 37, Issue 4, April 2010; https://www.proquest
.com/openview/765d7d1699fcebdb4f9f86d9bd04693a/1?pq
-origsite=gscholar&cbl=38018; accessed June 25, 2023.

4. Antonio Damasio, *The Feeling of What Happens: Body and Emotion in the Making of Consciousness* (New York: Mariner Books, 2000).

5. Brené Brown, *Atlas of the Heart*; Wholehearted School Counseling, https://wholeheartedschoolcounseling.com/free-resource-library/; *Creative Therapy Associates*, http://www.ctherapy.com/; accessed June 27, 2023. Noma Nazish, "How to De-Stress In 5 Minutes According to a Navy Seal," *Forbes*, May 30, 2019; https://www.forbes.com/sites/nomanazish/2019/05/30/how-to-de-stress-in-5-minutes-or-less-according-to-a-navy-seal/?sh=7331d8963046; accessed June 27, 2023.

6. Christine Brennan, "Heartbroken After Finishing Ninth, Olympic Champion Simone Manuel Reveals Why She Struggled," *USA Today*, June 18, 2021; https://www.usatoday.com/story/sports/christinebrennan/2021/06/18/simone-manuel-reveals-olympic-swimming-trials-why-shes-struggling/7742497002/; accessed June 26, 2023.

7. Loehr and Schwartz, *The Power of Full Engagement* (2006), 199-216.

8. James M. Tyler and Kathleen C. Burns, "After Depletion: The Replenishment of the Self's Regulatory Resources," *Self and Identity*, Volume 7(3), (2008), pages 305-321; https://www.tandfonline.com/doi/abs/10.1080/15298860701799997; accessed June 26, 2023.

9. Phillippa Lally, et.al., "How are habits formed: Modelling habit formation in the real world," *European Journal of Social Psychology*, Volume 40(6), October 2010, pages 998-1009; https://onlinelibrary.wiley.com/doi/abs/10.1002/ejsp.674; accessed June 26, 2023.

10. Caroline Leaf, *Switch On Your Brain: The Key to Peak Happiness, Thinking, and Health* (Grand Rapids, MI: Baker Books, 2013).

11. Rachel Dekel and Hadass Goldblatt, "Is There Intergenerational Transmission of Trauma? The Case of Combat Veterans' Children," *American Journal of Orthopsychiatry*, Volume 78(3), July 2008, pages 281-289; https://onlinelibrary.wiley.com/doi/abs/10.1037/a0013955; accessed June 26, 2023.

12. Leanne M. Williams, "Defining biotypes for depression and anxiety based on large-scale circuit dysfunction: A theoretical review of the evidence and future directions for clinical translation," *Depress Anxiety*, 34(1), pages 9-24, September 2016; https://www.ncbi.nlm.nih.gov/pmc/articles/PMC5702265/; accessed June 26, 2023.

3 THE SOLUTION—STRESS RESET

1. Brené Brown, "The Most Dangerous Stories We Make Up," *BreneBrown.com*, July 27, 2015; https://brenebrown.com/articles/2015/07/27/the-most-dangerous-stories-we-make-up/; accessed June 26, 2023.

2. Bessel van der Kolk, *The Body Keeps the Score: Brain, Mind, and Body in the Healing of Trauma* (New York: Penguin Books, 2014).

3. Bruce D. Perry and Oprah Winfrey, *What Happened to You? Conversations on Trauma, Resilience, and Healing* (New York: Macmillan, 2021).

4 THE RULES

1. A great book on this subject of emotional literacy: Brené Brown, *Atlas of the Heart: Mapping Meaningful Connection and the Language of Human Experience* (New York: Random House, 2021).

5 THE FIGHTER

1. Robert M. Sapolsky, *Why Zebras Don't Get Ulcers: The Acclaimed Guide to Stress, Stress-Related Diseases, and Coping* (New York: Holt Paperbacks, 2004).

2. Brené Brown, *Atlas of the Heart*; Wholehearted School Counseling, https://wholeheartedschoolcounseling.com/free-resource-library/; *Creative Therapy Associates*, http://www.ctherapy.com/; accessed June 27, 2023.

3. Noma Nazish, "How to De-Stress In 5 Minutes According to a Navy Seal," *Forbes*, May 30, 2019; https://www.forbes.com/sites/nomanazish/2019/05/30/how-to-de-stress-in-5-minutes-or-less-according-to-a-navy-seal/?sh=7331d8963046; accessed June 27, 2023.

4. Audrey Bergouignan, et.al., "Effect of frequent interruptions of prolonged sitting on self-perceived levels of energy, mood, food cravings and cognitive function," *International Journal of Behavioral Nutrition and Physical Activity*, 13(1), November 3, 2016, pages 1-12; https://ijbnpa.biomedcentral.com/articles/10.1186/s12966-016-0437-z?affinity=anthem; accessed June 27, 2023.

5. Janet Nikolovski and Jack Groppel, "The Power of an Energy Microburst," White Paper, *ResearchGate*, January 2013; https://www.researchgate.net/profile/Janeta-Nikolovski/publication/280683168_The_power_of_an_energy_microburst/links/55c10cd308ae9289a09cff0f/The-power-of-an-energy-microburst.pdf; accessed June 27, 2023.

6 THE RUNNER

1. Jasper van Oort, et.al., "How the brain connects in response to acute stress: A review at the human brain systems level,"

Neuroscience & Biobehavioral Reviews, 83, (2017), pages 281-297; https://www.researchgate.net/publication/320591574_How_ the_brain_connects_in_response_to_acute_stress_A_review_at_ the_human_brain_systems_level; accessed August 16, 2023.

2. D.N. Stewart and D. Winsor, "Incidence of Perforated Peptic Ulcer: Effect of Heavy Air-Raids," *The Lancet*, February 28, 1942; page 259; https://www.thelancet.com/journals/lancet/article/ PIIS0140-6736(00)57843-X/fulltext; accessed June 27, 2023.

7 THE WORRIER

1. Brown, *Atlas of the Heart*, 2021.

2. Jasper van Oort, et.al., "How the brain connects in response to acute stress: A review at the human brain systems level," *Neuroscience & Biobehavioral Reviews*, 83, (2017).

3. Amishi P. Jha, et.al., "Does mindfulness training help working memory 'work' better?" *Current Opinion in Psychology*, Volume 28 (August 2019), pages 273-278.

4. Kate Sweeney, et.al., "On the Experience of Awaiting Uncertain News," *Sage Journals*, Volume 27(4) (August 3, 2018), https://journals.sagepub.com/doi/ abs/10.1177/0963721417754197?journalCode=cdpa; accessed June 28, 2023.

5. Kim Pratt, "Psychology Tool: Schedule Worry Time," *healthypsych* (May 11, 2014); https://healthypsych.com/psychology-tools- schedule-worry-time/; accessed June 28, 2023. Sarah Kate McGowan, et.al., "A Preliminary Investigation of Stimulus Control Training for Worry: Effects on Anxiety and Insomnia," *Sage Journals*, Volume 37(1), (September 12, 2012); https:// healthypsych.com/psychology-tools-schedule-worry-time/; accessed June 28, 2023. "How to Worry More Effectively,"

PsychCentral (reviewed February 1, 2015, by Paul Jozsef); https://psychcentral.com/blog/how-to-worry-more-effectively#1; accessed June 28, 2023).

6. Luis Carlos Delgado, et.al., "Treating chronic worry: Psychological and physiological effects of a training programme based on mindfulness," *Science Direct, Behaviour Research and Therapy*, Volume 48, Issue 9 (September 2010), pages 873-882; https://www.sciencedirect.com/science/article/abs/pii/S0005796710001087; accessed June 28, 2023.

7. Lesley Bannatyne, "The Improvising Brain," *The Harvard Gazette, Health & Medicine*, (February 5, 2009); https://news.harvard.edu/gazette/story/2009/02/the-improvising-brain/#:~:text=Berkowitz%20and%20Ansari%20were%20interested%20in%20the%20brain,of%20piano%20training%20as%20subjects%20for%20the%20study; accessed June 28, 2023.

8. Ibid.

9. James E. Loehr and Sheila Ohlsson Walker, *Wise Decisions: A Science-Based Approach to Making Decisions* (Hoboken, NJ: Wiley Publishing, 2022). Amy Morin, "The Biggest Mistake Most People Make When it Comes to Taking Risks, According to a Psychotherapist," *Business Insider* (January 23, 2020); https://www.insider.com/psychotherapist-most-people-make-same-big-mistake-when-taking-risks; accessed June 28, 2023.

8 THE FREEZER

1. Sapolsky, *Why Zebras Don't Get Ulcers*, 2004.

2. *Psychology Today* staff, "Compartmentalization," *Psychology Today*, 2022; https://www.psychologytoday.com/us/basics/compartmentalization; accessed June 28, 2023.

3.   Perry and Winfrey, *What Happened to You?* (2021).

4.   Gordon MacDonald, *Ordering Your Private World* (Nashville, TN: Thomas Nelson, 2017).

5.   Johann Hari, *Lost Connections: Why You're Depressed and How to Find Hope* (New York: Bloomsbury Publishing, 2019). Emily Nagoski and Amelia Nagoski, *Burnout: The Secret to Solving the Stress Cycle* (New York: Ebury/Random House Publishing, 2019).

9 THE PLEASER

1.   Jenny Blake, *Free Time: Lose the Busy Work, Love Your Business* (San Francisco: Influential Marketing Group, 2022).

2.   Terry M. Metzger, "I Was Weary and Knew I Needed Something," *AASA*, June 2021; https://my.aasa.org/AASA/Resources/SAMag/2021/Jun21/Metzger.aspx; accessed June 29, 2023.

3.   Ja-Hyun Baik, "Stress and the Dopaminergic Reward System," *Experimental & Molecular Medicine* 52 (2020), pages 1879-1890.

4.   Melissa Urban, *The Book of Boundaries: Set the Limits That Will Set You Free* (New York: The Dial Press, 2022).

5.   Jim Collins, *Good to Great: Why Some Companies Make the Leap and Others Don't* (New York: Random House, 2009).

10 THE NEGATIVE SELF-TALKER

1.   Jackie K. Gollan, et.al., "Twice the negativity bias and half the positivity offset: Evaluative responses to emotional information in depression," *ScienceDirect, Journal of Behavior Therapy and Experimental Psychiatry*, Volume 52 (September 2016), pages 166-

170); https://www.sciencedirect.com/science/article/abs/pii/S0005791615300252; accessed June 29, 2023.

2. J.J. Ponzetti, ed., *Evidence-based Approaches to Relationship and Marriage Education* (New York: Routledge, 2016).

3. Frances Cohen, et.al., "Differential Immune System Changes with Acute and Persistent Stress for Optimists vs Pessimists," *Brain, Behavior, and Immunity*, Volume 13(2), (1999), pages 155-174.

4. Tiffany Ito and John Cacioppo, "Variations on a human universal: Individual differences in positivity offset and negativity bias," *Cognition and Emotion*, Volume 19(1), (2005); https://www.tandfonline.com/doi/abs/10.1080/02699930441000120; accessed June 29, 2023.

5. Elke Smeets, et.al., "Meeting Suffering With Kindness: Effects of a Brief Self-Compassion Intervention for Female College Students," *Journal of Clinical Psychology*, Volume 70(9), September 2014, pages 794-807.

6. Susan David, "Courage in the Face of Fear," *Emotional Agility Community Newsletter* (May 6, 2022); https://www.susandavid.com/newsletter/courage-in-the-face-of-fear/; accessed June 29, 2023.

7. Tara Swart, *The Source: Open Your Mind, Change Your Life* (New York: Vermillion, 2020).

8. Brené Brown, *Braving the Wilderness: The Quest for True Belonging and the Courage to Stand Alone* (New York: Random House, 2017).

9. Robert Burton, "The Certainty Bias: A Potentially Dangerous Mental Flaw," *Scientific American*, October 9, 2008.

11 THE DISTRACTED

1.   Wanda Thibodeaux, "Why Working In 90 Minutes Intervals is
     Powerful for Your Body and Job, According to Science," *Inc.com*;
     January 27, 2017; https://www.inc.com/wanda-thibodeaux/why
     -working-in-90-minute-intervals-is-powerful-for-your-body-and
     -job-according-t.html; accessed June 30, 2023.

2.   Matthew A. Killingsworth and Daniel T. Gilbert, "A Wandering
     Mind Is an Unhappy Mind," *Science*, Volume 330 (November
     12, 2010), page 932; https://www.science.org/doi/10.1126/
     science.1192439; accessed July 1, 2023.

3.   Roger E. Beaty, et.al., "Robust prediction of individual creative
     ability from brain functional connectivity," *Proceedings of the
     National Academy of Sciences*, 115(5), January 30, 2018, pages
     1087-1092; https://pubmed.ncbi.nlm.nih.gov/29339474/;
     accessed June 30, 2023.

4.   Tarek Amer, et.al., "Cognitive control as a double-edged sword,"
     Trends in Cognitive Sciences, 20(12), November 15, 2016, pages
     905-915.

5.   James Loehr and Tony Schwartz, "The Making of a Corporate
     Athlete," *Harvard Business Review* 79(1), (2001), pages 120-129.

6.   When the body starts moving, the brain "lights up" in almost all
     areas, and the result is improved cognition, creativity, and problem-
     solving (John J. Ratey and James E. Loehr, 2011, "The positive
     impact of physical activity on cognition during adulthood: a review
     of underlying mechanisms, evidence and recommendations");
     https://pubmed.ncbi.nlm.nih.gov/21417955/; accessed June 30,
     2023.

7.   May Rostom, "Four Ways Cold Showers Can Get Your Day
     Started Right" *Entrepreneur*, February 23, 2020. Andrew
     Huberman, "Using Cold Exposure for Health and Performance,"

Lab Podcast #66, 2022, *YouTube.com*; https://www.youtube.com/
watch?v=pq6WHJzOkno; accessed June 30, 2023.

12 THE THRIVER

1. Abiola Keller, et.al., "Does the perception that stress affects
    health matter? The association with health and mortality," *Health
    Psychology*, 31(5), (2012), pages 677-684; https://psycnet.apa.
    org/record/2011-30116-001; accessed June 30, 2023. Kelly
    McGonigal, "How to make stress your friend," *TedTalks*, 2013;
    https://www.ted.com/talks/kelly_mcgonigal_how_to_make_
    stress_your_friend/c; accessed June 30, 2023.

2. Swart, *The Source*, 2020.

3. Susan Fowler, *Why Motivating People Doesn't Work, and What
    Does* (Oakland, CA: Berrett-Koehler Publishers, 2017).

4. Daniel J. Siegel, et.al., editors, *The Healing Power of Emotion* (New
    York: W.W. Norton & Company, 2009).

5. Jeff V. Butler, et.al., "The role of intuition and reasoning in driving
    aversion to risk and ambiguity," *Theory and Decision*, 77 (2014),
    pages 455-484.

6. D.S. Yeager, et.al., "The far-reaching effects of believing people can
    change: Implicit theories of personality shape stress, health, and
    achievement during adolescence," *Journal of Personality and Social
    Psychology*, 106(6), (2014), page 867; https://psycnet.apa.org/
    doiLanding?doi=10.1037%2Fa0036335; accessed July 1, 2023.

7. Victor E. Frankl, *Man's Search for Meaning* (New York: Simon and
    Schuster, 1985).

13 THE INTERACTION

1. Charles Duhigg, "What Google Learned From its Quest to Build the Perfect Team," *The New York Times Magazine*, 26 (2016).

2. Margaret Heffernan, "Forget the pecking order at work," *TEDWomen 2015*; https://www.ted.com/talks/margaret_heffernan_forget_the_pecking_order_at_work/transcript; accessed July 1, 2023.

3. Stephanie Harrison, "Use these 9 little phrases to "instantly brighten" someone's day, says happiness expert," November 22, 2022, *CNBC Online*; https://www.cnbc.com/2022/11/22/say-these-little-phrases-to-instantly-brighten-someones-day-according-to-happiness-expert.html; accessed July 1, 2023.

14 THRIVER ACCELERATORS FOR EVERY STRESS PERSONALITY

1. Paul J. Zak, "Why inspiring stories make us react: The neuroscience of narrative," *Cerebrum*, January-February 2015; https://www.ncbi.nlm.nih.gov/pmc/articles/PMC4445577/; accessed July 1, 2023. Amy Banks and Leigh Ann Hirschman, *Wired to Connect: The Surprising Link Between Brain Science and Strong, Healthy Relationships* (New York: TarcherPerigee, 2016).

2. Jeremy Dean, "Why 'Thank You' Is More Than Just Good Manners," *PsychCentral*, September 2010, https://psychcentral.com/blog/why-thank-you-is-more-than-just-good-manners#1; accessed July 1, 2023.

3. Blake, *Free Time*, 2022.

4. Jim Loehr, *The Power of Story: Change Your Story, Change Your Destiny in Business and in Life* (New York: Simon and Schuster, 2008).

5. Qian Lu and Annette L. Stanton, "How benefits of expressive writing vary as a function of writing instructions, ethnicity and ambivalence over emotional expression," *Psychology & Health*, Volume 25 (6), 2009, pages 669-684; https://www .tandfonline.com/doi/abs/10.1080/08870440902883196; accessed July 2, 2023. Karla J. Gingerich, et.al., "Active Processing via Write-to-Learn Assignments: Learning and Retention Benefits in Introductory Psychology," *Society and the Teaching of Psychology*, Volume 41(4), 2014; https://journals.sagepub.com/doi/ abs/10.1177/0098628314549701?journalCode=topa; accessed July 2, 2023. Karen A. Baikie and Kay Wilhelm, "Emotional and Physical health benefits of expressive writing," *Advances in Psychiatric Treatment*, Cambridge University Press, January 2, 2018; https://www.cambridge.org/core/journals/advances-in -psychiatric-treatment/article/emotional-and-physical-health -benefits-of-expressive-writing/ ED2976A61F5DE56B46F07A1CE9EA9F9F; accessed July 2, 2023.

6. Boris B. Baltes, Cort W. Rudolph and Hannes Zacher, eds., *Work Across the Lifespan* (Salt Lake City, UT: Academic Press, 2019), 17-45.

7. Nathaniel F. Watson, "Recommended Amount of Sleep for a Healthy Adult: A Joint Consensus Statement of the American Academy of Sleep Medicine and Sleep Research Society," *NIH National Library of Medicine; Sleep*, June 1, 2015; https://pubmed .ncbi.nlm.nih.gov/26039963/; accessed July 2, 2023.

8. Nagoski and Nagoski, *Burnout*, 2020.

15 THE BOTTOM LINE

1. Andrew Prince, "Experience, Training Make for Smooth River Landing," *NPR*, January 16, 2009; https://www.npr.org/2009/01/16/99476650/experience-training-make-for-smooth-river-landing; accessed July 2, 2023. "US Flight 1549 Actual Footage of the Incredible Water Landing on January 15, 2009"; YouTube (2022); https://www.youtube.com/watch?v=QsHuJrNvPVE; accessed July 2, 2023.

2. BJ Fogg, *Tiny habits: The Small Changes That Change Everything* (New York: Eamon Dolan Books, 2019).

3. Madhuleena Roy Chowdhury, "The Science & Psychology of Goal-Setting 101," *PositivePsychology.com*; last modified February 2023, https://positivepsychology.com/goal-setting-psychology/; accessed July 2, 2023. Tara Swart, *The Source*, 2019. Johns Hopkins University "Separating Trash From Treasure: How the Brain Assigns Value to Objects," *NeuroscienceNews*, February 9, 2018; https://neurosciencenews.com/object-value-8469/; accessed July 2, 2023.

ABOUT THE AUTHOR

Lauren Hodges is passionate about watching others reach their highest potential, whether at work in their roles, or at home in those relationships that matter the most. Growing up, she always had an interest in human performance: she was an athlete, a personal trainer, a group exercise instructor, a boot camp owner, and an adjunct college professor. After ten years of living and working within the confines of higher education, fitness, and health, she realized her purpose was to serve others by helping them thrive in body, mind, and spirit so that their organizations could thrive, too.

Lauren is a speaker, facilitator, instructional designer, and learning sciences expert. She is an established thought leader in these spaces. She is also the owner of Performance on Purpose, LLC, a performance coaching company focused on advancing leadership and performance potential.

Lauren earned her doctorate in curriculum design from The University of Central Florida (Charge on, Knights!). She also has certifications in coaching, strength and conditioning, performance nutrition, and an advanced certificate in Neuroscience for Business from MIT Sloane School of Management.

Her most important role, though, is being mom to her two boys, Jake and Ryder, and partner to her husband, Daniel. She lives on the Florida coast and spends as much time as possible outdoors. As often as she can, she hikes, surfs, travels, exercises, and competes in triathlons.

CONTACT

LAUREN HODGES, ED.D.

www.performance-on-purpose.com/about

 laurenhodgestrainining@gmail.com

FOLLOW LAUREN:

 www.linkedin.com/in/drlaurenhodges/